Praise for
Carpe Diem Regained

'Brilliant. One of those rare books that forces you to ask what the hell you're doing with your life.'

George Monbiot, *Guardian* columnist and author of *Feral*

'Inspiring, bracing and elegant: a timely corrective to contemporary follies, from mindfulness to workaholism. *Carpe librum*!'

Sarah Bakewell, author of
At the Existentialist Café and *How to Live: A Life of Montaigne*

'The media tells us that we are forever young, but this wise and uplifting book is the perfect reminder that life is short and fragile, and that we need to seize the day to avoid living with regret.'

Philippa Perry, author of *How to Stay Sane*

'I read this book with a mixture of wonder and recognition. The sound of the galloping hooves of the horses of oblivion have always stalked me in case, for a moment, I should be distracted by the temptations of a life lived passively. In *Carpe Diem Regained*, Roman Krznaric has written a hugely important book for anyone who seeks to have agency in their life. It is a profound, playful book for wannabe grown-ups who love life.'

Sir Tim Smit, Founder of the Eden Project

'Stunningly good. Roman Krznaric has written a modern classic of contemporary philosophy. Seize it immediately.'

Julia Hobsbawm, author of
Fully Connected: Surviving and Thriving in an Age of Overload

'Insightful, inspiring and instructive. Anyone who feels like time is moving too fast and things are out of their control will be reinvigorated by ~~this~~ ~~~~

~~~~, author of
~~~~ *from Venus*

About the Author

Roman Krznaric is a social philosopher whose books, including *Empathy*, *The Wonderbox* and *How to Find Fulfilling Work*, have been published in more than twenty languages. He is the founder of the world's first Empathy Museum and of the digital Empathy Library. He is also a founding faculty member of The School of Life and on the faculty of Year Here.

Roman has been named by the *Observer* as one of Britain's leading popular philosophers. His writings have been widely influential amongst political and ecological campaigners, education reformers, social entrepreneurs and designers. He is an acclaimed public speaker, and his talks and workshops have taken him from a London prison to Google's headquarters in California.

After growing up in Sydney and Hong Kong, he studied at the universities of Oxford, London and Essex, where he gained his PhD in political sociology. Roman has worked as an academic, a gardener and a human rights campaigner. He is also a fanatical real tennis player and has a passion for making furniture.

By the Same Author

Empathy
The Wonderbox
How to Find Fulfilling Work
The First Beautiful Game

Carpe Diem Regained

The Vanishing Art of Seizing the Day

Roman Krznaric

Unbound

First published in 2017 by Unbound

This edition published in 2018 by Unbound

Unbound
6th Floor Mutual House, 70 Conduit Street, London W1S 2GF
www.unbound.com

© Roman Krznaric, 2017

While every effort has been made to trace the owners of copyright material
reproduced herein, the publisher would like to apologise for any omissions and
will be pleased to incorporate missing acknowledgments in any further editions.

Horace: Complete Odes & Epodes, translated and edited by David West
(Oxford World's Classics, 2008): Ode XI lines 1–8 plus 3 lines.
By permission of Oxford University Press.

Excerpt from Keith Johnstone's *Impro: Improvisation and the Theatre,*
Copyright © 1979. Reproduced by permission of Faber and Faber.

Text Design by PDQ

A CIP record for this book is available from the British Library

ISBN 978-1-78352-358-0 (trade hbk)
ISBN 978-1-78352-360-3 (e-book)
ISBN 978-1-78352-359-7 (limited edition)
ISBN 978-1-78352-493-8 (paperback)

Printed in Great Britain by Clays Ltd, St Ives Plc

1 3 5 7 9 8 6 4 2

Dear Reader,

The book you are holding came about in a rather different way to most others. It was funded directly by readers through a new website: Unbound. Unbound is the creation of three writers. We started the company because we believed there had to be a better deal for both writers and readers. On the Unbound website, authors share the ideas for the books they want to write directly with readers. If enough of you support the book by pledging for it in advance, we produce a beautifully bound special subscribers' edition and distribute a regular edition and e-book wherever books are sold, in shops and online.

This new way of publishing is actually a very old idea (Samuel Johnson funded his dictionary this way). We're just using the internet to build each writer a network of patrons. Here, at the back of this book, you'll find the names of all the people who seized the day and made it happen.

Publishing in this way means readers are no longer just passive consumers of the books they buy, and authors are free to write the books they really want. They get a much fairer return too – half the profits their books generate, rather than a tiny percentage of the cover price.

If you're not yet a subscriber, we hope that you'll want to join our publishing revolution and have your name listed in one of our books in the future. To get you started, here is a £5 discount on your first pledge. Just visit unbound.com, make your pledge and type seizetheday in the promo code box when you check out.

Thank you for your support,

Dan, Justin and John
Founders, Unbound

There is only one day left, always starting over: it is given to us at dawn, and taken away from us at dusk.

Jean–Paul Sartre

Contents

1

Carpe Diem from Horace to #yolo

On a summer morning in 2014, eighty-nine-year-old Bernard Jordan decided to escape. The former British naval officer was determined to go to Normandy to celebrate the seventieth anniversary of the D-Day landings with other World War Two veterans. But there was a problem: he was trapped in a care home in the English seaside town of Hove, without permission to travel. What could he do? Bernard came up with a cunning plan. He got up early and put on his best suit, making sure to pin on his wartime medals, then covered his outfit with a grey raincoat and sneaked out of the home. Now free, he tottered down to the railway station nearly a mile away, and took the next train to Portsmouth. Once there, he bought himself a ticket for the ferry to France and, on board, joined up with a party of war veterans who took him under their wing for the rest of the trip.

As soon as the care staff realised he was missing, a frantic police search began on the streets of Hove and in local hospitals. But by then it was too late. Bernard was already across the Channel, surrounded by marching bands and dancing girls. 'I loved every minute of it and would do it again tomorrow – it was such an exciting experience,' he said on his return. 'I expect I will be in some trouble with the care home, but it was worth it. I was naughty but I had to be there.'[1]

The story of Bernard's great escape took the British media by storm, knocking the sober anniversary speeches by world leaders and royalty off the front pages. The ferry company even offered him free travel to the Normandy beaches for the rest of his life. But Bernard was never able to take up that offer: six months later, he died.

Why did Bernard's adventure capture so much public attention? It was not just nostalgia for the wartime spirit or his venerable age. People also admired his courage to seize a window of opportunity that might never come again. The chance was there, and he took it. As one person commented in an online forum just after his death: 'RIP, am doubly glad he escaped and got to go to the anniversary… *carpe diem*'.[2]

Carpe diem – seize the day – is one of the oldest philosophical mottos in Western history. First uttered by the Roman poet Horace over 2,000 years ago, it retains an extraordinary resonance in popular culture. The heavy metal band Metallica has rocked audiences around the world with their song 'Carpe Diem Baby', while the actress Judi Dench had 'CARPE DIEM' tattooed on her wrist for her eighty-first birthday. Ask someone to spell out their philosophy of life and there's a good chance they will say something like 'seize the day' or 'live as if there's no tomorrow' – even if they appear to be trapped by routine or paralysed by procrastination. It's a message found in Hollywood films like *Dead Poets Society*, in one of the most successful brand campaigns of the last century ('Just Do It'), and in the social media hashtag #yolo ('you only live once'). Almost every language has an equivalent expression for the original Latin phrase. In Japanese it's 今を楽しめ ('enjoy now'), while wise Slovak grandmothers advise the young to *ži naplno* ('live fully'). Carpe diem has been a call to arms for everyone from the Jewish sage Hillel the Elder, who in the first century BCE asked, 'If not now, when?', to the Rastafarian sage Bob Marley, who sang out, 'Wake up and live!' If Horace were transported to the present, he would probably be surprised to discover that there is a heaving nightclub in Croatia named Carpe Diem, and dozens of fashion companies with carpe diem clothing lines – including a T-shirt that commands us all to CARPE THAT F*CKING DIEM.

It is remarkable that an expression from a long-dead language generates more than 25 million online search results. But just as striking is the fact that while most people can explain what carpe diem means to them, the answer varies greatly from one person to the next. For some, it's about that Bernard Jordan attitude of grasping a once-in-a-lifetime opportunity. Yet others associate it with wild hedonistic blowouts, or immersing themselves calmly in the present moment. This range of responses is reflected in the diverse translations of carpe diem that abound: while usually rendered as seize the day, it is sometimes translated as harvest, pluck, or enjoy the day. We might casually use the term carpe diem when chatting with a friend, but how aware are we of its many personalities hidden beneath the surface?

This book is my attempt to unravel how we think about carpe diem – to explore its various meanings and messages, its dangers and contradictions, its role in both personal life and social change. It might sound strange to talk about carpe diem as if it were an abstract noun like 'love' or 'truth', but I consider it to be a philosophical ideal that embodies a vision of how to live, similar to concepts such as happiness or freedom, and so I write about it in a comparable way. I want to understand what really motivates it, and what can make it such a difficult ideal to follow. Is carpe diem ultimately about the fear of death: a remedy for that instinctive –

but often fleeting – awareness so many of us have that life is short and our time is running out? Or is it just as much about expressing our desire for freedom and being the author of our own life?

My approach is necessarily eclectic, taking in everything from medieval carnival tradition to the neuropsychology of risk, from the history of opium addiction to existentialist thought. I will be delving into the lives of great seize-the-day practitioners, including nightclub dancers, war photographers, and committed revolutionaries. While mainly drawing on examples from the Western world, this is a journey that will take us from the streets of ancient Kyoto to the streets of contemporary Rio. To my knowledge, this is the first ever cultural and philosophical biography of carpe diem – which is astonishing given its bumper-sticker ubiquity in everyday life.

In the course of writing this book I have made two discoveries. First, that carpe diem has been hijacked, and as a result its potential to transform our lives is rapidly slipping away from us. Second, that humanity has, over the centuries, found five distinct ways to seize the day – and if we want to win back carpe diem from the hijackers, we need to revive them. My hope is to wake us up to the promise of Horace's maxim. The prize it offers is great: nothing less than the gift of radical aliveness or, to borrow a phrase from Henry David Thoreau, the possibility 'to live deep and suck out all the marrow from life'.[3] If, however, we fail to heed its call, we may end up reaching our final days and looking back on life with regret, viewing it as a series of paths not taken. The time has come to reclaim carpe diem.

THE VANISHING ART OF SEIZING THE DAY

The hijack of carpe diem is the existential crime of the century – and one that we have barely noticed. It might seem odd to claim that a phrase from a dead Roman poet has been 'hijacked', but the evidence is compelling. Who, or what, are the hijackers in question? First, the spirit of 'seize the day' has been surreptitiously hijacked by consumer culture, which has recast it as Black Friday shopping sprees and the instant hit of one-click online buying: in essence Just Do It has come to mean Just Buy It. Alongside this is the growing cult of efficiency and time management that has driven us toward hyper-scheduled living, turning the spontaneity of Just Do It into a culture of Just Plan It. A third hijacker is 24/7 digital entertainment that is replacing vibrant life experiences with vicarious, screen-based pleasures, and contributing to a new age of distraction. Rather than Just Do It, we increasingly Just Watch It instead. Finally – and though it might seem counterintuitive – carpe diem has been hijacked by the booming mindfulness movement. While practising mindfulness has many proven benefits, from reducing stress to helping with depression, one of its unintended consequences has been to encourage the idea that seizing the day is primarily about living in the here and now. Just Do It has become Just Breathe.

Confronted by these four hijackers, the art of seizing the day is vanishing before our eyes and we urgently need to do something about it, or else risk losing touch with the carpe diem wisdom of humanity that has accumulated over the past two millennia. I will be exploring in detail how this cultural hijacking has happened, and how we might best respond.

What about my second discovery? Curious to find out more about the different meanings people give to carpe diem, I decided to dig deeper and embark on a study of the way that phrases such as 'carpe diem', 'seize the day' and 'seize the moment' have been used across the arts, sciences, literature, popular culture and media. This involved analysing hundreds of original sources going back to the sixteenth century, with the help of a crack research team and some big databases in Oxford University's Bodleian Library.[4] A fascinating pattern soon began to emerge, revealing five essential interpretations of carpe diem through the centuries; an ensemble of ways that humankind has developed to seize the day.

The most popular of these interpretations I call *opportunity*, which concerns taking windows of opportunity that may never be repeated, whether it's the career break of a lifetime or the chance to rescue a crumbling relationship. A second strategy is *hedonism*, where we seize the day through sensory pleasures, from free love to gastronomic exploration. Another is *presence*, which includes mindfully entering the present moment through methods such as meditation, but also extends to more vigorous activities such as the intense rush of extreme sports or getting entranced in dance. Fourth is *spontaneity*, which involves throwing plans and routines to the wind and becoming more experimental in the way we live. Finally, there is the approach that is most often ignored or forgotten: *politics*. This is the realm of collective carpe diem, such as taking to the streets to topple a dictator or mobilising a social movement to tackle climate change.

These five paths cannot be found neatly laid out in any one spiritual tradition or philosophical doctrine, and we are mostly unaware of them. Although sometimes overlapping, they represent a distinct range of cultural tendencies, each of them a strategy that human beings have invented to inoculate themselves against the reality of death and to make the most of their brief moment of earthly existence. And why do they matter? Because it is precisely these rich approaches that have been hijacked. The challenge is to reclaim our cultural inheritance by reviving this quintet of ways to seize the day and harnessing their insights for the art of living.

This is an important historical moment for doing so. Despite living longer and more materially prosperous lives than at almost any moment in the past, and enjoying the benefits of handy iGadgets, cheap flights, and perfectly brewed gourmet coffee, Western societies seem to be failing to deliver personal wellbeing. There is an epidemic of mental illness – especially anxiety and depression

– and record figures of job dissatisfaction. In most countries levels of 'life satisfaction' have remained stagnant even when incomes have been rising. The arrival of efficient online dating has been accompanied by divorce rates of around 40%.[5] More and more of our time is taken up managing a deluge of emails, texts and tweets that keep us checking our phones, on average, 110 times a day, and which leave us in a state of continuous partial attention.[6] All this is compounded by a sense that society is malfunctioning on a broader level, visible in increasing inequality, the rise of extremism, corrupt and ineffective politicians, and impending ecological collapse.

It is no surprise then that the self-help industry is in such excellent health, and now valued at over $10 billion annually in the US alone: the search is on for new routes to a more fulfilling and meaningful life.[7] The happiness gurus have been out in force proposing alternatives to the increasingly obsolete model of consumer culture that has brought comfort and pleasure to some but left so many others wondering if it was really worth working so hard, or getting into so much debt, to taste its delights. We might turn to positive psychology or life coaching, or maybe holistic medicine or voluntary simplicity. We could join a therapy group, try a stress management course, or take solace in that ancient method known as religion. But amongst all these options, there is one that appears to have been largely overlooked: carpe diem. If we can rescue it from the hijackers, we might come to see it as a way to cut through the confusing array of possibilities by focusing our attention not so much on *what* we choose but *that* we choose.

We should be hopeful about the power of carpe diem, yet not become ideological zealots who believe that pursuing any one of its five forms will miraculously and automatically boost our wellbeing. It's important to find the right balance between them and recognise when *not* to cultivate them. Seizing the day can, at times, be reckless, dangerous, or even immoral. It might be rash to leave a steady job to open up your dream café if you've got a big mortgage to repay. Hedonism can easily turn into excess, evident everywhere from gluttony amongst the ancient Romans to the Neknomination online binge drinking craze, where kudos comes from being filmed downing whole pints of spirits.[8] Think how many carpe diem love affairs have led to broken marriages and divided families. And what about the bankers who seized opportunities for financial speculation that allowed them to make a killing while sparking the 2008 global financial crisis?

Seizing the day can also become an elite pursuit, open to the privileged few who have the economic means for risky decisions and adventurous choices. When my father was an immigrant refugee from Poland to Australia after World War Two, struggling to make ends meet, carpe diem living was a luxury he could not afford: it was security and stability that mattered to him. We also see certain differences across cultures. Decades of survey data reveal, for instance, that Swedes, New Zealanders and Mexicans place more value on personal autonomy, and having the opportunity for self-expression and for making choices in their lives, than Bulgarians, Chinese and Moroccans, who show a greater preference for economic and physical security. Such differences are due to many factors, such as poverty and inequality levels, religion, and political ideologies.[9]

And let's face it, seizing the day might be just too overwhelming or exhausting to keep up all the time. We all need distractions – even trashy TV – to help us unwind after a frustrating day at work or to keep our minds off relationship worries. Procrastination has its virtues too, shielding us from unwise and impulsive decisions that could wreak havoc with our lives. Seize-the-day passion and intensity may need to be tempered with a quieter, less zealous approach to life. As T.S. Eliot wrote in his *Four Quartets*, 'Human kind cannot bear very much reality.'

Yet it was a yearning to engage with reality that originally sparked my desire to write this book. It all began after an epiphany on the stairs. I was going up to my attic study with a biography of the travel writer Patrick Leigh Fermor, eager to dive into his spirited and daring life, which included walking across Europe from the Hook of Holland to Istanbul in the early 1930s. From the moment he set out, carrying a copy of Horace's *Odes* in his pocket, he felt an intoxicating sense of freedom. 'Living in a yeasty ferment of excitement,' he wrote, 'I grudged every second of sleep.'[10] I too wanted a taste of that exuberant freedom in my mouth. Half-way up the stairs, I was stopped still by a cascade of questions that unexpectedly flooded my mind. Why was I so keen to *read* about his passionate, carpe diem life rather than *live* such a life for myself? Was my own life too full of vicarious, second-hand experiences? If seizing the day is so good for us, why don't we do it more? In fact, what does it really mean? Of course, the irony hasn't escaped me that I have opted to answer these questions about carpe diem – a subject that more than most should inspire us to action – by sitting in my study and writing a book on it.

There was another underlying motive. Like most people, as I get older I can't help but hear the clock ticking. My mind keeps returning to a single, stark question: How can I make the most of the time I've got left? I have no desire to live in the shadow of regret like Tolstoy's Ivan Ilyich, who realised, on his deathbed, that he'd wasted his life on vain and superficial pursuits. Our lives are like that of the sparrow that the Venerable Bede wrote about in the eighth century, which flies momentarily through the hall of a great king on a stormy night:

> The sparrow, I say, flying in at one door, and
> immediately out another, whilst he is within, is safe
> from the wintry storm; but after a short space of fair
> weather, he immediately vanishes out of your sight,
> into the dark winter from which he had emerged.
> So this life of man appears for a short space, but of

what went before, or what is to follow, we are utterly ignorant.[11]

We are all sparrows, flitting into the warmth and light for an instant, then disappearing out into the darkness. In Bede's account, a missionary concludes that we should therefore believe in God, to stave off the uncertainty. My own conclusion is that we should seize the day, spreading our wings in full flight in the fleeting moments that we have.

I don't believe there is any ultimate meaning of life, whether written in scripture, the stars or our DNA. If it is meaning we seek, we can – and must – create it for ourselves. As the psychiatrist R.D. Laing noted, 'If there are no meanings, no values, no source of sustenance or help, then man, as creator, must invent, conjure up meanings and values, sustenance and succour out of nothing.'[12] Ways to do this have emerged in all human societies, ranging from supporting a cause and following a religion to focusing on family relationships and striving to use our talents.

But there is another approach whose possibilities remain untapped, and whose potential is fast disappearing: carpe diem. When we make a conscious choice to seize the day, even when our options are limited by circumstance, we are making a commitment to being active rather than passive beings, to pursuing our own path rather than one determined for us, to living in this moment rather than waiting for the next. And through that act of decision, we gain a sense of purpose by becoming the author of our own life. I choose, therefore I am.

THE BIRTH OF CARPE DIEM

The following pages will reveal the world of carpe diem in all its guises. We will delve into its various forms and the psychological barriers to practising them. We will come face to face with its hijackers, pinpoint its ethical weak spots, and ask whether it can be scaled up to become a force for social and political change. But there is something we must do first, to provide a foundation for everything that will follow: we must discover its backstory. Where and when was the idea born, and how did it develop its many personalities? The history of carpe diem begins quite simply: with a poem.

Its author was Quintus Horatius Flaccus – better known to us today as Horace – a leading lyric poet during the reign of the Roman Emperor Augustus, who wrote it while living comfortably on his beloved farm in the Sabine hills near Rome in around 23 BCE. The poem, Ode XI, from his first book of Odes, is a mere eight lines long, yet the whole carpe diem culture industry can be traced back to it. From the Renaissance right through to the twentieth century, being able to quote even a few lines of it was considered a mark of good education for a budding European gentleman.[13] Other writers both before and after Horace – such as the ancient Greek philosopher Epicurus – may have tried to express the sentiment of seizing the day, but it was Horace's phrase 'carpe diem' in the final line that captured the Western imagination.

Reciting Latin verse is hardly fashionable today, but Ode XI is still a subject of hot dispute amongst literary scholars, generating more than its fair share of clever critiques and barbed comments in learned academic journals. Some of the debate revolves around matters that would only excite – or be understood by – devoted classicists, such as Horace's use of the Greater Asclepiadean metre, the positioning of choriambic units and his radical introduction of the perfect subjunctive. But for the rest of us, the really crucial dispute is about interpreting what the famed Roman lyricist meant by 'carpe diem'. To untangle the meaning, it's worth looking at the poem as a whole. In this modern translation, which uses 'harvest' rather than 'seize' the day, Horace begins by addressing Leuconoe, a young woman – possibly a servant girl – in his company:

Don't you ask, Leuconoe – the gods do not wish it
    to be known –
what end they have given to me or to you, and don't
    meddle with
Babylonian horoscopes. How much better to accept
    whatever comes,
whether Jupiter gives us other winters or whether
    this is our last
now wearying out the Tyrrhenian sea on the
    pumice stones
opposing it. Be wise, strain the wine and cut back
    long hope
into a small space. Even as we speak, envious time
flies past. Harvest the day and leave as little as
    possible for tomorrow.[14]

If you would like to impress your friends, you could learn the final two sentences in the original: *Dum loquimur, fugerit invida aetas: carpe diem, quam minimum credula postero.*

I have to admit to being a little disappointed when I first read Ode XI. It hardly seemed to have the uplifting effervescent quality that I associated with seizing the day. Still, given its iconic status in Western culture for so many centuries, it certainly deserves our attention. So what might Horace be trying to tell us?

The most common way of reading this poem today is as a fervent call to grasp the fleeting opportunities that life offers. Time is flying, so don't wait for life to happen to you, get on with it now. Take some risks and do things you've never done before, because you only live once. 'Leave as little as possible for tomorrow,' Horace advises: don't procrastinate, just do it. Sources ranging from newspapers and novels to memoirs and song lyrics reveal that this has been the most widespread interpretation of 'carpe diem' or 'seize the day' for at least the last 200 years. If you search through copies of *The Times* going back to the nineteenth century, you will find that three-quarters of the references to these phrases concern the idea of taking advantage of windows of opportunity.[15]

This is certainly how carpe diem is understood in the film that has done more than any other to popularise it as a philosophy of living: *Dead Poets Society*. The late Robin Williams, playing the maverick English teacher John Keating at an elite boys' boarding school in 1950s New England, explains its meaning to his young charges in a poetry class. 'We are food for worms, lads,' he tells them. 'Because believe it or not, each and every one of us in this room is going to stop breathing, grow cold, and die.' He then takes them to look at fading photos of former alumni:

> Did they wait until it was too late to make from their lives even one iota of what they were capable? Because you see, gentlemen, these boys are now fertilizing daffodils. But if you listen real close, you can hear them whisper their legacy to you... Carpe diem. Seize the day, boys, make your lives extraordinary.[16]

A group of students then take carpe diem as their credo. It propels them to sneak out of school in the dead of night to chant poetry in a cave deep in the woods, and impels one of them to pluck up the courage to ask a girl on a date. But the feel-good, somewhat saccharine tone of the film is disrupted when one character, Neil, seizes the day by taking a part in a school play, in defiance of his overbearing father's wishes. After his evening as Puck in *A Midsummer Night's Dream*, the dream comes to an end. Neil's father announces that he's sending his son to a military academy, and that he will never act again. That night, Neil kills himself. Carpe diem has led to tragedy.

Robin Williams as school teacher John Keating in the 1989 film *Dead Poets Society*. The carpe diem theme was familiar to the actor: three years earlier he had played the lead role in a film adaptation of Saul Bellow's 1956 novel *Seize the Day*.

A very different view of Ode XI is to emphasise its sensual, hedonistic message. We should take the imperative 'carpe' to mean 'enjoy' the day. Clearly Horace is urging us to get ourselves merrily drunk ('strain the wine', sometimes translated as 'pour the wine'), make love and enjoy the good times before our inevitable end.[17] This perspective became particularly prevalent in the seventeenth century, when the 'carpe diem poem' emerged as a literary genre. Amongst the most renowned examples is Andrew Marvell's 'To His Coy Mistress', an erotic rendering of Horace's ode that celebrates the pleasures of the flesh (from a rather male perspective). With the prospect of 'time's winged chariot hurrying near', the poet impatiently implores the lady, 'And now, like amorous birds of prey,/ Rather at once our time devour' and 'tear our pleasures with rough strife/Through the iron gates of life'.[18] Hot stuff. Some modern commentators suggest that this is just what Horace wanted to convey. The poem, they say, is addressed directly to Leuconoe, a young girl who he is trying to seduce. She's resisting his advances and he's doing his very best to lure her into his bed chamber. Let's stop wasting time by talking ('even as we speak, envious time flies past') and get on with it, right now.[19]

No, no, no, respond others. Horace was not an advocate of hedonism but a critic of it. He was a believer in the Aristotelian middle way and his message is that we should live a life of moderation, quietly appreciating the beauties of nature and savouring the tastes of simple food and drink. Wasn't it Horace who elsewhere commended 'the virtues of plain living'? Instead of aggressively 'seizing' the day, we should gently 'pluck' it like the most delicate flower, and value each and every moment of our existence, no matter what life happens to throw at us ('accept whatever comes'). Don't fritter away your precious time speculating about the future. Instead, 'cut back long hope into a small space' and cultivate a sense of presence. Be here in the eternal now, in *this* day, rather than in any other. To really understand Horace's poem, we should focus on the *diem* not the *carpe*.[20]

This interpretation of carpe diem has become prominent in the media and public culture since the turn of the millennium, in large parts thanks to the mindfulness movement. Indeed, my research reveals that for around one-fifth of people today, carpe diem means immersing yourself in the present moment, as opposed to, say, seizing a window of opportunity.[21] This is an historically unprecedented development: few people in the nineteenth century would have associated carpe diem with what the contemporary mindfulness expert Jon Kabat-Zinn calls 'present-moment awareness'. Yet, as we will discover, this is precisely the kind of language with which it is now often described.

Another popular approach has been to adopt carpe diem as a motto for more spontaneous living. This seems especially pertinent given that cultural historians such as Barbara Ehrenreich have identified a long-term decline of spontaneity in Western society.

She argues that we may have been at our most spontaneous in the late Middle Ages, which was not simply a time of fear and misery, but also 'one long outdoor party' of raucous street carnivals, dancing, games and boozing interspersed with periods of hard labour.[22] We began to lose touch with our spontaneity in large part due to the Protestant Reformation and the Industrial Revolution, which ushered in a more controlled approach to everyday life dominated by the tempo of the factory clock. Today it struggles to emerge in the face of digital information overload and an obsessive time-management culture that result in people tightly planning their schedules days and weeks in advance. We might strive to seize the day by discarding our timetables, and becoming experts at improvised, spur-of-the-moment living.

A final strain of thought emerging from Ode XI concerns politics. Horace was not himself a highly political figure. Although holding a senior rank in the military and later becoming a supporter of Augustus' regime, he generally stayed out of public affairs. So it may well be too much to advocate reading his poem as a political manifesto. But at least since the eighteenth century, the terms 'carpe diem', 'seize the day' and 'seize the moment' have been commonly used to refer to making the most of political openings or possibilities.[23] In 1933, newspaper reports described the uncertain political situation in Spain as a chance for leftist forces to 'seize the moment and start their own revolution'.[24] When Richard Nixon made his historic visit to China in 1972, he declared that China and the United States should 'Seize the hour! Seize the day!', while Bill Clinton used 'seize the day' eleven times in public speeches on the final day of his 1996 campaign for re-election.[25] When tens of thousands of Germans breached the Berlin Wall on the night of November 9th, 1989, it was widely described as one of the great seize-the-day moments of recent history. In 2011 Occupy Movement protesters in the British industrial city of Sheffield received a visit from an anarchist band whose radical songs might have sent a shiver down Horace's conservative spine. The band's name? Seize The Day.[26]

Horace was a poet rather than a philosopher, more interested in aesthetic expression than presenting his ideas with analytical rigour and definitional precision. It may be unsurprising, then, that people have interpreted his poem in such different ways. Carpe diem clearly comes in many flavours, so if someone urges you to 'seize the day' you have good grounds for asking them exactly what they mean. Are they talking about grasping personal opportunities or enjoying hedonistic pleasures? Are they referring to presence, spontaneity or politics? In later chapters I will explore each of these five approaches, and how they offer different ways of confronting the shortness of life. But first I want to discuss what unites them: the fear of death. At the psychological root of carpe diem living is the knowledge that we are, as Mr Keating (and also Shakespeare) put it, food for worms. While we expend much of our energy attempting to deny this reality, a taste of death on our lips may be just what we need to truly appreciate the wisdom of Horace's ancient ideal and bring it into our lives.

2

Dancing with Death

I am sitting in a tiny, sparse stone hut at the top of a North Devon cliff, overlooking the sea, engulfed in swirls of wind and rain. Outside is an enticing sign: 'Ronald Duncan's Writing Hut is Open'. This is where the West Country poet and playwright – best known for writing the libretto for Benjamin Britten's opera *The Rape of Lucretia* – used to spend his working days. His former home, West Mill, where I am currently staying, is just down the steep coastal path.

Leafing through his autobiography, *All Men Are Islands*, I realise that what interests me about Duncan is not his literary friendships with people like T.S. Eliot, Ezra Pound and Gerald Brennan, but his adventurous streak and voracious appetite for living. After leaving Cambridge in the early 1930s, he pawned his clothes, bought himself a second-hand coat and slouch hat, then trudged across the slag heaps of Chesterfield in search of work in a coal mine. Being mistaken for a gypsy due to his dark complexion, and claiming he had worked with horses in a circus, Duncan landed himself a job looking after thirty-five pit ponies at the bottom of a shaft. This month-long immersion in working-class life – reminiscent of George Orwell's excursions 'down and out' on the streets of East London – was an unusual escapade for a budding aesthete descended from wealthy Austro-German aristocrats.

Duncan then set off for India, where he lived on an ashram with Gandhi. During World War Two, this experience not only inspired him to become a conscientious objector, but to conduct an experiment in utopian living, running his farm at West Mill as a commune. Unfortunately several of the poets and pacifists who joined him were more interested in writing verse and squabbling than milking cows, and the venture faded into failure. Despite this, it was emblematic of Duncan's efforts to take action rather than merely pontificate about his political ideals.

What really motivated Ronald Duncan? What was at the psychological root of his being? I find the answer buried in the middle of his book, where he spells out his philosophy of life – or rather death. It is one of the most evocative descriptions I have ever read of what it can mean to seize the day:

> I was, and am, acutely aware that life is ephemeral, limited and brief. I never wake up in the morning without being surprised at being alive: I never go to sleep without wondering whether I shall wake up. Death to me was the reality. Yet everybody I met and saw seemed unaware of it. They seemed to live as if they would live for ever. How else could they spend forty years marking exercise-books, going to an office to earn the money which would enable them to go on going to an office to earn the money which would enable them to –. I could see a skull beneath every bowler hat... I was obsessed with the feeling that I was a small boat floating on an ocean, and the ocean was death.[1]

As I sit in Duncan's former cliff-top writing hut, making notes on this passage, there is a sudden knock at the door. A woman in sensible walking shoes peers inside and sees me at the old desk with my fingers poised on my laptop, staring out across the Atlantic. She looks me up and down and asks, hesitantly, 'Are you Ronald Duncan?'

I'm not. And neither are most people, in the sense that relatively few of us feel such a daily proximity to death, and such an affinity with it. Yet recognising the ephemeral nature of existence, and being able to look death in the eye or float on its ocean, is perhaps the most crucial ingredient of carpe diem living. Some people – like Ronald Duncan – appear to be born with this capacity for death awareness, or may have absorbed it from their religious education, as is the case with many Catholics and Buddhists. Others, however, have to make a conscious effort to bring the reality of mortality into their minds, so it can spur them to wake up and grasp the possibilities of life. As Albert Camus scribbled in one of his notebooks, 'Come to terms with death. Thereafter anything is possible.'[2]

The challenge is that both the human psyche, and the societies we live in, do their very best to shield us from thinking about death. So in this chapter, with some help from a Californian tech entrepreneur, a bored Japanese bureaucrat and a Russian social climber, I want to explore how we can bring death closer to our lives so it can stir us to seize the day. Over the centuries, humankind has invented a number of ways to do this, which take the form of imaginative thought experiments that I call 'death tasters', serving to remind us of our mortality. Some of them, such as the Stoic maxim 'live each day as if it were your last', should be approached with caution. But there are lesser-known alternatives that we ought to recognise as ingenious mental devices to ensure that we don't reach the end of our days burdened by the ultimate regret: that we have wasted our lives and lived in vain. Before revealing them, however, it is essential to understand how death denial surreptitiously colonises our minds.

WHEN DEATH BURNS THE LIPS

Given that the one certitude of life is our inevitable death, it is curious that we don't dedicate more of our time to seizing the day. It is extraordinary that we are willing to give over so many hours to watching television, flicking idly through Facebook updates, following random web links to videos of cats turning on light switches, keeping up with celebrity gossip, or just generally mooching about in our dressing gowns. Think of those who died tragically young – a budding teenager destroyed by leukaemia, a talented ballet dancer killed in a car accident – and how much they would give to be granted just one extra day of being alive. Don't we owe it to them to make more of the precious gift of human existence?

Then again, maybe we should not be surprised by how easy it is to put carpe diem on the existential backburner. Most cultures today have lost the preoccupation with death that was so prevalent in medieval and Renaissance societies, when church walls were covered with frescoes of dancing skeletons, and people kept human skulls on their desks – known as *memento mori*, Latin for 'remember you must die' – as a reminder that death could take them at any moment. It was an age of deadly plagues, shocking child mortality and endemic violence for which we should hardly be nostalgic. At the same time, knowing that their mortal existence might be only the briefest of candles propelled people to live with a passion and intensity that we no longer possess – evident, for instance, in pre-industrial Europe's vibrant carnival tradition. That is why the historian of death Philippe Ariès concluded, 'the truth is that at no time has man so loved life as he did at the end of the Middle Ages'.[3]

Modern society, by contrast, is geared to distract us from death. Advertising creates a world where everyone is forever young. We shunt the elderly away in care homes, out of sight and mind. Dying in hospital, covered in tubes and wires, has eclipsed the old custom of dying at home, which is one of the reasons that children so rarely come face to face with death. The question 'Are you afraid of dying?' is hardly a favoured conversation topic on TV talk shows. Discussing death is not completely off the agenda: the dilemmas of euthanasia and palliative care are making their way into public debate, and there is a recent trend of Death Cafés in cities from Boston to Beijing, where people gather to ponder mortality and the meaning of life over tea and cake: since 2011 over 3000 meetings have taken place in more than thirty countries.[4] But in general, death remains a topic as taboo as sex was during the Victorian era.

'The word death is not pronounced in New York, in Paris, in London, because it burns the lips,' wrote the Mexican poet and essayist Octavio Paz in the 1950s. 'The Mexican, in contrast, is familiar with death, jokes about it, caresses it, sleeps with it, celebrates it; it is one of his favourite toys and his most steadfast love.'[5] This was probably something of an exaggeration, even back then, but it is fascinating how some cultures display an openness about death that is absent in many others. When Mexico holds its annual Day of the Dead festival, families conduct all-night vigils by their relatives' graves and children play with papier-mâché skeletons and eat Pan de Muerto – 'dead bread' in the shape of human bones. Go to an Irish wake or a New Orleans jazz funeral and you will also find vibrant and open attitudes toward death. This all contrasts with my own experience growing up in Australia. After my mother died of cancer when I was ten, she was barely spoken about in our family and I didn't visit her grave for twenty years. The veil of silence around her death, and my personal struggle to engage with it, was the by-product of a culture that censors conversations about death and shuns public grieving.

On a more subtle level, much of social life can be interpreted as an elaborate means of shielding us from our inherent anxiety about death. I spoke about this with psychologist Sheldon Solomon, who has spent three decades researching how fear of mortality motivates an extraordinary amount of our everyday behaviour, even if we don't consciously think about death that often:

> Literally hundreds of experiments have shown that when people are reminded of their mortality – such as by being interviewed in front of a funeral parlour or having the word 'death' flash on a computer screen so fast that they cannot see it – they respond by behaving in ways that bolster faith in their cultural worldviews and fortify their self-esteem. For example, after being reminded of death, materialistic people become more interested in owning high status luxury items like fancy cars and watches, and people who derive self-esteem from their personal appearance report that they intend to spend more time in a tanning booth and use less powerful sunscreen at the beach.[6]

Other studies by Solomon and his colleagues show that the more people think about death, the more likely they are to want to have children, and people who are obsessive compulsive wash their hands more often when presented with death prompts. Their findings have profound implications, suggesting that so much of what we do and what we strive for – such as social status and career success – are at the deepest level ways of protecting us from our existential fears and keeping the spectre of death at bay.[7] As the psychiatrist Irvin Yalom writes, 'The terror of death is ubiquitous and of such magnitude that a considerable portion of one's life energy is consumed in the denial of death.'[8]

Religion remains the most common way of confronting this terror. Belief in the afterlife and the immortality of the soul helps many to override the fear of everything coming to an abrupt end upon drawing their final earthly breath. Christianity, Judaism and Islam have all developed alluring visions of everlasting existence in a heavenly Paradise as a reward for the devout, while Buddhism, Hinduism and other faiths offer reincarnation as an alternative means of understanding and coming to terms with death. Such doctrines have millions of adherents: three-quarters of Americans, for instance, believe in heaven and an afterlife.[9] Those who lack faith can now turn to science instead: for $80,000 you can have your brain frozen, with the hope that in future decades or centuries molecular nanotechnology will come to your rescue and bring you back to life.[10]

Few people would openly admit that their lives are driven by a fear of death. Yet the prospect of death is always on our minds, if not always on our lips. We may have to live through the death of a parent or close friend, we worry that our children might get hit by a car, or we face personal health scares. Our impending mortality can even become disconcertingly real when we look in the mirror and suddenly see ourselves ageing (that shocking first grey hair, the deepening wrinkles), or notice that we can no longer walk up a hill without pausing to catch our breath. Moreover, while around 70% of people claim they are not afraid of dying, our dreams are suffused with images and symbols of death. Studies reveal that close to one-third of all dreams contain overt anxiety about death, and that dreaming of death is most pronounced amongst those whose conscious death anxiety is either very high *or* very *low*.[11] The nightmare of death haunts us like nothing else, even when we try to deny it.

When it comes to thinking about our own deaths, most people live in a twilight between knowing and not wanting to know. Like the Sword of Damocles, death hangs in the air ready to pierce us. But allowing this thought to inhabit our minds is simply too much for our psyches to bear. So we bury it, we deny it, we distract ourselves with the challenges and joys of everyday living or the solace of religion. Yet in doing so, we may rob ourselves of the most exquisite existential elixir: a taste of death that inspires us, or even compels us, to make the most of the limited time we've got before the Grim Reaper takes us away to heaven, hell or oblivion.

This leaves us with a delicate task: to bring the reality of death close enough to wet our lips without burning them. We need to become like the young woman in Gustav Klimt's 1916 painting *Death and Life* who seems willing to stare death in the face with her eyes wide open, apparently unperturbed. She, alone amongst the other figures, has the courage to begin a dance with death.[12] The question is how to think about our mortality in ways that open us to seizing the day. For this we can turn to an intriguing range of

carpe diem thought experiments, or death tasters, which have emerged over the past 2,000 years. We will begin our journey by exploring the best-known – yet perhaps the most flawed – of them all: to live each day as if it were our last.

SHOULD WE LIVE EACH DAY AS IF IT WERE OUR LAST – OR OUR FIRST?

Generations of scholars and sages have meditated upon death and the shortness of life, from the ancient Chinese philosopher Lao Tzu to the medieval theologian the Venerable Bede, from the Renaissance essayist Michel de Montaigne to the anthropologist Ernest Becker. One of the most recent figures on the scene – arguably a sage of the digital age – is Steve Jobs.

In 2005, the Apple founder gave a commencement speech at Stanford University that rapidly went viral on YouTube under the title 'How to Live Before You Die'. Jobs spoke about being diagnosed with a rare form of pancreatic cancer a year earlier. Having survived this near-death experience (in fact, a relapse of the cancer took his life in 2011), he told the audience that he uses his own mortality as a tool to help him make major life choices. The prospect of death not only makes our everyday fears and embarrassments fall away into insignificance, but can propel us to follow our dreams and intuition, to take risks, and defy convention. He also offered them a handy maxim for the art of living: that he lives each day as if it were his last.

Without ever using the phrase 'seize the day' itself, Jobs was expounding a carpe diem philosophy of life that has echoed through the centuries. Two millennia earlier, the Roman Emperor Marcus Aurelius pronounced that 'perfection of character is this: to live each day as if it were your last, without frenzy, without apathy, without pretence'.[14] Similarly, another Stoic thinker, the philosopher Seneca – born just a few years after Horace's death

– lamented that so many people squander their lives on wine and lust, greed and ambition. The problem, he wrote, 'is not that we have a short space of time, but that we waste so much of it… there is nothing the busy man is less busy with than living'. The wise man, by contrast, 'plans out every day as if it were his last'.[15]

Steve Jobs: a firm believer in the ancient Roman ideal of living each day as if it were his last.

What is the underlying message of 'live each day as if it were your last'? For a start, it shouldn't be taken too literally. The point is not to act as if we have no future whatsoever, running around as if there's only twenty-four hours left on our personal clock. Steve Jobs isn't saying that we shouldn't plan for our retirement or bother to have children. Rather, for him it's about retaining the big perspective that we don't live forever and should focus on doing what really matters, staying true to our values and personal vision. We can think about it as an existential check-in. For the Stoics, the emphasis is slightly different: it's more about appreciating each day to its fullest. As the philosopher William Irvine writes, 'when the Stoics live each day as if it is their last, it is not because they plan to take steps to make it their last; rather, it is so they can extract the full value of that day.'[16]

Although living each day as if it were your last might at first glance appear to be a wise ideal, it contains some questionable assumptions. While just a figurative expression, its framing encourages a short-termist attitude to life, directing our attention more to the present day and instant gratification than to the long view. It might, for instance, tempt some people to blow their savings in a spending spree or blow their relationship in an affair – even if this isn't what the Stoic philosophers originally intended. And why should the unit of measurement be a single day? Why not a year, or ten years? If it were phrased instead as 'live each *decade* as if it were your last' it might lose its sense of immediacy and urgency, yet could do more to inspire us to embark on meaningful long-term projects (such as learning flamenco guitar or writing a book) that require sweat and struggle today in exchange for benefits at some distant date.

Moreover, why should the focus be on treating each day as if it were our *last*? Why not live every day as if it were our *first*? Perhaps this would fill us with a profound sense of awe and wonder at the world, so we become like children who are astonished to touch snow for the first time or delighted to discover that giraffes are real living creatures. We might make more effort to appreciate the warmth of the sun on our skin or a kind gesture from a stranger.

A more fundamental problem is that Steve Jobs speaks as if there is no such thing as society, just a world of individuals whose actions have no apparent impact on one another. It might be *your* last day but that doesn't mean it is everybody else's too. Living as if there were no tomorrow is exactly the kind of worldview that is sending humanity hurtling toward its own destruction. We chop down rainforests, burn fossil fuels and pollute our rivers and oceans with far too little thought for the future inhabitants of our one and only fragile planet. Apple might be one of the most innovative tech companies of our time, but it was responsible for 34 million tons of greenhouse gas emissions in 2014 (roughly the same amount as the whole of Croatia), most of it from manufacturing plants in China.[17] The tragedy of our age is that we mainly have our eyes set on the present, our imaginations trapped in a mindset of seize-the-resource plundering and partying that will leave us with a planetary hangover from which society may never recover. We might be wise to learn from the Iroquois Great Law of Peace – known as the Kaianerekowa – a set of traditional indigenous principles that advises making decisions based on thinking ahead seven generations.[18] That's more like seizing two centuries than seizing the day.

So should we really try to live each day as if it were our last? For some people it's a potentially attractive ideal, particularly if they are searching for the confidence to overcome fears, to challenge conventions, and to live a life of their own making. I find it most useful when I'm with my ageing father and step-mother, who I usually only see for a few weeks each year when they are visiting from Australia. I'm acutely and painfully aware that they won't be around forever, so I try to treat each day I spend with them as if it might be our last together. It helps me to listen with more attention, to laugh with more abandon, to show my love and to receive it.

For other people, however, the idea of living each day as if it were our last may fail to resonate, for reasons such as its excessively short-term and individualistic vision. The good news is that there are alternative and possibly more effective ways to check in with death, each with its own unique twist.

THE HIDDEN MEANING OF A TOKYO PLAYGROUND

A curious new term came into popular usage in December 2007: 'bucket list'. Its origin coincides with the release of the comedy-drama film *The Bucket List*, starring Jack Nicholson as corporate billionaire Edward Cole, and Morgan Freeman as working-class mechanic Carter Chambers. These two very different characters meet while sharing a hospital room and discover that they have one thing in common: they both have terminal illnesses and less than a year to live. So they write down all the things they had always dreamed of doing before they kicked the bucket, and spend the rest of the film ticking off items on their list.

Over the next few months, the incongruous pair go skydiving, race Shelby Mustangs around a speedway, fly over the North Pole, eat dinner in a Michelin-starred restaurant on the Côte d'Azur, gaze at the Taj Mahal, ride motorbikes on the Great Wall of China, take in an African safari, and make it to Everest base camp. Finally, atop the Great Pyramid in Egypt, they both realise that having all these amazing experiences is not nearly as fulfilling as they had hoped it would be. What really matters to each of them is their personal relationships. Cole wants to be reconciled with his only daughter, who refuses to see him, and Chambers hopes to rediscover his love for his wife. In a predictably emotional yet happy Hollywood ending, this is just what happens before both men die.

Since the film's release, the idea of creating a bucket list has become an online craze. You can now find innumerable top 10s, 100s and even 1000s on blogs, digital magazines and YouTube. Despite the movie's message about the ultimate importance of family relations and emotional connection, most bucket lists look like brochures for adventure holidays and exotic travel breaks, and are often plastered with advertising from travel companies. Typical items include scuba diving in Costa Rica, climbing Kilimanjaro, bungee jumping and staying in Sweden's Ice Hotel. Some people favour more standard fare like visiting the Vatican or spending a romantic weekend in Paris, highly recommended by guides such as *1000 Places to See Before You Die*. The overriding characteristic of bucket lists is to approach life as a self-indulgent shopping trip where the aim is to accumulate as many perfect experiences as possible and buy yourself the greatest sensory pleasures on offer – and without any thought to your carbon footprint. The more items you can tick off your list, the happier you will be. The bucket list phenomenon is a result of our hyperindividualistic YOLO culture that places value on fleeting novelty and hedonistic thrill-seeking above all else.

Yet there is an interesting existential question hovering behind the film and the frenzied online cult it has spawned: what would you do if you knew you had only a set period left to live, such as six months or a year? It is, of course, a very real question for many people diagnosed with terminal illnesses. But it is also a classic carpe diem thought experiment, or 'death taster', that deserves serious contemplation at any stage of life.

The most profound cinematic exploration of this question is not *The Bucket List*, but a much more nuanced and powerful film from the Japanese director Akira Kurosawa. Released in 1952, *Ikiru* ('To Live') tells the story of Kanji Watanabe, a middle-aged, mid-level bureaucrat in post-war Tokyo. For the last three decades Watanabe has been working as the Section Chief of the municipal Public Affairs Department, shuffling papers, stamping documents and saving his pennies. And he's bored senseless. In fact, 'he might as well be a corpse... this man has been dead for more than twenty years now,' according to the film's narrator.[19] But his life changes in an instant when he discovers he has stomach cancer and just six months to live. So here's his dilemma: faced with this final window of opportunity, what is he going to do?

At first Watanabe feels the terror and isolation of his new situation. He sobs under his bed covers, contemplates suicide, and confronts the truth that he has wasted his days. The solution to his existential angst comes when he decides to do something meaningful by helping a group of poor mothers create a playground for their children. In complete contrast with his formerly downtrodden and self-serving character, Watanabe battles the petty bureaucrats with all his determination, and overcomes the intransigence of local politicians and threats from gangsters to

31

achieve his aim. In the end, he succeeds, performing a single act for the public good that gives his life meaning. He dies happy in the new playground on a swing, singing a song whose refrain echoes through the winter air – 'Life is brief'.[20]

The movie puts a subtle twist on the Stoic slogan to 'live each day as if it were your last', shifting the time frame to offer a compelling alternative: 'live as if you've got just six months left'. This shift makes a difference. It directs our mental gaze away from short-term thinking and pleasures, and encourages us to embark on potentially significant projects that might require sustained attention and effort – but without offering so much time that we are tempted to endlessly put things off or feel no sense of urgency. I have found myself taking this death taster rather literally since first watching *Ikiru*: it stimulates me to try my hand at new challenges every half year or so – the most recent was to start singing lessons despite being convinced I have an irredeemably awful voice – and

Kanji Watanabe deeply content in his playground, singing 'Life is brief' moments before his death.

to pragmatically abandon those pursuits and experiments after roughly six months if they haven't worked out.

Confronting our mortality, as Kanji Watanabe did, can wake us from our existential slumber, help us reassess our priorities, and spur us to seize the day and make something more of our lives. The task we face is to invent meaningful acts and projects for ourselves without falling back on the easy option of ticking off a bucket list of hedonistic pleasures that might still leave us wondering, 'What's it all for?' While the causes we choose to dedicate ourselves to might require a degree of struggle and suffering on our own part, we need to remember Nietzsche's dictum, 'He who has a *why* to live for can bear with almost any how.'[21] The ultimate act of creation is to conjure up this 'why' in our imaginations. This leaves each of us with a question: What is our own equivalent of Watanabe's playground?

THE BENEFITS – AND BURDENS – OF LIVING MORE THAN ONCE

'Live as if you were living already for the second time and as if you had acted the first time as wrongly as you are about to act now.'[22]

This mind-bending advice is courtesy of the Austrian existential psychotherapist and Auschwitz survivor Viktor Frankl. He saw it as a way of confronting ourselves with 'life's finiteness' and of encouraging us to take responsibility for our actions. But what does it really mean, and what light does it shine on seizing the day?

One interpretation appears in the 2013 film *About Time*, directed by Richard Curtis, which at first comes across as a typical romantic comedy but turns out – in my view – to be a fascinating exploration of Frankl's idea. It concerns a young man, Tim, who on his twenty-first birthday is told by his father that, like all men in his family, he has an inherited ability to relive (and even revise) the past by transporting himself back in time to any date and place in his memory. After overcoming his disbelief, Tim first uses his new power to get a girlfriend. But the film becomes far more interesting toward the end, when Tim's father is dying of cancer and reveals his secret to leading a happy life: live each day as normal, with all its tensions and worries, then go back and live it again, but this time making an effort to notice all the beautiful moments and small pleasures life has to offer.

Tim tries this himself, but then discovers an even richer philosophy that doesn't require any time travel at all: 'I just try to live every day as if I've deliberately come back to this one day, to enjoy it.' We see him putting it into practice – kissing his wife tenderly as she wakes in the morning instead of rushing out of bed, having fun with his kids while he makes them breakfast before school, making an effort to look the cashier in the eye and smile when buying his lunch. The carpe diem lesson here is about being in the now, being attentive and present, noticing the sweetness of the world. As Richard Curtis said in an interview, the 'movie is saying that we should relish every normal day and live it just for the day itself, not for what the day might achieve'.[23]

Frankl would probably have felt uncomfortable with this interpretation of his maxim, as he believed it was important to focus on future goals in life rather than give priority to dwelling in the present moment (an issue I will explore in a later chapter). I think he treated it more as a helpful tool for avoiding regret. The message is essentially this: whatever you are about to do, imagine you are probably going to make the wrong choice and regret it, so make sure you get it right this time. You might feel tempted to repeat an old pattern of unleashing your aggressive or sarcastic side during a tense family discussion. Invoking Frankl's idea could give you pause for thought. Or you may have a tendency to avoid taking on challenging work assignments due to a lack of self-confidence, and find yourself frequently regretting your decision. So next time this kind of opportunity arises, trying his thought experiment might inspire you to take on the task.

The philosopher Friedrich Nietzsche offered an even more radical death taster. It is known as 'eternal recurrence', and ranks as one of the most dazzling doctrines to have emerged from the Western philosophical tradition. Nietzsche himself considered it to be the most important discovery of his career and referred to it as his 'formula for greatness'. It is not about imagining living the days of your life for a second time, but living them over and over again forever. This is how he put the idea:

> This life, as you live it at present, and have lived it, you must live it once more, and also innumerable times; and there will be nothing new in it, but every pain and every joy and every thought and every sigh, and all the unspeakably small and great in thy life must come to you again, and all in the same series and sequence.[24]

Scholars have spent decades debating whether Nietzsche believed eternal recurrence to be a reality.[25] I think it is more helpful to view it as a provocative thought experiment. It initially looks like the opposite of carpe diem thinking: Nietzsche's vision is to contemplate life as unending rather than limited, a kind of endless loop of reincarnation. But there is a powerful seize-the-day message at the core of eternal recurrence: if you are not willing to live your life over and over again, then you're probably not living it wisely and should make a change.[26] Why are you spending years staying in a job that pays well but leaves you completely stressed out and with little free time, if you would not be willing to do so again in a subsequent life, ad infinitum? Why lose yourself in jealousies, grudges or self-pity unless you are prepared to do so for eternity? Or just imagine condemning yourself to watching TV game shows for aeons.

In Nietzsche's view, the test of whether we are making the right choices is if we are willing to bear with their consequences in a world of eternal recurrence. For some people this might be too much of a burden, with all our suffering and selfishness coming back to haunt us. For others, it could be a liberation, offering a useful rule of thumb for making life choices. It is the very fact that life is finite and doesn't recur (as far as I know) that makes it so important to get it right first time, and eternal recurrence is our clever device to ensure we do so.

Nietzsche's canny concept is part of a long intellectual tradition of playing with the theme of repetition, ranging from Camus' antihero Sisyphus who endlessly pushes a stone up a hill only to have it roll back down once he has reached the top, to Bill Murray eternally returning to the small-town nightmare of Groundhog Day. It undoubtedly takes us in a very different direction to an adage like 'live each day as if it were your last'. Rather than making choices as if there were no tomorrow, eternal recurrence asks us to imagine a thousand tomorrows, and to live with the consequences of our decisions throughout our lives.

LITTLE DEATHS, MANY LIVES

The Japanese Buddhist monk Kamo no Chōmei, born in 1153, began his career as a court poet and musician in Kyoto. But the older he became, the more he wanted to escape worldly affairs into monastic seclusion. Finally, at age sixty, he built himself a tiny wooden hut, ten feet by ten feet, at nearby Mount Hino. Like the naturalist Henry David Thoreau over 600 years later, Chōmei approached it as an experiment in self-sufficient simple living, surviving on nuts gathered from the mountainside and weaving his own clothes from arrowroot. Surrounded by the sound of cuckoos and cicadas, he wrote *Hōjōki* ('An Account of My Hut'), an essay whose opening lines have become a classic statement of the Buddhist concept of impermanence or *mujō*:

The current of the flowing river does not cease, and yet the water is not the same water as before. The foam that floats on stagnant pools, now vanishing, now forming, never stays the same for long. So, too, it is with the people and dwellings of the world.[27]

Chōmei's remarkable work chronicles the disasters he witnessed during his lifetime. He recalls the devastating fire of 1177 that burned Kyoto to ashes, a typhoon that flattened everything in its path, a violent earthquake that destroyed the homes of both rich and poor, and the terrible famine of 1181 that left tens of thousands dead and so many corpses on the streets that carriages could not pass by. He ponders the meaning of all this death and destruction from the vantage point of his mountain retreat:

Nor is it clear to me, as people are born and die, where they are coming from and where they are going. Nor why, being so ephemeral in this world, they take such pains to make their houses pleasing to the eye. The master and the dwelling are competing in their transience. Both will perish from this world like the morning glory that blooms in the morning dew... When, after a boat passes, the white waves immediately fade away, I see my own transient experience in that.[28]

So we are immersed in a universe of impermanence. There is no escape from the fleeting nature of existence. We spend our lives striving to create permanence – the homes we build, the careers we pursue – but this pursuit, Chōmei believes, is ultimately futile. Why become attached to material wealth or strive for prestige when, in the end, it is all destined to disappear? Instead, he prefers to spend the remaining days of his life praying to the Buddha and playing his koto alone in his hut, trying to imitate the sound of the wind as it passes through the pines.

The idea of impermanence has resonated across human cultures, in both East and West, for more than two millennia. Like Chōmei, the ancient Greek philosopher Heraclitus turned to the metaphor of a river, remarking, 'everything changes and nothing remains... you cannot step twice into the same stream'. Recognising the ephemeral nature of life and that everything is in flux offers an important way of tasting death. It suggests not just that our own lives are transient, but that they are composed of an infinite number of 'little deaths' or moments that pass into nothingness. A wind comes then passes, never to be felt in exactly the same way again. Our children grow up just once, and if we don't pay attention we miss their precious early years. Like Shakespeare's Seven Ages of Man, our own lives are episodic: we may have our years of teenage discovery and angst, followed by our footloose twenties, which then die and pass into sensible middle age, when our mind matures but our vigour typically declines until, in the end, we are 'sans teeth, sans eyes, sans taste, sans everything'. We are constantly dying from the moment we are born.

For Chōmei, viewing life in this way leads him to renounce worldly goods in accordance with the Buddhist principle of non-attachment, and to live in the absolute present as far as possible, appreciating the sublime and transient beauties of nature. I am reminded of a plumber I know who, when he sees flowers blooming by the roadside, stops his van and gets out to smell them. 'You've got to stop,' he tells me, 'because they're just not going to be around tomorrow.' But a 'little deaths' philosophy could take us in many other directions. Sex and drugs and rock 'n' roll for instance. If all is impermanence, and the past and future are mere constructs of our minds, then why not follow in the footsteps of the opium addict Samuel Taylor Coleridge and give yourself a one-way ticket to Kubla Khan's stately pleasure-dome where you can drink the milk of paradise?

I see another approach to impermanence in the many lives of David Bowie. Throughout his career he was known for his capacity to reinvent himself, especially through the creation of new public stage personas. These had complex origins, including in his study of Kabuki theatre and the influence of his first dance teacher, Lindsay Kemp.[29] After starting out as a straight acoustic rocker in the 1960s, he exploded onto the stage in 1972 with his alter ego Ziggy Stardust, a bisexual alien rock superstar. He reinvented himself again with personas such as Aladin Sane and the Thin White Duke, then emerged in the 1980s as a peroxided pop idol who made albums like *Let's Dance*. At the same time, Bowie turned himself into an actor, taking leading roles in films such as *The Man Who Fell to Earth* and theatrical productions like *The Elephant Man*.

The enigmatic nature of his shape-shifting was commented on by Bowie himself in 1976 in a classically elliptical statement: 'Bowie was never meant to be. He's like a Lego kit. I'm convinced I wouldn't like him, because he's too vacuous and undisciplined.

David Bowie becoming Ziggy Stardust in a backstage dressing room, 1973.

There is no definitive David Bowie.'[30] Whether made from a Lego kit or not, Bowie's many public lives can be viewed as a series of 'little deaths', where new Bowies were regularly being born as old Bowies died. As a performer, he was always in a state of transience, personifying the idea of impermanence – a theme reflected in his song 'Changes'. In the end he did leave the stream of impermanence, dying of liver cancer, but not before seizing the day and making a final album, *Blackstar*, where he even sings about his own death. Many people have had their lives changed by David Bowie in different ways, but I think one of his legacies is to offer inspiration to those who can feel many selves bustling within their being, waiting to burst out – from the teenager who dreams of coming out into the open about their sexuality, to the frustrated accountant who wants to lead a more creative and adventurous life. The philosophy of little deaths can galvanise us to seize the moment, put an old role behind us, and invent ourselves anew.

THE DEATHBED TEST

'What if my whole life has really been wrong?'[31] These are the agonising words of Ivan Ilyich on his deathbed, tormented by the idea that he has lived his life in vain. The protagonist in Tolstoy's novella *The Death of Ivan Ilyich* is a judicial prosecutor who has dedicated his career to rising through the legal ranks and helping his family achieve a place in respectable bourgeois society. His professional success has given him social standing, he has a beautiful home with antique furniture and gloved servants, he throws intimate and exclusive dinner parties for all the 'right people', and his daughter is set to marry a prosperous magistrate. What more could he want?

But as he lies dying at the age of forty-five, having mortally injured himself in a fall while hanging curtains in his aristocratic St Petersburg apartment, he comes to realise that his aspirational life has been worthless. 'I was going up in public opinion, but to the same extent life was ebbing away from me,' he reflects bitterly.[32] He might have had the perfect curtains, but his marriage was loveless and he had no true friends. As a judge he was powerful and respected, but his work ultimately left him feeling hollow and bored. His best memories were far away in his childhood. And so he dies, in pain, lonely and alone in the face of death, convinced that he has wasted his life.

Tolstoy's story provides us with a final carpe diem death taster: if we project our mind to the end of our life, when we are lying on our deathbed, how would we feel about it looking back? Would we be proud of our achievements? Would we feel that we had sucked the marrow from life? Or might we, like Ivan Ilyich, be filled with regret?

While fictional characters can help us ponder such difficult questions, it may be even more useful to discover what real people who are near death tend to think about how they lived. What are the most common regrets of the dying? When an Australian palliative care nurse, Bronnie Ware, explored this question with her patients, who had between three and twelve weeks left to live, particular themes kept recurring. One of the most common – especially amongst men – was 'I wish I didn't work so hard'. People deeply regretted dedicating so much time to the treadmill of work, and felt they had missed their children growing up and their partner's companionship. Another was 'I wish I'd had the courage to live a life true to myself, not the life others expected of me.' Further common regrets, found in many studies of the terminally ill, include people wishing they had made more effort to stay in touch with their closest friends, and that they had been more emotionally open and honest with people they loved – in one case a young man dying of HIV/AIDS lamented that he had hidden his homosexuality from his parents all his life.[33] In the end, when people look back on their lives, they are rarely concerned with worldly achievements such as career success or reputation. What seems to matter above all is intimate relationships.

There is, however, a certain bias in these studies. By focusing on people in their final moments, this is just when they are most likely to feel frightened and alone and in need of close personal connection and comfort. It doesn't mean that emotional attachment is unimportant, just that it might be exaggerated in relation to other issues, such as whether people felt they had 'made a difference' during their lives, or been able to fully pursue and express their talents and passions.

So I think we should supplement such studies by conducting some of our own, more personal, thought explorations that help us look back on our lives. Psychotherapists sometimes refer to these as 'guided fantasies', which are designed to help us reflect on life (and death). One common exercise is to imagine yourself at the end of your life and to write your own obituary (or even to write two of them, one 'real' and one 'ideal'). Another is to imagine your own funeral and the eulogies that people might deliver. Are they talking about someone who had lived with integrity and made a difference in the world? Or maybe, reading between the lines, a person who had been a little too self-obsessed and a bit of a slacker? A more structured approach used by some therapists is to have you draw a straight line on a sheet of paper, which represents your birth at one end and death at the other. You then place an X to indicate where you are now. The task is simply to meditate on this for five minutes.[34]

These exercises can help us think seriously about our own lives in retrospect and whether we might, in the end, find ourselves consumed by regret. Although artificial, for some people they can be an incentive to reassess priorities and take new pathways. In other words, to seize the day. Out of the many ways of envisioning ourselves at the end of life, my personal favourite – which I find both playful and profound – is inspired by a thought experiment from the neuroscientist David Eagleman.[35]

Imagine yourself at a dinner party in the afterlife. Also present are all the other 'yous' who you could have been if you had made different choices. The you who studied harder for exams. The you who walked out on your first job and followed your dream. The you who became an alcoholic, and another you who nearly died in a car accident. The you who put more time into making your marriage work. You look around at these alternative selves. Some of them are impressive, while others seem smug and annoying. A few make you feel inadequate and lazy. So which of them are you curious to meet and talk to? Which would you rather avoid? Which do you envy? And are there any of these many yous whom you would rather be – or become?

ROLLING THE DEATH DICE

Maintaining an awareness of death can be difficult when both our own minds and everyday culture are so good at distracting us from the stark and elemental fact that our time on earth is ephemeral, limited and brief. The various death tasters I have explored each, in its own way, acts as an enlightening aide-mémoire, reminding us to honour Horace's carpe diem credo, and that we are like the Venerable Bede's sparrow with just a few moments to spread our wings in the warmth and light before we fly out of the hall into the darkness.

In the spirit of that old line 'life is a gamble', just for fun I've made myself a Death Dice, on each side of which is one of the death tasters. Keeping one of these in your pocket is a modern equivalent of the medieval practice of placing a human skull on your desk – though somewhat less conspicuous, and hardly as macabre. Whenever I have to make a difficult choice, or feel frustrated or stuck in some way, I can simply take out my dice and give it a roll. I can't say that I always strictly follow the instruction on the side that lands up, but it does serve as a prompt to new thoughts and perspectives that help me to avoid the perils of regret. As my Death Dice is probably not yet available in your local gift shop, I have created a do-it-yourself cut-out version that you can make in your own home with nothing more than scissors, glue and a little patience.

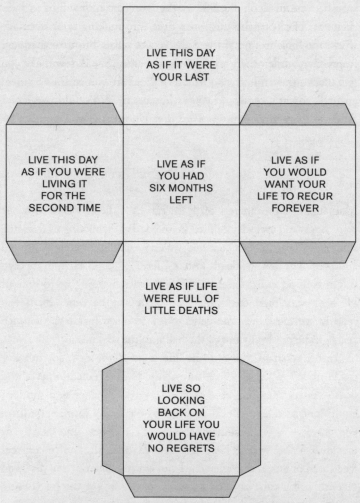

LIVE THIS DAY
AS IF IT WERE
YOUR LAST

LIVE THIS DAY
AS IF YOU WERE
LIVING IT
FOR THE
SECOND TIME

LIVE AS IF
YOU HAD
SIX MONTHS
LEFT

LIVE AS IF
YOU WOULD
WANT YOUR
LIFE TO RECUR
FOREVER

LIVE AS IF LIFE
WERE FULL OF
LITTLE DEATHS

LIVE SO
LOOKING
BACK ON
YOUR LIFE YOU
WOULD HAVE
NO REGRETS

Make your own Death Dice. Cut out and form into a cube. Roll daily, or when making major life decisions. Follow the instruction. Parental supervision not required.

Tossing the dice of death is only the beginning of a carpe diem journey. The death tasters do not in themselves tell us precisely how we should go about seizing the day. They could drive us toward hedonism as much as mindful presence, or might provoke us to take risky opportunities, to revel in spontaneity, or enter the fray of political action. So we still need to delve into these different ways that human beings have found to seize the day and discover what role they might play in our lives. But before doing so, we must confront a fundamental barrier that Horace could never have foreseen: the hijacking of his most famous idea.

3

How Carpe Diem Was Hijacked

It isn't easy to steal a philosophy of life, but there is no doubt that it has been done, and from right under our noses. Carpe diem has been hijacked.

At first glance it seems unlikely. Both 'carpe diem' and 'seize the day' remain popular everyday catchphrases with a global reach: if you go to the tiny village of Shi Ban Qiao near Guilin in southern China, you might stumble across a hostel named Carpe Diem. The original Latin motto has been joined by modern equivalents such as YOLO – you only live once – which has become a widespread lifestyle meme and social media hashtag since the Canadian rapper Drake made it fashionable in his 2011 song 'The Motto'. Spontaneous, seize-the-day living also appears to be on the rise: more than half of British holidaymakers book short breaks with less than a week's notice thanks to smartphone technology and websites such as lastminute.com.[1]

So carpe diem looks to be in good health. But scratch below the surface and a different, more troubling picture begins to appear. We are well aware of some of the persistent barriers to seizing the day, many of which have existed since Horace wrote his celebrated ode: a lack of self-confidence that derails our resolve, our inbuilt aversion to risk that breeds cautious decision-making, burdens of debt that chain down our lives, and exhausting jobs with long hours that leave us with little leftover diem to carpe.

More startling, however, is the emergence of a crafty triumvirate of hijackers that have – without us even noticing – distorted the way we think about and practise seizing the day, and drawn it into the realm of relatively trivial and superficial choices. The hijackers in question? The cult of efficiency inherited from seventeenth-century Christianity and the Industrial Revolution; the rogue ideology of consumer capitalism that developed after World War One; and that deceptively pleasurable cultural addiction known as television, which has colonised our lives since the 1950s and remains dominant in the era of 24/7 digital entertainment. Together, these deep-rooted forces have ousted the carpe diem ideal Just Do It and supplanted it with a new set of aspirations: Just Plan It, Just Buy It and Just Watch It. In a later chapter we will also discover that there is a fourth hijacker – the mindfulness movement, which sends us the message to Just Breathe.

Once we grasp the extent of this hijacking, we will have gained the insights and inspiration we need to win back the seize-the-day ethos and embrace it in our lives.

Just Plan It: How the Cult of Efficiency Took Over Our Minds

During a recent trip to Brazil I was struck by the spontaneous, carpe diem feel of everyday life. Friends randomly drop in on each other and sit chatting for hours. A bunch of kids in a favela suddenly start up an improvised high-velocity football match in the middle of the street, seemingly oblivious to the passing traffic. Someone brings out a guitar at a community barbecue and within moments everyone is singing along to the tune. People stay out dancing until the early hours even if it means oversleeping and turning up late for work. Buses still run, shops open and children go to school, but somehow it appears to be a nation without a To Do list, where the electronic calendar has failed to cast its long digital shadow.

I was aware that I was falling for a romanticised version of Brazilian spontaneity: I met many stressed-out, uptight people too, who were constantly rushing to meetings and spent more time looking at their phones than at the world around them. Even so, upon returning to my home in Oxford I resolved to bring a little bit of the idealised Brazil into my life. But all my efforts to promote carpe diem living failed dismally. One Saturday I tried inviting several friends over for a last-minute Sunday lunch (with Brazilian cocktails on tap), but everyone was predictably busy busy busy. I tried knocking on my neighbours' doors to drop in for a friendly afternoon chat, but typically felt I was imposing. I attempted to arrange spontaneous playdates for my kids but discovered that they needed scheduling two weeks in advance. I called three people to join me when I found out one of my favourite musicians was playing in town that night: one of them had to do his tax return, and the other two were dealing with a backlog of work emails. There was only one conclusion to draw: I was enveloped by a culture of Just Plan It, not Just Do It.

It wasn't always thus. According to cultural historian Barbara Ehrenreich, the amount of free, spontaneous, seize-the-day living and festivity that existed in medieval and pre-industrial Europe 'is almost beyond our imagining today'.[2] There were harvest festivals and Saints' Days full of feasting, games and revelry, and country fairs with puppetry, comedy and raucous boozing. At carnival time men dressed up as women or wild beasts, and peasants put on the robes of priests or lords in mockery of their masters. Carnival may have been a regularly scheduled tradition, but it was full of unpredictable effervescence. A dance craze swept across the continent in the thirteenth and fourteenth centuries. 'People danced in both churches and cemeteries in the Middle Ages, especially on holidays such as the Feast of Fools,' according to one chronicler, while another recorded that, in 1278, 200 people kept dancing all day on a bridge in Utrecht until it collapsed (and all of them were drowned).[3] Right up to the eighteenth century working hours were hardly regular for most labourers. There were plenty of holidays, and many professions such as weavers and cobblers never worked on a Monday, which was known as 'Saint Monday' or 'Cobbler's Monday'.[4] There is no doubt that daily existence was full of drudgery and destitution, misery and fear, but it was punctuated by pulses of exuberance and festivity that make contemporary life look embarrassingly dull.

How did we lose this Dionysian lust for life? The German sociologist Max Weber pointed the finger at the spread of Protestant ideals in the sixteenth and seventeenth centuries. Puritan asceticism 'descended like a frost' on social life in England and other countries, and 'turned with all its force against one thing: the spontaneous enjoyment of life and all it had to offer'.[5] Church authorities abolished carnivals and festivities, while thousands of laws were introduced to ban fairs and dances, sports and theatre.

Monks on the dance floor. In this Dutch painting by a follower of Hieronymus Bosch (c.1600–20), the man playing the bagpipes on the raised table represents the figure of Carnival. The woman carrying the fishes is Lent, with everyone else engaged in carpe diem revelry before fasting begins.

In their place came a new and methodical uniformity of life that frowned upon free and exuberant living. People were expected to keep their heads down, get on with their work and attend church. 'Wasting time' was elevated into a deadly sin and punctuality became a virtue.[6] This repressive ideology chimed perfectly with an older Christian idea, going back to St Augustine in the fifth century, that happiness was not to be enjoyed in this life but was rather a reward granted by God to true believers in the next life. In other words, we are condemned to suffer during our time on earth and should be content with delayed gratification.[7] The promise of jam tomorrow should be enough to keep us happy.

Carpe diem was not extinguished by Christianity alone. A more powerful and pervasive force was the spread of industrial capitalism and its greatest weapon: the factory clock. From around the eighteenth century, the growth of urban industrialisation engulfed millions of workers in a more controlled and regimented way of life that served the interests of bourgeois business. The clock punished labourers who turned up late by docking their pay, and kept them confined in textile mills and coal mines until the final whistle. Between 1780 and 1830, wrote the historian E.P. Thompson, 'the "average" English working man became more disciplined, more subject to the productive tempo of "the clock", more reserved and methodical, less violent and less spontaneous'.[8] This discipline was reinforced by Henry Ford's innovation of the moving assembly line in 1913, and the introduction of 'time and motion' studies that ratcheted up the pace of factory work in an effort to increase productivity and efficiency.

This might all sound like history, but its legacy permeates our minds today. It explains why a friend of mine greets me by asking, 'Have you had a productive morning?' It's why we often feel guilty about 'wasting time', as if we have some Puritan preacher inside our brains nudging us not to be idle. It's one of the reasons why we schedule so many activities for our kids after school and on weekends, robbing them of free and self-directed play. It's why we are constantly checking the time on the clocks that have colonised our phones, wrists, bedside tables, computers, microwave ovens and city streets. It's why another friend consults the calendar on her phone when I suggest meeting up for a coffee and says, only half-joking, 'I'll see if I can fit you in.' Most of us are too busy to seize the day, and we hardly notice what we are missing. The freedoms of the pre-industrial past seem to have been erased from our cultural memory.

We live in what the French philosopher Michel Foucault called a 'disciplined' society, where order and control – much of it self-imposed – are far more pervasive than we care to admit.[9] In the last two decades, the drive for discipline and efficiency has been reinforced and exacerbated by what I think of as an 'info bomb' that has exploded on our screens and inside our minds.[10] In 1621 the writer Robert Burton, who had 1,700 books in his capacious library, complained about the problem of growing information overload: 'new books every day, pamphlets, currantoes, stories, whole volumes of all sorts, new paradoxes, opinions, schisms, heresies, controversies'.[11] But nobody could have prepared him for the digital glut today – millions of Wikipedia entries and YouTube videos, billions of tweets, Facebook updates and cc'd emails. Through the Tardis-like portal of our phones we can access a world resembling the universal library that Jorge Luis Borges described in his 1941 story 'The Library of Babel', which contains every book in every language, the faithful catalogue of the library and every false catalogue, commentaries on the gospels and commentaries on those commentaries.

Discipline is currently imposed on us not just by the legacy of the factory clock and the pious preacher, but by digital overload. We attempt to invent efficient systems to deal with it all – smart ways of filtering our emails, rationing our social media time, apps to help us tag and organise articles we want to read, catching up with podcasts while jogging and newsfeeds on the toilet (75% of people use their phones there) – but it is hard not to feel overwhelmed.[12] Multitasking is a common strategy to deal with the overflow of bits and bytes filling our lives, but we are less adept at it than we think: typically we switch rapidly between tasks rather than do them simultaneously, and become less efficient in the process, in part because the quick switching triggers production of the stress hormone cortisol. This can generate some scary statistics: knowing there is an unread email sitting in your inbox while you are focusing on another task can reduce your effective IQ by ten points.[13]

The end result is that we spend an enormous amount of time and energy trying to manage the flood of information, and all the choices and decisions that it generates. We no longer just choose – we choose *how* to choose, becoming metamanagers of our digital selves.[14]

Why do we find it so difficult to handle the info bomb? One reason is that our brains are not well calibrated to deal with such electronic abundance. The prefrontal cortex has a novelty bias, so we are easily distracted by a new text message or video that pops up on the screen and issues its siren call 'click me'. Attending to them releases a burst of feel-good opioids that rewards us for diverting our focus (even if at the end we curse ourselves for what might turn into a twenty-minute digression of following links).

According to Tristan Harris, a former 'design ethicist' at Google, part of the problem is that digital technology is designed so it 'hijacks our psychological vulnerabilities'. One way this is done is through offering 'intermittent variable rewards', which is how slot machines create millions of addicts: you pull the lever and immediately either win an enticing reward or receive nothing, and get addicted by the hope that next time might be your lucky day. In effect, says Harris, 'Several billion people have a slot machine in their pocket.' We take out our phone and press refresh, hoping we have new email, or tap a social media icon to check if we have new notifications. And then we can't help going back for more, just in case we win.[15] If you think you're not a victim, download an app named Checky, which tells you how often you unlock your phone each day – and get ready for a nasty shock.

In the face of all these emails, messages and other digital offerings, we may strive to be efficient, schedule our time meticulously, and feel a surge of satisfaction when we tick items off our To Do list. But there is a cost to this apparently benevolent management mentality: it is squeezing more and more carpe diem spirit out of our lives, with the result that we just plan it instead of just do it. We have almost forgotten how to be free and spontaneous, to grasp the moment and immerse ourselves in the present like our dance-crazy medieval forebears. This is an astonishing cultural loss that amounts to a surreptitious hijacking of our seize-the-day souls.

Just Buy It: How Nike Taught Us to Seize the Credit Card

They don't wear balaclavas. They don't have guns or issue ransom notes. You know them by their clever aliases – 'brand strategist', 'planner', 'creative' and 'e-commerce manager'. Yes, it's the advertising and marketing industry. And they are out to hijack your carpe diem.

Since the rise of psychoanalysis in the 1920s, the brains behind the brands – along with psychologists in their pay – have attempted to trigger our emotions, stimulate our unconscious desires and spark our psyches so that we buy more stuff and fuel our turbo-charged consumer culture. One of the most potent strategies used by the hijackers has been to create environments and messaging that tap into our seize-the-day instincts. Shopping is deliberately structured to encourage the human propensity for impulsive behaviour and the desire for instant gratification that exist alongside our more risk-averse and cautious selves.

A good example is what marketing experts call 'store positioning'. At almost every supermarket checkout you will find snack foods, discount goods and celebrity gossip magazines, placed specifically to induce a seize-the-day impulse purchase. We are especially prone to this, argue psychologists, because an exhausting supermarket trip during which our brains often make hundreds of decisions as we go up and down the aisles can lead to what is known as 'decision fatigue'. By the time we reach the checkout, our limited store of willpower has gone and we just can't resist popping a chocolate bar into the cart. It's a case of seize the sugar.[16] These positioning strategies help explain why around 40% of people spend more than they had planned in stores, and one-third report making a sizeable impulse purchase every week, averaging $30 in value. In the United States, impulse buying generates over $4 billion in sales annually.[17]

Another method is the use of language designed to channel our carpe diem instincts by signalling windows of opportunity – what in marketing jargon is known as the 'scarcity sell'. Think of those sales signs blaring out 'While Supplies Last!', 'Going Out of Business Sale!' or the slogan 'When It's Gone It's Gone!' used by Tesco supermarkets and other retailers (by the way, red and yellow signs apparently work best). The invention of Black Friday has taken it all further, with frenzied crowds rushing into stores offering 'for one day only' mega sales.

These strategies are far from new, and go back to the emergence of seasonal sales in department stores such as Selfridges, Macy's and Bon Marché after World War One.[18] The founder of Selfridges, Harry Gordon Selfridge, would be impressed by the way today's technology has transformed retailing and created new opportunities for impulse buying. How many of us can resist the quick and easy convenience of online shopping and the temptations of that one-click button, with the added bonus of super-fast delivery options? One need look no further than Amazon's extraordinary sales statistics for evidence. More than 304 million people worldwide now have Amazon accounts, while the number of Amazon Prime customers – who pay a premium for high-speed shipping and other benefits – has reached 54 million in the US alone, with each of them spending on average $1100 per year.[19]

Shopping both online and offline can often feel like an exciting or spontaneous seize-the-day experience, although I doubt whether Horace wrote Ode XI to inspire us to get a bargain down at the Forum. Yet this only touches the surface of the way that consumer culture hijacks the carpe diem ideal. To explore how this happens at a deeper, more systemic level, it's worth looking at the ultimate just-do-it company: Nike.

Throughout the 1980s Nike was losing ground against its corporate rival Reebok, which was dominating the booming aerobics and fitness market. But between 1988 and 1998 Nike managed to turn the tables, increasing its share of the US sports-shoe business from 18% to 43%, and boosting worldwide sales from $877 million to $9.2 billion. Within just ten years – and despite vigorous campaigning against its reliance on sweatshop labour – the company convinced millions of people to start wearing sports shoes and athletics clothing not simply for jogging or playing basketball, but as everyday fashion items. By the early 1990s the average American owned four pairs of athletics shoes, and the typical boy had more than double that number.[20] An estimated 80% of Nike sneakers were never used for the activities for which they were designed: they were worn far more to pad around shopping malls than to race on running tracks.[21]

How did Nike manage this spectacular marketing achievement? The key was their new carpe diem advertising slogan: Just Do It. Launched in 1988 and still going strong today, Just Do It is regularly rated as one of the most successful brand campaigns of all time. Targeted not only at athletic males – the focus of Nike's early advertising strategy – the new campaign sought to attract everyone from working women and pot-bellied dads to insecure teenagers and high-style fashionistas. The slogan cleverly tapped into both the emerging obsession with personal health as well as an expanding desire for personal growth in every aspect of life. Using celebrity sporting heroes like Michael Jordan covered with the Nike swoosh logo, it sent the message that whoever you are and whatever you do, with grit and determination you can overcome the odds and achieve greatness. Soon posters could be found in gyms, college dorms and workplaces, showing a runner on a country road accompanied by the message: 'There are clubs you can't belong to, neighborhoods you can't live in, schools you can't get into, but the road is always open. Just do it.'[22] The advertising campaign not only enthused couch potatoes to take up marathon running, but sparked some people to leave their abusive relationships, and even attempt heroic rescues from burning buildings.[23] And of course it sold a lot of shoes: by the turn of the millennium Nike was selling around 100 million pairs a year.[24] Just Do It had become Just Buy It.

The genius of Nike's strategy was that it was not ingenious at all. It was simply based on one of the mainstays of the growth of consumer capitalism, which has been to link the act of shopping with the transformation of the self. For nearly a century advertising has focused on selling us not just products but lifestyle aspirations and the promise of personal change.[25] Forget Gandhi's advice to be the change you want to see in the world – advertising convinces us to buy the change we want to see in ourselves. By paying $100 for a pair of shoes, you too could reinvent who you are, becoming faster, stronger, more successful, and better than the rest. You could become just a little bit like Michael Jordan, Tiger Woods or Maria Sharapova. That's an almost irresistible bargain. This kind of celebrity-led strategy certainly worked on me. I remember getting my first pair of Nike tennis shoes as an aspiring junior player, and not just experiencing a feeling of athletic speed and lightness but literally feeling *more confident* – as if I could step in and return serve like my Nike-sponsored idol John McEnroe.

By offering a formula for refashioning the self, Nike's strategy – like all advertising that invites us to reinvent who we are, whether through the clothes we wear or the car we drive – drew a growing share of our life choices into the realm of material consumption. This was part of a larger cultural process evident since the 1970s in which we increasingly sought out self-esteem, social recognition, personal expression and a sense of belonging through our consumer purchases. A new philosophy of life was starting to dominate Western society: I shop, therefore I am. The cultural critic John Berger commented on this development in his 1972 book and documentary film *Ways of Seeing*:

> Publicity is not merely an assembly of competing images: it is a language in itself which is always being used to make the same general proposal. Within publicity, choices are offered between this cream and that cream, that car and this car, but publicity as a system only makes a single proposal. It proposes to each of us that we transform ourselves, or our lives, by buying something more.[26]

The consequences for seizing the day have been devastating. If we accept consumerism as a key to self-transformation, then this is where we are likely to focus more and more of our carpe diem energies. In doing so, we end up turning our backs on life experiences that cannot be easily found in retail outlets or online shopping emporiums. As the social commentator George Monbiot puts it: 'How many [of our ancestors] would have guessed that people possessed of unimaginable wealth and leisure and liberty would spend their time shopping for onion goggles and wheatgrass juicers? Man was born free, and he is everywhere in chainstores.'[27]

For the first time in history, shopping has become one of our most popular leisure activities, so instead of seizing the day we're busy seizing the credit card.[28] Consumer culture has crowded out a huge range of vibrant, exciting and potentially meaningful pursuits: not only epic personal adventures like mountain climbing, but also more everyday experiences like joining a jive class or playing Ultimate Frisbee with friends. And what has consumerism replaced these with? A bland version of liberty that redefines freedom as a choice between brands. In the 1990s it was Nike or Reebok. Today it is more likely Nike or Adidas, iPhone or Samsung, or that old favourite dilemma of Coke or Pepsi.[29] As our attention gets distracted by a daily assault of billboard advertising, pop-up ads and TV commercials, we begin to lose touch with what is really valuable in life, and our seize-the-day vitality becomes enmeshed in a multitude of relatively trivial choices.

Now wait a moment. Isn't this just a rehashing of the old Marxist critique of consumer capitalism that we are all dupes whose minds are manipulated by clever and devious marketing executives who in effect make our purchasing decisions for us, devise cunning ways to tap into our impulsive instincts, and get us to buy things we don't really need? Aren't there very good and relatively innocent reasons why we might want to buy a pair of Nike sneakers – because, for instance, they are a superior product, and we need them to go running? And what's wrong with buying stuff anyway if it makes you feel good about yourself?

I happen to think that critics like John Berger and George Monbiot are largely correct. Nobody really believes the official industry line that advertising is a neutral medium that simply provides us with objective information to help us make better choices. Marketing and brand specialists are incredibly successful at creating needs we never knew we had and getting us to buy their products – does anyone really need onion goggles? The reason they spend billions of dollars on advertising each year, and hire in psychologists as highly paid consultants, is because it works. Few of us like to admit that we are personally prone to their tactics. We wish to believe that our consumer choices are of our own free will

Consumerism redefines freedom as a choice between brands.

and reflect our personal aesthetic. So you decide to buy that great art deco lampshade or new armchair with the 1960s retro look you really love. But then why do remarkably similar items appear in the homes of three of your friends? Because the brains behind the brands have made some of our choices on our behalves. We call it, somewhat innocently, fashion.

I'm certainly not saying that all our consumer purchases are the product of psychological manipulation – quality, convenience, beauty and sheer usefulness dictate much of what we buy. Your iPhone not only looks cool but allows you to find your way when you're lost, get an emergency pick-up when your car breaks down, or film your child taking her first tottering steps. The point, however, is that there is more hidden persuasion going on than we think.[30] Anyone who is serious about carpe diem needs to step back and consider the ways their life is shaped by consumer society, and not succumb to the comforting belief that everyone but themselves is influenced by it.

As the merry-go-round of commerce keeps turning, and we spend more and more of our lives working hard to buy all the things that we believe will bring us happiness, we should stop to think about whether seizing the credit card or the shopping trolley is really the best way to seize the day. We might wish to bask in the pleasures of consumer choice. But what is the value of being able to choose amongst sixty-three models of Nike Air Max shoes (yes, sixty-three), seventeen types of coffee at a corporate coffee chain, or over thirty kinds of garden spade on Amazon? Is this the kind of freedom that really matters? The great tragedy we must face is that, over the past century, our lives have been increasingly enveloped by a culture of consumer-infused carpe diem where the way we just do it is to just buy it. It's time to break free of the chain stores.

JUST WATCH IT: HOW THE PLEASURES OF TELEVISION PRODUCED AN ERA OF PROXY LIVING

I loved television as a kid, fitting in an hour before school each day (*Thunderbirds*, *Superheroes*) and at least an hour-and-a-half before dinner (5.30: *Wheel of Fortune*, 6.00: *The Goodies*, 6.30: *Dr Who*). Ask people what they get out of it, and you will receive a variety of answers that help explain why it is the most popular leisure pursuit in the Western world. It helps us relax and unwind after a stressful day at work. It offers an escape into inaccessible worlds: the romance of a period drama, the excitement of an action thriller, an adventurous trek through the jungles of Borneo. It's a cure for loneliness, especially for the elderly and isolated. Exhausted parents know that it's a great way to keep the kids quiet while they make dinner or put their feet up for half an hour. Families can bond in front of the set, chatting and catching up during the ads. And viewers can find plenty of programmes that are educational and informative: news, nature shows, history documentaries.[31]

What I didn't realise as a teenager, as I sat on my beanbag in suburban Sydney making the agonising decision whether to break tradition and watch *Gilligan's Island* instead of *The Goodies*, was that I was absorbed in a ritual that ranks as one of the most momentous cultural transformations ever experienced by humankind. Within less than fifty years of the first ever television demonstration in Selfridges department store in London in 1925, around 99% of Western households had a set in their homes. Today the typical European or American watches an average of around three hours per day, whether it's on flat screen TVs, computers, phones or other devices (most people, by the way, greatly underestimate how much they actually watch). This is apart from time spent engaged in digital pursuits such as internet surfing, social media, texting or video games. So television takes up a full 50% of our leisure time, and more time than we spend doing any other single activity apart from work or sleep.[32] Perhaps the best way to grasp how much TV has colonised our lives is to tape the following statistic to your remote control: assuming your viewing habits are somewhere near average, if you live to seventy-five, you will have spent around *nine years* of your life watching television.

Let me try that again. Imagine being on your deathbed, gazing back at your life – the successes and failures, the loves, the regrets, the good times and bad. Nearly a decade of it will have been spent staring at the tube. I doubt many of us will look back and treasure the memories of watching reruns of *The Big Bang Theory*.

In a digital world of smartphones and iPads, you might have thought that television no longer retains such a hold on our lives, and if there is anything that threatens to hijack carpe diem, it is more likely to be all that time we spend fiddling with our phones and checking our social media feeds. But the time-use data reveals that TV remains by far the dominant force in our 24/7 digital existence. According to one of the most detailed studies of how much time US adults spend using different electronic devices, 12% of the daily total is using a smartphone, 9% on a PC, 4% with a tablet and 18% listening to the radio. And the figure that dwarfs them all? Television, at 51%, which we watch at scheduled times and for which we increasingly use 'on demand' or 'catch-up' services.[33] It is true that people aged eighteen to thirty-five tend to watch less TV than the average, and that much of the time people are watching they are also multitasking on other devices. But in general, even those addicted to checking their phones end up giving a sizeable chunk of each day to John Logie Baird's wondrous invention of television. As a seminal report on teenage media use concluded, 'even in this new media world, television viewing – of one form or another – continues to dominate media consumption.'[34]

So here's the question we need to ask: How does the absolutely staggering amount of time we grant to watching TV – however and wherever we do it – impact on our capacity to seize the day?

Ever since it became a globally dominant cultural force in the 1970s, television has attracted serious critiques. Does TV violence breed violence in society? Is corporate media distorting the news? Are fast food commercials turning our kids into obese junk-food addicts? Most criticism and debate has concerned the content. My interest, however, is in the medium itself rather than the message.

If I were to ask you to seize the day, right here and now, it is unlikely that you would switch on the television and start flicking through the channels. Most people recognise TV is a step removed from real-life experience. Carpe diem is about seizing experiences for yourself, not gazing at others seizing them on a screen. There is a big difference between going to a tango class and watching celebrities tango on *Strictly Come Dancing*. Similarly, your palms might sweat watching an exciting tennis match on TV, but it's nothing like the sweat you get from running around a court yourself.

This point was powerfully made in the classic 1978 book *Four*

Arguments for the Elimination of Television, written by the former TV advertising executive Jerry Mander. 'In one generation, out of hundreds of thousands in human evolution,' he wrote, 'America had become the first culture to have substituted secondary, mediated versions of experience for direct experience of the world.'[35] Mander was keen to emphasise that mediated experience was not in itself a new development. With the expansion of literacy in the eighteenth century, for instance, books became a major conduit through which we gained knowledge or were entertained. But in Mander's view, television submerged us in artificial environments like never before, accelerating the spread of mediated experience and ushering in a new age of proxy living. It became normal to sit in front of a screen and spend a substantial portion of each day watching other people live their lives – or actors pretending to be other people – instead of living our own. In historical terms, this was nothing short of bizarre.

Wasn't Mander going too far by branding television as an artificial activity distinct from genuine life experience? It is certainly true that watching TV is an experience of sorts. We engage our senses (at least our eyes and ears), and it can be a communal pastime – like when we go to a bar to watch a World Cup final or the Super Bowl. Also, due to digital recording and streaming technology, we now actively choose what to watch and when to watch it more than ever before.

In general, however, it is an unusually passive way of engaging with life. Sure, we might sometimes press a button that allows us to vote in a reality TV show, but most of the time we are just gazing at the screen, interrupted by snatched conversation during commercial breaks or sending a quick text to a friend. Unlike many other digital activities such as Skyping with your mum or playing online Scrabble against your best friend who lives in a different city, television offers little scope for participation or interaction, placing it at the far end of the spectrum of passive experience.

TV might be a great way to relax, it might make you laugh or cry, and it can certainly be more informative or enlightening than scrolling through Facebook updates. But it is a poor surrogate for the pulsating sense of aliveness and active engagement that is the essence of seizing the day. We experience the world filtered through a prism of electronic flickers of light, through a two-dimensional model of reality created for us by sitcoms, news features, cartoons, crime series and reality TV programmes (which, as we all know, are full of fabricated moments and artificially induced drama). As the cultural critic Guy Debord prophetically put it in the late 1960s, we have immersed ourselves in a 'society of the spectacle' where 'everything that was directly lived has moved away into a representation'.[36] Well, not everything. Only nine years of it.

For all the pleasures that television brings, it is difficult to avoid the conclusion that the sheer volume of second-hand experience that has come to occupy most people's lives – irrespective of class, race, gender or age – represents a colossal hijacking of our carpe diem potential. While our medieval ancestors threw themselves into Carnival, we are now satisfied with watching a thirty-minute documentary about it. What is more, the three hours we dedicate to TV each day robs us of precious time that we could be using to do a multitude of other activities, whether it is learning to play the ukulele, training your dog to catch a frisbee, doing a daily meditation session, or inventing a new kind of solar panel in your back shed. You are unlikely to make much progress in any of these if your default evening activity is settling down in front of the television. Would history's greatest carpe diem adventurers, from Marco Polo to Amelia Earhart, have been TV addicts? I doubt it. They were addicted to the heady business of experiential living (though I'm sure Marco Polo would have been blogging and tweeting on his journeys).

Might not a travel show inspire us to embark on a cycling expedition across the Sahara, or a creative children's programme show kids how to make a fort out of lollipop sticks?[37] Can't TV motivate us to get up off the sofa and propel ourselves into life? Yes... but only occasionally. Decades of research shows that television generally acts as an experiential soporific. Switching on the TV tends to switch us off from so much else. For a start, it's bad news for our sex life: people with a television set in their bedroom have half as much sex as those who don't.[38] It makes us less active: heavy TV viewers tend to do less sport or physical exercise, especially if they are women.[39] High television consumption is associated with low levels of civic and political engagement, for example in volunteering, voting and protesting.[40] And it isn't great for kids: pre-schoolers who spend lots of time looking at screens spend less time in creative play and constructive problem-solving.[41]

One other small point I forgot to mention: television will kill you. During the course of my research I came across a startling article in the respected *British Journal of Sports Medicine* that concluded: 'On average, every single hour of TV viewed after the age of 25 reduces the viewer's life expectancy by 21.8 minutes'.[42] If anything was going to stop you seizing the day – or doing anything else – it would be premature death. But could this statistic possibly be true? Was watching an hour of *Sherlock* a veritable death sentence? What I discovered was a whole field of public health research, based on the study of tens of thousands of people, proving over and again that TV viewing, and other forms of sedentary behaviour such as sitting at a computer all day, go hand in hand with increased risk of death, particularly from cardiovascular disease. Experts in preventative medicine are starting to recognise that human beings simply aren't designed for long periods of sitting still. Doing so may, for instance, have a detrimental effect on how our bodies process fats and other substances, leading to greater risk of serious heart problems.[43]

The curious thing about the above arguments is that they are unlikely to convince you to watch less television. The reason is that TV has such powerful addictive qualities. People can have a strong sense that they should be watching less but find themselves unable to reduce their viewing time: surveys reveal that 40% of adults and 70% of teenagers say they watch too much TV, and 10% of adults describe themselves as addicts. Researchers in Germany found that people who try to resist the urge to watch television fail around half the time, and are much better at resisting the desire to nap or snack. Other studies show that the longer people watch, the less enjoyment they get from it – yet they don't have the willpower to switch it off even if the programme is boring.[44] Think how many times you've come to the end of a programme or film and thought to yourself, 'Why did I just waste my time watching that junk?' It happens to me more often than I'd like to admit.

Simultaneously stimulating and relaxing, watching television develops into an almost physiological craving: we become desperate for an injection on a daily basis.[45] The addictive nature of television makes it disconcertingly similar to the happy drug soma used to dope up the inhabitants of Aldous Huxley's *Brave New World*.

Of course we all need regular doses of relaxation. But might there not be other ways of relieving tension and anxiety – like a massage from your lover (if you can get it) or a long candlelit bath (if you can't)? Isn't it more fun to laugh with your friends than with the studio audience on TV? Aren't there better ways of keeping up with world events than an evening news programme that offers only a handful of two-minute stories that are carefully selected for their visual interest, dramatic content and 'packagability' as much as newsworthiness?[46] Wouldn't we be better off engaging in activities involving some skill or effort (from gardening to woodworking), which research reveals to provide far more satisfaction than watching TV?[47] Ultimately, is it really worth granting nine years of our precious existence to the second-hand pleasures of television when we might be having more direct experience of the world?

I'm not suggesting that we ought to abandon television entirely. Ever since the ancient Greeks invented public theatre, human beings have loved being entertained – that's why I've just binged on the superb six-part BBC drama *Wolf Hall*. TV can be far more than entertainment too: I'm sure I learned a lot more about American society from watching *The Wire* than reading a bunch of sociology textbooks, and I wouldn't want to give up the holy father–son bonding ritual of watching test cricket with my dad. But if we hope to bring more carpe diem into our lives, there may be no more obvious action to take than this: cut back the television hours and win back the seize-the-day opportunities that have been hijacked from us.

While television remains dominant in our increasingly screen-based lives, other forms of digital media also pose challenges for carpe diem living. We may need to devise strategies to regulate our exposure to all of them. Some people put themselves on a digital diet, using apps such as Anti-Social, which switches off access to tempting websites you specify such as YouTube, Facebook or Netflix. Others go cold-turkey by using Freedom, which turns off internet connectivity completely for a set time period. When it comes to the television set, you could try keeping it in a cupboard at the top of the house and only bring it out if you really want to watch something (it's an extreme measure, but it worked for me). A less eccentric option would be to ration yourself a set number of viewing hours each week.

The evidence suggests that one of the best ways to break the habit is to write down a list of easily available and enjoyable non-TV activities that you can consult each time you are about to perform the reflex action of switching on the television.[48] Stick them to the screen with a Post-it note if necessary. It will force you into making a genuine choice: is watching this programme what I really want to be doing with my life at this very moment (it could well be) – or is there some better alternative? This strategy sounds almost too artificial, but it could be the first tiny but significant step toward a life driven by a new habit: to just do it instead of just watch it. Dust off that ukulele and get ready to play.

THE ILLUSION OF CHOICE

So consumer culture, TV and digital media are hijacking our drive to seize the day – and we hardly even notice. How could we be so blind to this major existential crime? One reason is that we are bombarded with cultural messaging telling us that we live in an era of unprecedented choice. Experts ranging from economists and technology gurus to marketing professors and psychologists claim that greater choice is a defining characteristic of our times.[49] In some ways they are right. When I do my weekly online supermarket shop there are over 1,600 organic items alone that I can click on, while digital TV has exponentially expanded our range of viewing options, and the advent of cheap flights has opened the frontiers of travel to millions.

This apparent abundance of choices gives us the feeling that the possibilities for seizing the day have expanded too. If the range of pathways has multiplied and we have more freedom, then it stands to reason that there is more scope for being experimental with our choices, travelling in new directions and deciding to live in the moment.

But in truth, our age of choice is an illusion of near-mythic proportions. Due to the hijacking we've been looking at, in some of the most vital realms of life our choices have diminished, disappeared or been manipulated and trivialised into insignificance.

How can we win back carpe diem and outsmart the hijackers in the process? The trick here is not to approach our assailants head on by directly attempting to fight the cult of efficiency, overthrow the juggernaut of consumerism or eradicate our addiction to television. These would be losing battles. A wiser and defter strategy is to put something better in their place so that we are positively drawn to alternative choices and ways of living. We must create a picture of what seizing the day could really look like in today's world – an image of carpe diem to which we can aspire. It is time to turn to the five key ways that humanity has discovered over the centuries to seize the day: opportunity, hedonism, presence, spontaneity and politics. Their inspiration is our greatest hope for disarming the hijackers and reclaiming our freedoms.

4

The Art of Seizing Opportunities

Remember Bernard Jordan, the intrepid eighty-nine-year-old navy veteran who broke out of his care home to celebrate the seventieth anniversary of the D-Day landings? His daring escape to the beaches of Normandy was the perfect carpe diem crime. It also represented a very specific type of seizing the day: grasping a momentary window of opportunity that may pass and be lost forever. Since the eighteenth century, this has been the dominant meaning of carpe diem in popular culture, and far more common than alternatives like the pursuit of hedonistic pleasures or the ambition to live in the present moment.[1] Our language is now peppered with expressions that urge us to take the fleeting chances that life offers, from 'seize the opportunity' and 'opportunity knocks' to 'window of opportunity' and 'lost opportunity'.

Appropriately enough, given Bernard's seafaring background, the word 'opportunity' itself has maritime origins. It comes from the Latin phrase *ob portum veniens*, meaning 'coming toward a port', and referred to a favourable wind that would blow a ship into harbour. So we can think of an opportunity as a good wind blowing to our advantage. We are in the right place at the right time. The question is whether we are going to hoist our sails, point them in the appropriate direction and catch this propitious wind. And can we overcome our fear that in doing so we may not be brought safely into port, but dashed upon the rocks?

If we wanted a name for a person intent on taking opportunities and jumping at the now-or-never, the obvious contender would be 'opportunist'. Yet this is a term overlaid with negative connotations, typically referring to someone who takes advantage of situations – and of other people – for their own egoistic ends. It originally emerged from nineteenth-century Italian politics and the idea of *opportunismo*, where an opportunist was someone who was willing to give up their principles in the interest of political expediency.

It is curious that we don't have more positive, or at least neutral, terms to describe those whose lives are strongly driven by a carpe diem mentality of seizing opportunities, so in this chapter I will introduce six character types that capture some of the important ways that people do so. Alongside the self-seeking opportunist there is the experimentalist, the death gazer, the daredevil, the role breaker and the revolutionary. Each has their own motivations, worldviews and strategies. What they share is a talent for making choices – not the trivial choices we make at department store sales, but the more substantive decisions that provide existential sustenance and have the potential to take our lives in new directions. They are at the forefront of challenging the hijack of carpe diem by forces such as consumer culture. Through the choices they make, they set their sights on adventurous sailing that, though full of dangers, may blow them into unknown and even exotic harbours.

How to Wing It as a Nightclub Dancer

If there was a single thread running through the life of Maya Angelou it was her carpe diem approach to living. In her later years Angelou was best known as a writer and poet – a distinguished African-American woman-of-letters with over fifty honorary degrees. But by the age of forty, as she revealed in her seven volumes of autobiography, she had already had an astonishing range of jobs, including short-order cook, waitress, prostitute, madam (running a lesbian whorehouse, aged just eighteen), tram attendant, nightclub singer and dancer, actress, theatre director, political organiser for Martin Luther King and Malcolm X, journalist and newspaper editor in Egypt and Ghana, and TV script writer.

Maya Angelou, 1957. Amongst her many carpe diem careers was inventing herself as a nightclub dancer.

She lived with passion and verve, not only pursuing a huge array of careers, but constantly moving to new cities and countries, throwing herself into politics and love affairs, drinking plenty of whisky, and generally daring greatly until her death in 2014, aged eighty-six. 'Life loves the liver of it,' was her great mantra, which was not just about recognising windows of opportunity, but making a courageous effort to open those windows and walk right through them.[2] She was an 'experimentalist', someone who viewed life as a smorgasbord of possibilities and experiences there for the tasting, even when it involved risk and the prospect of failure.

Angelou elevated seizing opportunities into an art form. On seeing an advertisement for a Creole cook paying $75 a week, she waltzed in and announced she was an expert Creole chef despite having no experience whatsoever. When she chanced upon a man looking for someone to join his dance act, she pretended to have a professional dancing pedigree in order to land the job. Determined to make a career in showbiz, she heard about an opening as a singer at a San Francisco nightclub, and invented herself as a Cuban Calypso singer, having only ever sung in her church choir as a young girl (and she wasn't Cuban either).[3] Over and over again, Angelou took her chances and plunged herself into new jobs and experiences with a bravado that few of us possess.

A century of sociological research tells us that opportunity and privilege go hand in hand. There are relatively few opportunities – especially in the world of work – for those living on the social margins compared to people with financial means, expensive educations and good social connections. True enough: get yourself a degree from Harvard or Oxford and doors will open, especially if you are white and male. But Angelou's story adds nuance, revealing how even in conditions of poverty and adversity it can be possible to develop a carpe diem approach to living founded on seizing opportunities. Especially in her early life, she took opportunities as a matter of utter necessity rather than choice. Having grown up in a small town in Arkansas surrounded by everyday racism and prejudice, at the age of seventeen she found herself as a single mother with a child and having to make a living. So from that early age she grabbed every opportunity that came her way. 'The birth of my son,' she recalled, 'caused me to develop the courage to invent my life.'[4] As time went on, Angelou realised that her carpe diem outlook, originally motivated by the need to make ends meet, was actually giving her an incredibly vibrant existence. She came to cherish the freedom and excitement it offered, especially after getting married for the first time and discovering her distaste for domesticity. 'My life began to resemble a *Good Housekeeping* advertisement,' Angelou lamented.[5] She soon got out of it.

Yet for all the freedom she enjoyed, seizing opportunities did not come without costs. At the age of twenty-six, Angelou was suddenly offered a dream job to tour Europe as a dancer in a production of *Porgy and Bess*. With only four days' notice, she followed the call of carpe diem and left the United States, venturing abroad for a year. But to do so, she also had to leave behind her nine-year-old son to live with his grandmother. Her son was psychologically scarred by this enforced separation, which left Angelou consumed by guilt. Throughout his childhood he had to face the insecurities of his mother's freewheeling life that resulted in him attending nineteen different schools over a period of eleven years.[6] It is a reminder that seizing the day can be accompanied by serious collateral damage, not just for the person doing the seizing, but for the people who are touched by their decisions. Every choice comes with an inescapable responsibility.

There is no doubt that Maya Angelou had extraordinary courage and confidence, but she was quick to point out that most people have a capacity for daring once they recognise that the skills required for almost any career or activity can be learned on the job through determination and application. When offered a position as a newspaper editor in Cairo, she learned from others how to pen opinion pieces. Similarly, when asked to write a ten-part TV documentary on African-American culture, she took it on, believing that she could teach herself to write film scripts from books. 'With time and a kindly librarian, any unskilled person can learn how to build a replica of the Taj Mahal,' she wrote.[7] It's an inspiring idea, though one which surely risks having the building crumble around us.

There was, however, another secret to her carpe diem courage: Angelou became an expert at 'winging it' – a term that originally referred to actors who played a role without fully knowing their lines and received prompts from the wings of the stage.[8] She was regularly out of her depth and bluffing her way through her many roles. Sometimes she failed and fell flat on her face, but mostly she didn't and managed to make a success of her endeavours. There is good evidence that many more people are actually winging it in their jobs than we realise, from politicians and business professionals to civil servants and journalists.[9] While there are plenty of genuine experts around, there are just as many people who are secretly improvising and operating on the very edge of competence. This can be a frightening thought, but also a potentially liberating one. We might all join the ranks of those who are just winging it, and release more of our experimentalist side on the world.

THE WOMAN WITH THE CARPE DIEM TATTOO

Anyone who sees the 1971 cult film *Harold and Maude* would want to spend at least one day of their life with Maude. While Harold is a morbid, lost, wealthy young man struggling to find meaning in his existence, Maude is a free-spirited seventy-nine-year-old who lives with passionate abandon. She breaks into pet shops and liberates the canaries. She steals people's cars and drives them recklessly to beautiful hilltops where she frolics in the sunshine. She works as a nude model. She goes on the most hair-raising rides at the amusement park. She lives in a cluttered old railway car that looks like a pawn shop, full of banjos, flowers, sculptures, a portrait of herself making love with a swan, and an olfactory machine that pumps out the smell of snow in New York City.

They meet while engaged in a favourite pastime they share: attending the funerals of strangers. Maude's vivacious and extrovert approach to life blows Harold's introspective, self-obsessed world apart. 'I'm always looking for the new experience,' says Maude. 'Try something new each day. After all, we're given life to find it out. It doesn't last forever'.[10] Harold becomes infected by her lust for living. Together they kidnap a small tree dying of city smog and drive it – chased by the police – to a lush forest, where they replant it and give it new life in a gesture that serves as a metaphor for the film itself. As they fall in love – defying their six-decade age gap – they sing Cat Stevens's carpe diem anthem, 'If You Want to Sing Out, Sing Out'.

Where does Maude's extraordinary appetite for life come from? It remains a mystery for most of the film, but toward the end her secret is revealed. Some people miss it on first viewing. The couple are watching a sublime sunset together. Harold reaches down to take Maude's hand and for the briefest instant he sees a number tattooed on her arm: P-876854. It may be the most subtle yet powerful Holocaust moment in film history. Maude is a survivor of the death camps.

Maude is an example of a death gazer, someone who decides to seize the day after coming face to face with death. The encounter with their mortality wakes them up to the possibilities of human existence, helps them rethink what is really important, and compels them to seize opportunities and live life to the fullest. It can happen when someone discovers they have a terminal illness, but may also occur following a near-death experience – like surviving a car accident.

Are death gazers like Maude unusual in their response to death? Not at all. Psychologists have a name for it: 'post-traumatic growth'.

This expanding field of research looks at how traumatic events, particularly close shaves with death, can have a positive impact on people's lives. One of the major findings is that such events are more likely to trigger growth experiences than result in psychiatric disorders such as depression.[11] Some people become more caring and empathic, while others have spiritual awakenings. But one of the most prevalent effects is that it induces a carpe diem zest for life. People abandon their tedious jobs, embark on bonding travel adventures with their children or, like Maude, dedicate themselves to taking chances and squeezing every ounce of experience out of being alive. While for many individuals – perhaps around half – the traumatic event has no major impact on how they choose to live, for others it is a major turning point.[12]

A study of over 200 people who had survived life-threatening dangers such as drowning, traffic accidents, mountain climbing falls and serious illness revealed that around one in four of them developed a sense of the preciousness of life and a desire to live more fully, reassess their priorities and take more risks (including in social relationships).[13] Gazing at death made them realise that life was short and that they had been taking it for granted. A similar message appeared in a recent viral YouTube video featuring a woman who was diagnosed with brain cancer and given six months to live. 'Seize the day,' she urged. 'What's important to you? What do you care about? What matters? Pursue that. Forget the rest.'[14] Maude would surely have agreed.

Occasionally post-traumatic growth happens on a mass scale. The Roaring Twenties, known as a period of wild and exuberant living, flowered as a response to the horrors of World War One. Millions of soldiers had seen the face of death on an unimaginable scale in the trenches, and witnessed their compatriots suffer and die before their eyes. 'Here was a new generation,' wrote F. Scott Fitzgerald in *This Side of Paradise*, 'grown up to find all Gods dead, all wars fought, all faiths in man shaken'. The result was an outbreak of carpe diem vitality, where grabbing new opportunities and live-for-the-moment hedonism were the rule of the day.

Not everyone, however, was partying during the Jazz Age. Just as some 20% of US soldiers returning from Iraq and Afghanistan today suffer from post-traumatic stress disorder, World War One veterans had their own version, referred to with the inadequate term 'shell shock'. Many never recovered.[15]

So gazing at death can be a mixed blessing. But if, like Maude, you can psychologically survive the ordeal, it may open your mind to a new possibility: that life is not only full of individual moments of opportunity, but is itself a window of opportunity that flashes into existence just once and is there for the taking. After all, as Maude says, we're given life to find it out.

THE ADDICTIVE THRILL OF BEING SHOT AT

Vietnam, Cambodia, Congo, El Salvador, Uganda, Biafra, Northern Ireland, Lebanon, the Six-Day War. In a career spanning more than thirty years, British photographer Don McCullin took extraordinary risks with his life to cover some of the world's most dangerous conflicts. His images of the horrors and suffering of war, mainly published in the *Sunday Times Magazine* from the late 1960s to the early 1980s, were etched on the minds of a generation. He didn't go to Vietnam just once. He went more than fifteen times, somehow dodging the bullets as soldiers got blown to pieces around him, wading through canals filled with bloated corpses, and sleeping in rat-infested holes as sniper fire honed in on him. In Cambodia, under attack from the Khmer Rouge, he escaped with his life when an AK-47 bullet wedged itself into his Nikon F camera, just millimetres from his skull. In Uganda, he was imprisoned by Idi Amin's feared security forces and was lucky to be deported after four days while dozens of people in the surrounding cells were brutally executed.

McCullin approached photography as a carpe diem craft. His ambition was to seize opportunities to capture – with a click of his camera – fleeting moments of violence, terror, poverty, and sometimes love and comradeship. A man playing the mandolin over the body of a dead girl in Lebanon. A soldier throwing a grenade like an Olympic athlete, an instant before being shot. To catch the wind of opportunity, McCullin travelled to some of the most volatile and perilous places on the planet, drawn by an uncanny instinct that deposited him in the right place at the right time. In 1961 he sensed that Berlin was going to explode and immediately went there, arriving just in time for the Berlin Wall crisis, which became a turning point in the Cold War. Upon setting foot in a conflict zone he usually headed straight for 'where the close combat seemed to be at its bloodiest'.[16] In the Congo, he disguised himself as a mercenary to reach the killing fields of Stanleyville and could easily have been put in front of a firing squad when his high-risk deception was discovered by a local military commander. All in an effort to get the best pictures.

Don McCullin at an exhibition of his own war photographs, 2005.

McCullin was a seize-the-day daredevil, someone whose efforts to create and grasp opportunities involve courting death and danger. This contrasts with the death gazer, whose carpe diem mentality is born from an accidental or undesired encounter with death, rather than a willed intention to dance with it. But what drives a daredevil like McCullin? What rewards could possibly make it worthwhile to take such extreme risks? He describes it this way:

> When I go home and sleep in my own bed, I soon become restless… My wars, the way I've lived, is like an incurable disease. It is like the promise of a tremendous high and the certainty of a bad dream. It is something I both fear and love, but it's something I can't do without. I cannot do without the head-on collision with life I have when I am working.[17]

This is war as an addiction, a drug; the adrenalin rush that comes with danger and makes him feel fully alive. 'I wouldn't like to go through a year without being in a war,' he once said.[18] Although clearly driven by a humanitarian desire to expose the horrific reality of warfare, as well as a dose of career ambition, McCullin repeatedly uses the word 'excitement' to describe the attraction of his work. 'I thought it was an amazing kind of excitement to lay under a barrage of shells dropping on me or a sniper trying to get me,' he revealed in one interview.[19] Sometimes it would transform almost into a type of insanity. After two weeks in a deadly battle while embedded with US marines in Vietnam, 'in the end I became totally mad, free, running around like a tormented animal'.[20] The result was that he took some of his most celebrated photographs. For all his fame, the toll on his family life was severe. His first wife, Christine, always hated his job. 'Work was not only the enemy – it was the other woman, so to speak, as well,' he admitted. 'Christine was always there for me, but she couldn't win in the end.'[21] Their marriage eventually fell apart.

McCullin is long-retired and now haunted by what he witnessed in war, a living casualty of his own carpe diem drive. He is at the extreme end of the daredevil category, but is certainly not alone in his quest for excitement. Rock climbers, racing drivers, sky divers, polar explorers and many others take substantial risks in order to gain themselves a taste of intense aliveness. It is an ideal that goes back to pre-modern hunting culture, where the thrill of the chase – picture Native Americans pursuing bison herds on horseback across the Great Plains – was often just as much a reward as the meat it provided. As a carpe diem philosophy of life it may be best expressed by the high-wire walker Philippe Petit, who in 1974 traversed the forty-three metres between the Twin Towers in New York City on an inch-thick cable, devoid of any safety equipment:

> To me, it's really so simple, that life should be lived on the edge. You have to exercise rebellion. To refuse to tape yourself to the rules, to refuse your own success, to refuse to repeat yourself, to see every day, every year, every idea as a true challenge. Then you will live your life on the tightrope.[22]

Petit may encourage us to embrace risk as a part of life and not be afraid to take opportunities that induce fear and uncertainty. But don't we all naturally want to minimise risk and follow the safest path available? Not according to risk scholar John Adams. He argues that taking risks is part of what makes us human and that we all have an inbuilt 'need for excitement'. *Homo prudens*, zero-risk man, is just one element of our characters. '*Homo aleatorius* – dice man, gambling man, risk-taking man – also lurks in every one of us,' he writes. Even the most risk-averse person has it within themselves, having once been a toddler learning to walk, where each wobbling step was a gamble. And imagine a life without any risk whatsoever, whether in our relationships, at work or in our leisure activities. 'Too much certainty is boring, unrewarding and belittling,' says Adams.[23] It diminishes us and cossets us in a cotton-wool existence that robs us of the rewards of excitement and challenge.

This is not to say that we should all sign up to become tightrope walkers or war photographers, but that we ought to recognise that opportunities in life necessarily involve taking risks, and that too much caution might not be good for our existential health. It's a topic I will return to in a later chapter, when exploring the cognitive biases that draw us toward seeking security rather than risk. But for now it is worth recalling a phrase we often hear children saying to one another: 'I dare you'. Perhaps they understand something fundamental about the human condition and what makes us thrive, which many adults may have forgotten.

Having now met the daredevil, the death gazer and the experimentalist, it is time to announce the entrance of a fourth character who finds ways to catch the winds of opportunity: the role breaker.

PINK FLOYD AND THE FIRE-WALKING GRANNY

An ancient idea in Western social thought is to view society as a theatre in which human beings are like actors on a stage set, playing roles ranging from the comic to the tragic. This *theatrum mundi* tradition goes back to Plato and the idea that we resemble puppets whose lives are scripted by the Gods. Shakespeare developed the theme, declaring that 'all the world's a stage' on which each of us 'plays his part'. For the last half century sociologists specialising in 'role theory' have used the metaphor of social life as a drama to explore how we present ourselves to other people and get caught in particular narratives. This vision of ourselves as characters in a play resonates with the original meaning of the word 'person', which comes from the Latin *persona*, an actor's mask. We are all, in some sense, wearing masks.[24] And these masks, I believe, can affect our capacity to seize the day.

Stop for a moment and think of the different roles you play in daily life: the dutiful daughter, the perfect mother, the sober lawyer, the life of the party, the loyal friend, the sullen teenager, the maverick entrepreneur, the tortured artist, the good provider, the charming host, the chilled dude or the serious intellectual. You readily switch between roles, depending on whether you are at a work meeting, a stag night or playing with your children. Each role has its own socially recognised personality and expectations, and comes with specific ways of speaking, acting, body language, clothing and emotional expression. As the life of the party you're bubbly and chatty, telling jokes, filling up glasses and dragging people onto the dance floor. As the dutiful daughter you are the one who regularly visits your elderly mother in the care home (your siblings rarely bother). As the perfect mother you always put your kids before your career, and ensure they're looking immaculate for the visit to your in-laws. I know that when I go home to visit my parents in Sydney I quickly revert to an old childhood role in which I am uncharacteristically lazy and let my parents do most of the cooking and cleaning while I sit around watching more television than is good for me. It happens every time. And I'm forty-five.

There is nothing inherently wrong with playing roles, but it is important to notice when the roles start to play us. Over time, the different characters we inhabit sometimes seep into our unconscious, shaping the way we talk, think and act. A management consultant I met, who spent several years working at one of the world's top firms in his twenties, told me how his role began to take over his personality:

> I became completely trapped in the narrative of
> what it meant to be a management consultant. In

meetings when we were kickstarting a new project, I said what I was supposed to say about my personal development goals – 'in this project I want to be taking on more responsibility', things like that. Things that you didn't really believe or care about, but it was expected of you. Then like everyone else I started going skiing for my holidays, because that's what all the other consultants did. It was part of the image, being sporty and a bit macho. At first you know that you're playing a role but then the narrative becomes part of you and it all starts to become 'normal'.[25]

Similarly, someone playing the role of 'charming host' might typically greet people with a warm handshake and look them in the eye, ask them how their family is and chat amiably about holiday plans, while making sure not to reveal any personal distaste he might have for a particular guest and keeping any emotional turmoil going on in his life to himself. While the charming host would most likely deny that he is 'controlled' by his role and following a script, it is telling that an outside observer could probably predict most of this behaviour: it's the socially recognised formula of what a charming host does.

When such patterns of behaviour become so ingrained that we don't even notice them, an interesting question arises: How authentic are we being in the various roles we play? It was a question famously asked by Jean-Paul Sartre in his book *Being and Nothingness*, where he describes a café waiter who seems to be acting a role. His movements are exaggerated – he bends forward to his customers just a bit too eagerly – and his voice and facial expression are almost too solicitous. 'He is playing at being a waiter in a café,' writes Sartre, 'there is nothing there to surprise us.'[26] In other words, he is not really being himself. He is almost a caricature of a waiter. He is not free.

Most waiters I know are scarcely as fawning and role-bound as the Parisian variety encountered by Sartre, yet there is compelling evidence that social roles can powerfully shape our behaviour. Amongst the best-known examples of this is the Stanford Prison Experiment devised by the psychologist Philip Zimbardo in 1971. Twenty-four psychologically stable students were given roles of prison guard or prisoner in a mock jail, yet within just a few days the guards became sadistic (such as by physically abusing inmates) and the prisoners became acutely distressed, with some screaming or crying uncontrollably. It got so out of hand that the experiment had to be halted after only six days, rather than the planned two weeks. Although an extreme case, it is revealing of the way we readily internalise roles.[27]

But what does all this have to do with seizing the day? Allow Eve Hoare to explain. When in her seventies, she was interviewed for a project I ran in Oxford about how people change the course of their lives. 'The best years have been from the age of sixty to seventy,' she said. Why?

> I really grew, because when I was sixty-two I went on a life assessment course and suddenly realised I didn't know who I was. I had been the obedient child, worker, wife, teacher, mother. I was always my roles. It was a real shock.[28]

The training course involved physical challenges as well as offering tools for self-reflection. Participants had to descend several hundred feet down a steep cliff, cross a ravine, jump into the sea from about thirty feet, and do a fire-walk across twenty yards of burning coals. Eve, who eventually became an assistant on the course, did the fire-walk seven times. The real learning, though, was recognising that she had been playing roles that, on reflection, did not seem to be fully of her own choosing. From a young age she had been a dutiful carer for her unwell mother, and gave up a scholarship to study at Edinburgh University in order to look after her when she had a nervous breakdown. Eve became a shorthand typist, then a housewife for ten years, and later worked as a primary school teacher to support her family.

Following her revelation about roles, Eve's life began to open up and she started to seize the day with incredible vigour. She went to college and studied literature, took to writing poetry and painting, did volunteer work in Bosnia with children who had been injured in the war, and joined a friendship network to support terminally ill people.

> I came to realise that if you don't enjoy the way you live, you ought to change it straight away, which is why I retired from teaching... You can just see how some young people get the balance wrong, not realising they should make the most of their precious years. I feel I have a mission to make other people see that they should grab every opportunity there is, that life goes by so quickly.[29]

She likes to quote Pink Floyd's song 'Time', especially the part about how we can miss the starting gun in life. Eve Hoare took a long time to hear the starting gun, but once she did she sprinted. What broke the silence? Coming to understand how social roles had shaped her life, and limited her choices and personal vision. In the end, she became a role breaker and gave herself a new kind of freedom on a different stage.

THE MACHIAVELLIAN WAY TO SEIZE THE DAY

Amongst the most powerful cultural myths that emerged in the nineteenth century was the idea of the self-made man. One of its champions was Samuel Smiles, author of the 1859 bestseller *Self-Help*. Holding up figures such as Benjamin Franklin, he argued that success in life – whether as a businessman, politician, inventor or artist – was chiefly a matter of individual industry and application, perseverance and prudence, efficiency and self-improvement. 'The spirit of self-help is the root of all genuine growth in the individual,' wrote Smiles. 'Help from without is often enfeebling in its effect, but help from within invariably invigorates.'[30]

In what ways was it a myth? Look no further than the post-Civil War economic boom in the United States, in the decades immediately after Smiles published his book. The vast majority of those who achieved worldly success were not self-made but normally started with the advantages of wealth, education and social contacts: a study of 300 US textile, steel and railroad executives in the 1870s showed that 90% came from middle-class or upper-class families.[31] But it was also a myth that an essential ingredient of self-help success was to be what Smiles called a man of 'noble character' who embodied 'truthfulness, integrity and goodness'.[32] In reality, an overriding character trait of those who managed to rise to the top of the financial heap was that they were seize-the-day opportunists who were perfectly prepared to lie, bribe, steal, exploit and bend the rules in order to amass their personal fortunes. The most famous of them became known as the 'robber barons', who presided over an era of economic freewheeling and corruption that historians have referred to as 'bandit capitalism'.[33]

Chief amongst the bandits was the railway magnate Jay Gould, who in 1868 spent $1 million to bribe members of the New York legislature to legalise his issue of $8 million of so-called 'watered stock' (stock not representing real value) in the Erie Railroad. Gould's opportunism made him millions and gave him control of the company.[34] Then there was the banker J.P. Morgan, whose profiteering during the Civil War tarnished his later gentlemanly reputation: in a notorious deal, he was involved in purchasing 5000 rifles for $3.50 each from a Union army arsenal and selling them to a general from the very same army for $22 each – while omitting to mention that the rifles were defective and would shoot off the thumb of any soldier using one.[35] Morgan was later on the receiving end of such deception when Andrew Carnegie sold him his steel company in 1901 at a vastly inflated price by lying about its profits. As one historian points out, Carnegie cheated and lied 'egregiously, consistently, and continually' to become one of the world's richest men.[36] It was an approach to business well understood by Al Capone, who found his own way of expressing the carpe diem ideal: 'This American system of ours, call it Americanism, call it capitalism, call it what you like, gives to each and every one of us a great opportunity if we only seize it with both hands and make the most of it.'[37]

The bad behaviour of the robber barons does not surprise us today. We can all reel off lists of corporations and businessmen – from Enron to Jordan 'Wolf of Wall Street' Belfort – who have grabbed opportunities by using underhand methods ranging from accounting fraud and bribery to tax loopholes and making political donations to gain government favours. Such opportunists who sacrifice integrity for selfishness, greed and personal gain represent a dark side of carpe diem. They are the heirs of Machiavelli's *The Prince* – the first ever handbook on opportunism – which advised rulers to 'learn how not to be virtuous' in order to maintain their power.[38]

If ever we are tempted to indulge in a little opportunism of this kind ourselves, it is worth remembering that it is easy to get our fingers – or our wallet – burned, as happened to Tommy Wilhelm, the lead character in Saul Bellow's novel *Seize the Day*. His life is a mess. His marriage has fallen apart, he has failed in his acting career, he can't get on with his successful father and he is in a big financial hole. It's all sent him spiralling into malaise. But then he meets Dr Tamkin, a philosophical commodities trader who convinces him to bet all his savings on the stock market, encouraging him with carpe diem fervour: 'The past is no good to us. The future is full of anxiety. Only the present is real – the here and now. Seize the day... Grasp the hour, the moment, the instant.'[39] Tamkin, unfortunately, turns out to be an opportunistic conman rather than a saviour, and swindles Wilhelm out of every dollar he has. Bellow's story may be a carpe diem parable for us all.

A SHORT GUIDE TO ESCAPING A RUSSIAN PRISON

We should not forget a final persona who attempts to see beyond the straitjacket of the self in the search for windows of opportunity. This is the revolutionary, who doesn't just try to seize the day but aims to seize history itself and radically alter public life. From the rebel slave Spartacus who led a violent revolt against the Roman Empire to the rebel pacifist lawyer Gandhi who challenged the might of the British Empire, the great revolutionary figures of the past have looked to grasp opportunities for fundamental change and catch fresh political winds that blow away power and privilege.

One of the most fascinating – yet relatively unknown – exemplars of this tradition is the Russian anarchist and geographer Peter Kropotkin. He was born in 1842 into an aristocratic family that owned over 1,200 serfs and several estates, and educated at an elite military academy, where he was chosen as a personal *page de chambre* of Tsar Alexander II. Yet Kropotkin (unlike Tolstoy) completely abandoned his upper-class background, reinventing himself as a revolutionary activist and intellectual whose prophetic books challenged the image of anarchism as a nihilistic and violent ideology, giving it a serious philosophical and scientific basis. Amongst them was *Mutual Aid*, which contested Darwinism by arguing that cooperation was a stronger evolutionary force in nature than competition (an idea currently much in vogue), and *The Conquest of Bread*, which foresaw the totalitarian tendencies of Marxist socialism and argued that true freedom would only come from a society based around worker cooperatives and voluntary organisations (he was a great fan of what became the Royal National Lifeboat Institution).

In the 1860s Kropotkin held military appointments in Siberia, where he led surveying expeditions that established his reputation as a prominent geographer, and had his first direct contact with peasants living in extreme deprivation, which began to awaken his political consciousness. The death of his overbearing father in 1871 was a liberation; finally he felt free to live his own life. With carpe diem gusto he abandoned the steady job he had acquired in the Russian civil service and travelled to Western Europe, drawn by the political upheavals of the Paris Commune and the growing international workers' movement. He went to Switzerland, where he read every piece of radical literature he could get his hands on, and spent time with the poor watchmakers of the Jura region, whose political ideals were so inspiring that he adopted them as his own: he became a convinced anarchist, believing – in contrast with the socialists – that society could be organised without a dominant centralised state into a system of decentralised federations.[40]

Returning to Russia, Kropotkin saw that growing discontent with imperial rule was creating an opportunity for political change. He made an effort to seize it by joining a secret society, the Chaikovsky Circle, to spread revolutionary ideas amongst peasants and workers.[41] Constantly on the run from the Tsar's secret police, Kropotkin took enormous risks. For example, disguised as a peasant named Borodin, he spoke at clandestine meetings of weavers and cotton workers urging them to agitate and organise. But his luck didn't last. With members of the Chaikovsky Circle being arrested in early 1874, Kropotkin was about to flee St Petersburg but couldn't resist staying an extra week to give a scientific paper to the Geographical Society on glacial formation in Finland and Russia. Just hours after his presentation he was arrested. (Never seize the podium when you should be seizing the day.)

Kropotkin spent the next twenty-one months imprisoned in solitary confinement in the infamous Peter and Paul Fortress. Never a procrastinator, he took the opportunity to write a massive two-volume book on glacial periods in his tiny, damp cell. His vigorous intellectual activity did not protect him from contracting rheumatism and scurvy, and his health began to deteriorate rapidly. After being transferred to a prison hospital, he realised that the lax security offered the chance of escape, so he hatched a daring plan, smuggling secret messages to his supporters. He could easily have been shot but, as he wrote in his memoirs, 'against a certain death in prison, the thing is well worth the risk'.[42]

The day for the escape came. He went out for a walk in the prison yard at 4pm. Someone started playing a mazurka excitedly on a violin in a nearby house. That was the signal.

> I turned around. The sentry had stopped five or six
> paces behind me; he was looking the other way. 'Now
> or never!' I remember that thought flashing through
> my head. I flung off my green flannel dressing-gown
> and began to run.[43]

It was the perfect carpe diem window of opportunity. He dashed for the open gate with the guard now giving chase, trying to thrust his bayonet into Kropotkin's back. But Kropotkin just managed to fling himself onto a waiting cart, which quickly galloped away. That night police swarmed across St Petersburg looking for the escapee. But by then Kropotkin had shaved off his beard and, with seize-the-day panache, he went out with a friend for dinner in an elegant coat and opera hat at one of the city's fanciest restaurants, correctly guessing that the police would never think of looking for him anywhere so obvious.

After his time in prison, Kropotkin was ready to 'enjoy the full intensity of life'.[44] For most of the next forty years he lived in exile in Europe, constantly hounded by Russian spies, being thrown in jail for his political activities, and working around the clock to build up the international anarchist movement. He deeply believed that he was living at a moment in history when it was genuinely possible to create revolutionary change that would forge a more equal and free society. He might have been overly optimistic. But there is no doubt he thought that the best way to make it happen was to live a carpe diem life of jumping at the now-or-never. And this may be one of his most important legacies for the political and ecological activists of today.

SCREW IT, JUST DO IT?

We can now line up before us a parade of characters who reveal some – but by no means all – of the most essential ways of catching the winds of opportunity: experimentalist and death gazer, daredevil and role breaker, opportunist and revolutionary. Some of them you may admire, while others might attract your criticism. Would you really want a mother who suddenly disappears for a year to go dancing around Europe? Or a husband who has a compulsive need to risk his life in war zones while you stay at home looking after the kids? There are probably easier people to live with. Yet rather than judge them, I think their main role is to help us ask questions about who we are and who we want to be. Are we clinging too tightly to security when we might benefit from more winging it like Maya Angelou? Is it time to follow Maude's lead and let go of the small stuff, all the distractions filling our lives, the things that don't really matter? Do you identify with Eve Hoare, caught in the narrative of roles that lock you into a life that isn't really of your own making?

Seizing opportunities, in whatever form, inevitably involves making choices. It requires shaking off passivity and taking an active decision to shift our direction of travel. One challenge of doing so is that many of us are afraid. We live in fear of freedom. We would rather stick with the security of what we know than take a chance, or just go with the flow and have our choices made for us, and so evade the responsibility and anxiety of making decisions. Yet we cannot avoid this simple fact: not choosing is a choice in itself. To continue coasting along with our existing mode of living is a decision we make and, as Sartre insisted, we *must* take responsibility for it. 'What is not possible is not to choose', he wrote, and 'I must know that if I do not choose, that is still a choice.'[45]

All too often we coast along all the same, because the psychological barriers to carpe diem can be formidable, and in a later chapter I will be delving into the most important of them: procrastination, risk, apathy and overload. Right now, however, I would like to mention a much more practical barrier, over which we may have little control: money.

It is hardly an issue for some people, like the swashbuckling entrepreneur Richard Branson, whose seize-the-day philosophy of 'screw it, just do it' has sent him attempting to circumnavigate the globe in a hot air balloon, kitesurfing across the English Channel, and investing millions in space tourism. 'Most of Virgin's successes can be attributed to carpe diem moments spurred by optimism,' he tweeted to his 5.4 million followers in 2014, alongside a photo of himself beaming his winning smile in front of a Virgin jet.[46]

He makes it sound easy. But let's not fall for the self-help fantasy that we can all be whoever we want to be and seize whatever we want to seize. Our choices and opportunities are limited by circumstance. While it isn't hard to be a carpe diem optimist if you are a billionaire like Branson, the options are limited for the thousands of entrepreneurial refugees living in Britain and other countries who find it difficult to get a bank loan to start up a business, or whose family obligations mean they can't afford the risk of giving up their double-shift cleaning job to pursue their career ambitions. They're even limited for a recent middle-class graduate carrying the burden of £44,000 of student debt (Britain's national average).[47] How much freedom do they really feel to invent their lives?

While some people resemble Maya Angelou in possessing the confidence and determination to defy the limits of economic circumstance, the truth is that for many, it is most realistic to seize opportunities in realms that are not circumscribed by wealth or power, such as personal relationships, creative endeavours or political action. Even with an almost empty wallet it is generally possible to take the risk of making peace with a sibling you have been fighting with, or to stand up and sing at the open-mic night at your local pub, or to make your voice heard at a community meeting.

If we grasp the opportunities before us, we will be giving ourselves the greatest carpe diem gift imaginable, while at the same time keeping the shadow of regret at bay. Here we are at the cutting edge of our one and only life, this very second that is about to tip us into an unknown future. What are we going to do? What choices will we make?

Few people have understood the importance of such questions better than Henry David Thoreau, as revealed in a journal entry from April 1859. With its maritime metaphors, perhaps he knew that the word 'opportunity' came from a Latin phrase for a favourable wind that a ship might catch:

> Nothing must be postponed. Take time by the forelock. Now or never! You must live in the present, launch yourself on every wave, find your eternity in each moment. Fools stand on their island opportunities and look toward another land. There is no other land; there is no other life but this, or the like of this. Where the good husbandman is, there is the good soil. Take any other course, and life will be a succession of regrets. Let us see vessels

sailing prosperously before the wind, and not simply stranded barks. There is no world for the penitent and regretful.[48]

5

The Hidden Virtues of
Hedonism

'Life is short. Have an affair.' This is the carpe diem tagline of
Ashley Madison, the world's most famous website for arranging
an extra-marital fling. 'Thousands of cheating wives and cheating
husbands sign up every day looking for an affair,' the Canadian-
based site boasts, claiming that it has over 40 million users in
more than fifty countries, who it matches together for 'discreet
encounters'. In July 2015, however, the company's promise to
guarantee absolute secrecy received the ultimate blow: its data was
hacked and posted online. Suddenly anyone could check whether
their spouse had signed up and search their personal profile for
their wish-list of kinky turn-ons. The fallout has included a flood
of divorces, alleged suicides, shaming of public figures and an
epidemic of distrust, with suspicious partners starting to covertly
check the emails and texts of their significant other for evidence of
an Ashley Madison liaison.

Ashley Madison's membership figures have been shown to be
exaggerated, but there is clearly an enormous appetite for having a

fling: nearly 60% of men and over 45% of women have an affair at some point during their marriage.[1] Yet the set-up promoted by Ashley Madison and other similar companies is widely seen as immoral, irresponsible and indulgent. It's hedonism taken to the extreme – pleasure for pleasure's sake, regardless of the consequences – and contributes to the generally bad reputation of hedonism, whether it's extra-marital sex, binge drinking, taking drugs or gluttonous overeating. In many people's minds, hedonism is about sin, selfishness and deceit, anti-social excess, debauchery and addiction. The dominant image is that hedonism harms – sometimes ourselves, and often others.

In the nineteenth century, the historian Thomas Carlyle condemned the philosophical ideal of utilitarian hedonism – maximising pleasure as the chief purpose of life – as a 'doctrine worthy only of swine'.[2] The self-help industry today takes a similar position. Pick up a typical book on happiness or wellbeing and I can almost guarantee it will not suggest downing a couple of tequila slammers, devouring a large slice of chocolate cake, having

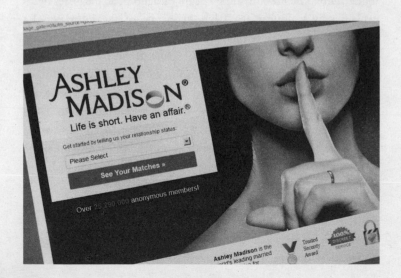

an affair or smoking a joint under the stars. Instead you are likely to be offered a healthy diet of positive thinking exercises, advice on breathing techniques to hone your meditation skills, and top tips on time management to destress your life. This kind of guidance reflects a growing puritanical streak in the modern happiness movement, which focuses on promoting moderation and self-control while leaving hedonism off the agenda. It is usually only discussed in pejorative remarks about what psychologists call the 'hedonic treadmill' – the idea that we get caught in cycles of seeking material pleasures, such as buying a fancy sports car or taking a luxury Caribbean cruise, which only give a temporary boost to our wellbeing and leave us hungry for more.

It is time to challenge this new puritanism and recognise that hedonism is a source of unexpected virtues. I'm not in favour of having secret affairs, buying a Lamborghini or becoming a strung-out coke addict. Rather, we need to appreciate that hedonism has long been central to human culture, personal expression and passionate living, and it is essential that we find a place for it in modern life. The life-affirming nature of hedonistic pleasures helps explain why hedonism itself has been one of the most popular interpretations of the carpe diem ideal for the last three centuries. 'Gather ye rosebuds while ye may,' wrote Robert Herrick in his 1648 carpe diem poem 'To the Virgins, to Make Much of Time', exhorting us – with a thinly veiled metaphor – to seize the sexual pleasures of the present while we still have youthful vigour. Even the King James Bible says: 'Let us eat and drink; for to morrow we die'. More recently, the heavy metal band Metallica gave an erotic spin to Horace's Ode XI in their 1997 song 'Carpe Diem Baby', which encourages us to 'squeeze' and 'suck' the day.[3]

While the self-help and psychology gurus have failed to see the positive role that hedonism can play in private life, they may have committed an even greater crime in remaining blind to its impact on political change. Hedonism has a distinguished history as a source of individual freedom, as a counter to authoritarianism and as a catalyst for social progress. Sound unlikely? As we explore how the Victorians discovered sexual freedom, the human desire for altered states of consciousness and the philosophy of gastronomy, these unsung political virtues of hedonism will begin to emerge.

THE LONG WAR AGAINST PLEASURE

As a first step to taking this more open-minded approach to hedonism, we need to ask why we tend to view it in such a negative light. Why are we so often suspicious of it? Well, in large part due to the legacy of Greco-Roman moral ideals and hair-shirt Christian teachings that have slowly infiltrated our minds. For 2,000 years there has been a long war against pleasure.

We tend to think of the ancient Romans as masters in the art of gratuitous hedonism. While the notorious *vomitorium* is a myth – it wasn't a place to make yourself sick so you could eat yet another course, but a passageway for the audience to 'spew out' of the amphitheatre – the Romans undoubtedly had indulgent culinary tastes. Caligula was said to be particularly fond of flamingo tongue ragoût, while dormice were a prized delicacy, the *foie gras* of the ancient world: they were kept in jars in the dark and fattened up on nuts until ready to fulfil their duty as a sumptuous dish like dormouse stuffed with minced pork and pepper. Public baths across the Empire were hot spots for steamy sex, with plenty of orgies and prostitutes on call. Throughout the year there were riotous festivals and nocturnal rituals in honour of Bacchus, the god of wine, intoxication, freedom and ecstasy, which probably arrived in Rome around 200 BCE as an import from the Greeks, who had long worshipped Bacchus under the name of Dionysus.[4]

Yet it would be utterly mistaken to view Roman social life as one long alcohol-fuelled, feast-laden sex romp. The most striking aspect of Roman society was not its hedonistic excesses but its conservatism and militarism that frowned upon such practices. A law introduced in 186 BCE was designed to crush the debauchery of the Bacchanalia and effectively bring it under the regulation of the Senate. According to some accounts, in the ensuing crackdown around 7,000 men and women were detained, with large numbers of them executed.[5] The Roman historian Livy was typical of the social conservatives who distrusted the Greek-inspired mystery religions and viewed the Bacchanalian cult as evidence of degeneracy that threatened social order. His description of the rituals – written long after they took place – were full of alarmist paranoia:

> The pleasures of drinking and feasting were added to the religious rites, to attract a larger number of followers. When wine had inflamed their feelings, and night and the mingling of the sexes and of different ages had extinguished all power of moral judgment, all sorts of corruption began to be practised... The violence was concealed because no cries for help could be heard against the shriekings, the banging of drums and the clashing of cymbals in the scene of debauchery and bloodshed... No sort of crime, no kind of immorality, was left unattempted. There were more obscenities practised between men than between men and women.[6]

In fact, there is little or no evidence that Bacchanalia was a violent affair: this was most likely an invention of Livy's fertile imagination. The truth is that the Roman elite – Livy included – simply feared a widespread social expression of hedonism that they could not control, and which outlived their attempts to ban it. The writings of the Stoics, the pre-eminent philosophical school in ancient Rome, were similarly scathing of hedonistic extremes. Seneca, for instance, was a champion of moderation and self-control. 'The happy man is content with his present lot, no matter what it is,' he wrote, while at the same time disapproving of 'those who have time for nothing but wine and lust; for none have more shameful engrossments'. His motto was unequivocal: 'nothing for pleasure's sake'.[7]

Seneca's views echoed those of the ancient Greek thinker Epicurus. That might sound surprising, since we usually think of an epicurean as someone devoted to sensory pleasures. Indeed, Epicurus himself said 'pleasure is the beginning and goal of a happy life'. But Epicurus never advocated hedonism, believing that we should aim to free ourselves from bodily pain and mental anguish not through 'drinking and revels' but 'sober reasoning'. He was an ascetic who argued that 'plain dishes offer the same pleasure as a luxurious table'. His standard diet was water and bread (though occasionally he permitted himself a few lentils), and he was a strict celibate who believed sex should be avoided because it led to unhappy feelings such as jealousy. Hence Seneca concluded that the 'teachings of Epicurus are upright and holy and, if you consider them closely, austere'.[8]

The early Christians are often blamed for the bad reputation of hedonistic indulgence, especially their fanatical condemnation of lust and gluttony, bodily pleasures which were thought to distract believers from spiritual union with God. However, the conservative Romans played a fundamental part in shaping these Christian ideals. Take, for example, the Seven Deadly Sins. These were not a biblical credo, as most people assume, but an invention of the fourth-century monk Evagrius Ponticus, and there is compelling evidence that Evagrius effectively imported them from Stoic thinking for a Christian audience. The obsession with sexual abstinence that developed in medieval Christianity can be traced back to Roman moralists such as Seneca, who believed we should use our willpower to overcome our sexual desires.[9]

Such attitudes were expressed most vehemently in the writings of St Augustine, the first intellectual superstar of Christian theology. Born in what is now Algeria in 354, St Augustine spent his early years 'in the shadowy jungle of erotic adventures' and 'hellish pleasures', and fathered a son with a woman he never married and then abandoned. As he wrote in his autobiographical *Confessions*, 'As a youth I had been woefully at fault... I prayed to you for chastity and said, "Give me chastity and continence, but not yet"'.[10] Following his conversion, aged thirty-two, he turned on his hedonistic past and the temptations of the flesh with unbridled vigour. His formulation of the doctrine of original sin made clear that ever since Adam's fall from grace in the Garden of Eden, humankind had been corrupted by the filthy allures of lust. Yet like Evagrius, St Augustine was profoundly influenced by Stoic thought, especially on the subject of ethics. Our passions are located in the mind not the body, he argued, and a good Christian must subject their hot-blooded physical cravings to the dictates of cool reason.[11] In other words, Ashley Madison is off-limits.

Over the centuries, Christianity developed into a potent force that did everything it could to dampen the hedonistic desires that continually reared up amongst even the most pious believers. These desires were vividly displayed in the blatant eroticism of Hieronymus Bosch's painting *The Garden of Earthly Delights* (c.1500), which depicted a carpe diem paradise of sensual pleasures and acrobatic fornication, including a man appearing to have sex with a giant strawberry, and others who were fondling animals or had flutes and flowers emerging from their backsides. It was precisely to quell such devilish impulses that, in 1532, the Holy Roman Emperor Charles V introduced a penal code that banned the use of contraceptive devices. The message was clear: you can no longer have sex for the fun of it. Half a millennium later, this kind of thinking remains at the root of the Catholic Church's official opposition to birth control, and the guilt many of today's Catholics still feel about having sex outside the strict limits of procreation.

In the emerging Protestant tradition, alcohol came to be seen as almost as threatening to devout belief as sex. Monks may have been brewing beer since the ninth century, but the demon drink became the focus of Christian condemnation, especially from the eighteenth century, when spirit drinking reached pandemic proportions amongst Europe's urban poor and even young children were given gin, rum and whisky by their parents. Popular medical works such as Dr Benjamin Rush's 1784 book *An Inquiry into the Effects of Spirituous Liquors on the Human Body* provided a scientific link between excessive drinking and moral decline. By the nineteenth century, Temperance campaigners in Britain and the United States had created a powerful lobbying machine intent on banning the consumption of alcohol. The prohibitionists scored a major victory in 1851, when Maine became America's first dry state, with fines for those caught drinking and prison for repeat offenders. Organisations such as the fanatical Women's Christian Temperance Union kept up the pressure until they achieved their ultimate goal:

The kinky hedonism of Hieronymus Bosch in *The Garden of Earthly Delights* (c.1500, detail). Salvador Dalí looks tame by comparison.

the Volstead Act of 1920, which made prohibition the law of the land.[12] Teetotalism had – at least in theory – triumphed.

Probably no piece of legislation in Western legal history has been a more spectacular failure. Just as the Church had never been able to stop people having sex simply for the pleasure of it, it was equally impossible to stop them boozing. America's experiment with prohibition, which lasted thirteen years, drove people to drinking not just sacramental wine but dubious spirit substitutes such as anti-freeze and embalming fluid. It spurred the creation of illegal distilleries and speakeasies, which in turn provided ripe pickings for criminal gangs and police corruption. The White House itself was overflowing with bootleg hooch, and part of the Senate Library was curtained off and transformed into a bar serving confiscated liquor.[13]

The ingenuity with which people circumvented the law is persuasive evidence that it is almost impossible to legislate away the desire for hedonistic pleasures. We are drawn to hedonism like moths to torchlight. Alongside our intellectual capacities and spiritual yearnings, we are physical beings with a sensory apparatus designed to ignite the multiple pleasure centres of the brain and trigger delicious biochemical reactions. 'The desire for pleasure is part of human nature,' points out neuroscientist Morten Kringelbach, and 'perhaps we have to learn to accept that the human brain makes us disproportionately interested in pleasure'.[14] And yet, in large part due to our cultural inheritance of ancient Roman and Christian ideals, the long war against pleasure persists, and hedonism's public reputation continues to be tinged with immorality and excess. The US government spends millions each year on (famously ineffective) abstinence-only sex education programmes in an effort to reduce teenage sex.[15] Religious groups like the Salvation Army persist in promoting teetotalism. The statute books are replete with laws that limit hedonistic pursuits, from age restrictions on purchasing liquor to bans on the sale of cannabis.

There are good reasons for such regulations: we all know people whose lives have been devastated by drug dependency or alcoholism. But even so, lust need not always get out of hand and drinking does not have to lead to drunkenness, just as indigenous Bolivians have been chewing coca leaves for centuries without bringing societal collapse upon themselves. We should develop a more nuanced approach to hedonism, one which recognises that it can – if managed wisely – be both personally and politically liberating. How to do so? We can start by exploring one of the most important inventions of Western culture since the eighteenth century: sexual freedom.

How the Victorians Discovered Erotic Sex

Flip through an ancient sex manual such as *Methods of Intercourse Between Yin and Yang*, written in China in the second century BCE, or later Indian equivalents such as the *Kama Sutra* or the *Koka Shastra*, with their helpful advice on the benefits of biting and scratching your partner, and it becomes clear that sex is one of the oldest forms of hedonistic pleasure. While there are certain gender differences – the most authoritative study reveals that men think about sex on average thirty-four times a day, compared with nineteen times for women – there is no doubt that sexual enjoyment is a carpe diem pastime that we have long found nearly irresistible.[16] There may be no more intense or electrifying way of feeling fully alive than experiencing that most remarkable evolutionary gift: the orgasm. The Romantic poet Shelley drew on the French euphemism for it, *la petite morte* ('the little death'), to declare orgasm to be the 'death which lovers love'. The allure of this little death helps explain the extraordinary ubiquity of sex in daily life – in office flirtations, secret affairs, relationship jealousies, advertising images, teenage sexual angst, prostitution and digital pornography.

Although we find it hard to stop thinking about sex, we rarely think of it as a political act. Yet the pursuit of erotic pleasure has been a powerful force for social equality and cultural transformation. The place to begin exploring this neglected virtue of sexual hedonism is not in the infamous Roaring Twenties or the free-love communes of 1960s California, but – perhaps surprisingly – in the apparently prim and proper Victorian era.

To set the scene, however, we must first return to the streets of seventeenth-century London. At that time carnal pleasure remained a largely male privilege, both inside and outside marriage. One need look no further than that fine and upstanding literary gent and public official Samuel Pepys – who also happened to be an aggressive and even violent sexual predator. One diary entry in February 1664, when he was thirty, is particularly revealing. Travelling in his coach up Ludgate Hill he noticed three men 'taking a pretty wench which I have much eyed lately… a seller of ribbons and gloves. They seemed to drag her by some force… but God forgive me, what thoughts and wishes I had of being in their place.' Pepys lived out such lustful fantasies, which bordered on rape, in his relationship with the attractive wife of a ship's carpenter who worked under him named William Bagwell. As his diaries reveal – using French for the more lurid details – over a period of five years he was continually forcing himself upon her with kisses and gropings, and repeatedly had sex with her against her will.[17]

This was seizing the moment in its darkest guise. Pepys was fairly typical of men of his era and class who sexually harassed and victimised women as a matter of course, viewing it as part of their patriarchal entitlement. This unbridled lechery was the reality of the libertine tradition, from rakes like John Wilmot, Second Earl of Rochester, to Casanova and the Marquis de Sade.

By the Victorian age a noticeable shift in sexual relations was getting under way, especially amongst the bourgeoisie. We love to depict the Victorians as prudish moralists who would blanche at the mention of sexual pleasure. Sex in marriage was for procreation not recreation. Husbands were stern and upright bastions of Christian virtue (although making occasional trips to prostitutes to vent their sexual energies). Wives were dutifully focused on cake-baking and child-rearing, and as tightly buttoned up in their attitudes as in their corsets.[18]

That might be the image, but it is far from the truth. In fact, the diaries and private letters of bourgeois women in the Victorian era reveal that a small but growing number of them were exploring erotic pleasures, especially in the privacy of the marital bedroom. This was the case not only in England but in North America where, as social historians point out, Victorian culture also extended its reach.[19] A celebrated example is the New England socialite Mabel Loomis Todd, an accomplished pianist, painter and editor who enjoyed an undoubtedly steamy sex life with her astronomer husband, David Peck Todd. Mabel's diaries are an unusually open record of what they got up to. An entry for early 1881, when she was twenty-four years old, reads: '8:30am. What a lifetime of happiness I have had since about 5 A.M.,' followed at the end of the day by '#16 (o)', her secret symbols denoting that it was the sixteenth time she'd had sex that year, and that it had been accompanied by an orgasm.[20] Their sexual athleticism, which relied on the classic contraception devices of the rhythm method and *coitus interruptus*, was signalled by euphemistic entries such as 'Oh! my oriental morning' or 'a little Heaven just after dinner'.[21] Married life for the Todds was also filled with sensual rituals. 'Every night,' Mabel wrote, 'he undressed me on the bright Turkey rug before the fire, & then wrapped me up to keep me warm while he put hot bricks in the bed.' In the morning would come 'the grapes or figs or apples on which he always regaled me before breakfast'.[22]

Mabel was a thoroughly modern woman who revelled in her sexual freedom. She not only, in her own words, 'flirted outrageously' with the young male students at Amherst College, where her husband taught – she also took a lover. For more than a decade she had an affair with a much older married man, Austin Dickinson, brother of the poet Emily Dickinson. Everyone knew about Mabel's man on the side, including her husband, but in their polite society nobody spoke about it publicly. The semi-clandestine relationship proved a strain on their marriages, but for Mabel it was a price worth paying for both exciting sex and emotional affection. David Todd's tolerance of the affair may have helped to cover up his own marital infidelities.[23] All this more than a century before Ashley Madison.

The increasing desire amongst some middle-class women for sexual equality in the bedroom was part of the broader movement for gender equality in Britain and the United States that helped to create what is known as 'first-wave feminism', referring to the struggle for legal rights such as women's suffrage in the late nineteenth and early twentieth centuries. In other words, sexual hedonism became an expression of political empowerment. More and more women, particularly those who were relatively wealthy and educated, were expecting and demanding equal treatment in both private and public life. They were out to overturn the subordination of women that characterised the age of Samuel Pepys, and what happened between the sheets was a vital aspect of this.[24] Of course, the sexual liberation of women like Mabel Loomis Todd, or others such as the writer George Eliot (who lived, as Mary Ann Evans, in scandalous unhallowed union with the philosopher G.H. Lewes), didn't immediately usher in an era of women on top. It was the early beginnings of a long period of social struggle and cultural change, spurred on by factors such as the gradual admission of women to universities, the arrival of the pill in 1960, and the challenge to patriarchy issued by books such as Germaine Greer's *The Female Eunuch* in 1970. In a world where domestic violence and rape remain all too common, it is a struggle that still continues.

Mabel's references to a 'Turkey rug' and her 'oriental morning' are revealing of another aspect of sexual life amongst the middle and upper classes in the nineteenth century: the craze for 'the East'. This was far more than the fad for Persian carpets and Japanese lacquer furniture: the Orient also evoked fantasies of erotic sensuality and passionate carpe diem living that were the opposite of sober Victorian Christianity. Such fantasies were encouraged by Richard Burton's

Mabel Loomis Todd displaying her taste for the exotic East, 1896.

notoriously explicit translation of the *Arabian Nights* in 1885, and of the fifteenth-century Arabic erotic manual *The Perfumed Garden*, with its risqué chapters describing sexual positions including 'frog fashion', 'the rainbow arch' and the intriguing 'screw of Archimedes'.[25] But the attractions of Eastern sensuality were nowhere better expressed than in the remarkable popularity of the *Rubáiyát of Omár Khayyám*, a long poem by the eccentric English scholar Edward FitzGerald, based on his loose translation of verses by the eleventh-century Persian poet and mathematician Omár Khayyám.

The initial publication of the *Rubáiyát* in 1859 went completely unnoticed: it didn't sell a single copy in its first two years. But by chance a remaindered copy of FitzGerald's twenty-page booklet was picked up for a penny by the Celtic scholar Whitley Stokes, who passed it on to Dante Gabriel Rossetti, who subsequently fell in love with it and sang its praises to his Pre-Raphaelite circle. In 1863 John Ruskin declared, 'I never did – till this day – read anything so glorious', and from there began a cult of Omár Khayyám that lasted at least until World War One, by which time there were 447 editions of FitzGerald's translation in circulation. The poem was memorised, quoted and worshipped by a whole generation. Omár Khayyám dining clubs sprang up, and you could even buy Omar tooth powder and playing cards. During the war, dead soldiers were found in the trenches with battered copies in their pockets.[26] The attractions of the *Rubáiyát* are revealed in some of its most famous lines:

> Then to the lip of this poor earthen Urn
> I lean'd, the Secret of my Life to learn:
> And Lip to Lip it murmur'd – 'While you live
> Drink! – for, once dead, you never shall return.'[27]

The carpe diem calling of the *Rubáiyát* was unmistakable.[28] It was an unapologetic celebration of hedonism, bringing to mind sensuous embraces in jasmine-filled gardens on balmy Arabian nights, accompanied by cups of cool, intoxicating wine. It was a passionate outcry against the unofficial Victorian ideologies of moderation, primness and self-control. But the message was even more radical, for the *Rubáiyát* was a rejection not just of Christian morality, but of religion itself.[29] There is no afterlife, Omár Khayyám seemed to be saying, and since human existence is transient and death will come much faster than we imagine, it's best to savour its exquisite moments. This heady union of bodily pleasures, religious doubt and impending mortality captured the imagination of its nineteenth-century audience, who were more used to singing pious hymns at church on a Sunday morning. No wonder the writer G.K. Chesterton declared that the *Rubáiyát* was the bible of the 'carpe diem religion'.[30]

The influence of the *Rubáiyát* on Victorian culture was especially visible in the works of Oscar Wilde, who described it as a 'masterpiece of art' and one of his greatest literary loves alongside Shakespeare's Sonnets.[31] FitzGerald's poem makes its clearest mark on Wilde's 1890 novel *The Picture of Dorian Gray*. The character of Lord Henry Wotton is a champion of hedonism who explicitly refers to the sensual allures of 'wise Omar', and tempts Dorian to sell his soul for the decadent pleasures of eternal youth:

> You have only a few years to live really, perfectly, fully... Time is jealous of you, and wars against your lilies and roses. You will become sallow, and hollow-cheeked, and dull-eyed... Live the wonderful life that is in you! Let nothing be lost upon you. Be always searching for new sensations. Be afraid of nothing... A new Hedonism – that is what our century wants.[32]

Yet the novel was not simply about the pleasures and follies of carpe diem hedonism, played out by Dorian remaining in perfect youth while his portrait ages into a horrible mask of creased and craggy callousness. It was about breaking social conventions and challenging the strictures of Victorian morality. This was most evident in the allegedly homoerotic passages (some of them removed by Wilde for later editions) that reinforced the growing public scandal of the author's homosexuality, and which played a part in his eventual imprisonment for two years for sodomy and gross indecency. Much of the critique focused on the adoration of the painter in the novel, Basil Hallward, for the beautiful young man Dorian, which many reviewers considered immoral filth. Wilde's real-life lover, Lord Douglas – a devoted fan of *The Picture of Dorian Gray* – was sixteen years his junior. During Wilde's trial in 1895, his literary depiction of relationships between older and younger men were used as part of the case against him, with passages of the book being read out in court.[33] In the end, Victorian society was not yet ready for the brand of sensual hedonism in Wilde's novel, or in his life, and ours is only beginning to be after decades of social struggle for gay rights. In Britain, homosexual relationships were not fully decriminalised until 1982, and it was only in 2000 that the Armed Forces removed its ban on LGBT individuals serving openly. Sodomy laws were not overturned in the US until a landmark Supreme Court ruling in 2003. Over seventy countries, mostly in Africa and Asia, retain laws criminalising homosexuality, while it still remains taboo in many religions.

Whether we look at the diaries of adventurous women like Mabel Loomis Todd, or peruse the pages of the *Rubáiyát* or *The Picture of Dorian Gray*, we can see that during the nineteenth century sexual hedonism was not just a matter of private pleasures: it was a potent way to defy social rules and break the boundaries placed on individual liberty and equality. The personal merged with the political. Today in the West, in our age of greater sexual openness and tolerance, this more political aspect of sexual hedonism may not seem so relevant. Yet I believe it is: notwithstanding serious issues such as sex trafficking, sex remains one of the most important realms of life for exploring and expressing freedom and equality that society has to offer. This idea was recognised back in the early 1970s when Alex Comfort, a physician and committed anarchist, wrote *The Joy of Sex*, a bestselling recipe book for what he called 'Cordon Bleu sex'. In the introduction, Comfort emphasised that we should view sex as 'a deeply rewarding form of play' and pointed out that:

> One of the most important uses of play is in expressing a healthy awareness of sexual equality. This involves letting both sexes take turns in controlling the game; sex is no longer what men do to women and women are supposed to enjoy... Sex is the one place where we today can learn to treat people as people.[34]

The Church may have spent centuries condemning lust, but if sexual hedonism can involve mutuality and reciprocity, then it shifts out of the strictures of individual indulgence into the realm of political equality. It becomes about both me and we, and enables women to be more than just passive objects of pleasure.

There is one other reason why sex has such carpe diem appeal: it's normally free. There are some exceptions, of course, but in general, sex doesn't require a trip to the ATM. Between consenting couples (or triples or more), it is free at the point of use. Unlike gourmet dining or binging on coke, sexual delight is known as much by the poor rural farmer as by the noble lord, giving it an egalitarian universality. This very fact means that sex is an inadvertent challenge to consumer society, which tells us that pleasure is something we need to buy in a shopping mall. If that were not enough, sex is pretty much carbon free – unless you happen to be doing it on a plane. It has all the credentials to be the recreation of choice for the global simple living movement.

While a mass outbreak of sexual passion is unlikely to bring down capitalism or solve the climate crisis, and making love has not yet stopped us from making war, sex retains untapped potential as a counter-culture force. So, in the name of carpe diem, gather ye rosebuds while ye may.

WELCOME TO THE PLEASURE DOME

It is a summer afternoon in our garden, and my three-year-old twins have made a startling discovery: spinning. They spin round and round on the grass, arms outstretched, laughing like crazy, staggering around in giddiness when they stop, then collapsing on the ground and watching in fascinated euphoria as the sky whirls in circles above them.

Spinning games are a near-universal phenomenon amongst infants, as are experiments with breath-holding, which can produce similar light-headedness. And it's not only children who understand the attractions. Exuberant spinning is part of the ritual dances of Sufi dervishes, as well as indigenous Amazonians and Pacific Islanders, with the power to induce a mental state that is almost hallucinogenic.[35]

The desire to whirl is striking evidence that human beings are drawn to entering altered states of consciousness. More commonly, many of us rely on alcohol and drugs to take us out of ourselves and help us step through the doors of perception. Such efforts have a long history. When the sixteenth-century Franciscan missionary Bernardino de Sahagún was in Mexico, he came upon a traditional Aztec banquet where the festivities began with the eating of a black mushroom, probably the super-powerful hallucinogen *Stropharia cubensis*. 'These mushrooms caused them to become intoxicated, to see visions and also to be provoked to lust,' he wrote, 'and when they began to feel excited due to the effect of the mushrooms, the Indians started dancing, while some were singing and others weeping.'[36]

Today we may be surrounded by rules and regulations to prevent 'substance abuse', but like the tripping Aztecs and our whirling childhood selves, we can't stop seeking altered states. Every morning millions of people give themselves a liquid injection of the world's most popular legal drug, coffee, containing an intense stimulant – caffeine – which accelerates cognitive function and augments the heart rate.[37] Legions of smokers can't get through the day without sucking nicotine into their lungs. Many people treat themselves to a beer or glass of wine at the end of a hard day at work to help their worries float away into a gentle haze. Then there are the multitudes who take pills like Prozac to rescue them from a depressive state or pump them up for a night of partying. In the West we are bound up in a habitually self-medicating culture that uses alcohol and drugs as a quick and easy way of escaping from daily anxieties, as a lubricant for sociability, and as a source of mental stimulation and ecstatic experience, as well as a form of pain relief.

Yet it can all easily lose its innocence, as revealed in stark and shocking detail in the cult film *Trainspotting*. Set amongst the poverty-stricken council estates of 1980s Edinburgh, it begins as an extremist homage to heroin use. What people forget, says the narrator Renton, 'is the pleasure of it… take the best orgasm you've ever had, multiply it by a thousand, and you're still nowhere near it.' But the film's opening song, Iggy Pop's 'Lust for Life', loses its lustre as the film progresses. Faced with bleak and meaningless futures, we see desperate addicts shooting up in the squalor of abandoned tenement buildings, wrecking their own and their families' lives, turning to crime and violence to feed their addictions, and ending up in prison or killing themselves with their habits. Just for good measure, there is also a psychotic alcoholic who disdains drugs but regularly goes on violent drunken rampages. It's hardly a great advertisement for hedonism.

So how can we negotiate our way between the mind-altering pleasures of drugs and alcohol, and their potential as a slippery slope to self-destruction? What role should artificially transforming our state of consciousness play in carpe diem living?

As a writer, I'm intrigued by the long tradition of literary figures who have turned to drugs and drink in the course of their often wayward careers. There's something dangerously alluring about knowing that Robert Louis Stevenson allegedly wrote his 60,000-word novel *The Strange Case of Dr Jekyll and Mr Hyde* during a six-day cocaine binge in 1885.[38] One of the first writers to reflect deeply on the experience of using drugs was the nineteenth-century poet and opium addict Thomas De Quincey. 'I am a Hedonist,' declared De Quincey in his *Confessions of an English Opium-Eater*, 'and if you must know why I take opium, that's the reason why.' He was enthusiastic about its benefits: it could 'tranquilise all irritations of the nervous system', 'stimulate the capacities of enjoyment', and 'sustain through twenty-four consecutive hours the else drooping animal energies'. After taking opium for the first time, on a wet Sunday afternoon in 1804 – apparently to relieve toothache – he was convinced he had discovered 'the secret of happiness'. Nothing could better it: 'I do not readily believe that any man, having once tasted the divine luxuries of opium, will afterwards descend to the gross and mortal enjoyments of alcohol'.[39]

But then there were the dreams. Horrible, haunting, excruciatingly vivid dreams stirred up by a habit that was the equivalent of the daily opium dose for over 300 hospital patients at that time. De Quincey found himself being 'kissed, with cancerous kisses, by crocodiles', chased by vengeful Hindu Gods through forests, sacrificed by bloodthirsty priests, and buried for thousands of years 'in stone coffins, with mummies and sphinxes, in narrow chambers at the heart of eternal pyramids'.[40] Such torturous dreamscapes were by no means a universal experience. For some literary users, opium dreams were a doorway to beautiful, voluptuous imagery that stimulated their creative imagination and poetic sensibilities. Probably the most famous opium dream of them all took place in the autumn of 1797, when Samuel Taylor Coleridge dreamed his sumptuously hedonistic poem *Kubla Khan*, while staying at a remote farmhouse in Porlock, near Exmoor in Somerset. In his own account of what happened, he began writing it down immediately upon waking, describing the enchanted land where Alph the sacred river ran, but was interrupted by a visitor. Returning to his desk, he found that the remainder of the poem had – to his utter annoyance and the literary world's eternal loss – disappeared from his mind.[41]

Before you stock up on laudanum, the tincture of opium that became Coleridge's constant companion and maybe even his inspiration, know first that it was this 'milk of paradise' that destroyed him. Once he was under its spell, the dazzling and excitable literary genius that he displayed in his youth went into sorry decline. Coleridge spent years fighting his addiction, which, by his early forties, became so acute that he even hired burly men to forcefully stop him from entering pharmacies. Over time, he became a self-absorbed, self-doubting and depressed man who could still be an entertaining talker (when on a drug high) but whose creative juices had long been spent. Although eventually gaining a public reputation as a philosophical sage, he spent his final years skulking around the back door of a chemist in Highgate desperate for his next fix.[42]

Despite such stories, I believe there should be a place for mind-altering stimulants in our lives, not just because of the pleasures they can bring, but because they can be such a powerful catalyst for social change. Think of the drug-fuelled counter-culture of 1960s America. While any hippy worth their salt was turning on, tuning in and dropping out on a psychedelic bus tour across the country, taking drugs was just as much an act of defiance against the political establishment. Anti-Vietnam protesters turned their backs on the draft and joined Berkeley sit-ins where they lit up joints instead. Experimenting with peyote while living on an ashram was a fun way to spend a summer of love but also a rebellious gesture aimed at a consumer society that wanted its citizens wearing business suits and buying a nice house in the suburbs in imitation of the American Dream. It was after taking LSD in 1966 that the visionary thinker and activist Stewart Brand was struck by a question: Why haven't we seen a photograph of the whole earth yet? It was the beginning of what became the *Whole Earth Catalog*, a publication that helped ignite the country's environmental and simple living movements.[43] While there is no need to romanticise the lives of self-destructive drug addicts like William Burroughs, there is no doubt that the anti-authoritarian and progressive politics of the 1960s was, to a significant degree, produced and sustained thanks to drug-induced hedonism. As the historian Eric Hobsbawm commented, Sixties drugs culture was a route to 'shattering bonds of state, parental and neighbours' power, law and convention... personal liberation and social liberation thus went hand in hand'.[44]

These liberating effects of drugs are perhaps best understood by the Dutch. The Netherlands has long had a pragmatic and tolerant approach to drugs, which was initially driven by commercial interests. In the nineteenth century the Dutch cultivated coca on the island of Java, and in 1900 the government even established its own cocaine factory in Amsterdam, the Nederlandsche Cocaïnefabriek, which enabled it to dominate the global cocaine market within just ten years.[45] While recreational drug use was banned for much of the twentieth century, popular pressure to legalise it emerged in the 1960s, driven by groups such as the radical Provo movement.[46] In 1975 the Dutch unveiled one of their greatest inventions since the telescope in the seventeenth century: the 'coffee shop', where anyone was free to buy and consume cannabis in its various forms. Today there are hundreds of them scattered around the country, used by locals and tourists alike.

The Dutch have developed a unique model of state-approved mind-altering hedonism, where the government effectively tolerates soft drug use. The policy, known as *gedogen* (legal toleration), generally works. Cannabis use in the Netherlands is around the European average (some 25% of people have tried it, with 7% being 'recent users'), and much lower than in North America, where there is far stricter prohibition. Also, while Holland has its fair share of addicts, Dutch cannabis users are less likely than their US counterparts to have tried hard drugs like cocaine and heroin.[47]

My own limited experience of Amsterdam's coffee shops – strictly for research purposes of course – has convinced me that the Dutch have got it about right. After my first small experiment, which involved puffing my way through a poorly rolled joint on a bleak autumn afternoon, I ventured out to visit some Van Gogh paintings. I normally get bored extremely quickly in art galleries, but not on this occasion. The colours, the frames, the people walking past them, all possessed an astonishing intensity of being, as if I had shoplifted the experience straight out of Aldous Huxley's *The Doors of Perception*, where he describes the 'Istigkeit' – the 'is-ness' – of everyday objects after taking mescalin in 1953.

As I drifted around with a somewhat inane smile on my face and a feeling of being absolutely in the moment, I mused that it would probably be a bit exhausting to be a top-flight Buddhist monk permanently in such a state of heightened awareness. Still, it was a useful reminder of how infrequently I give that much attention to the present, or to anything really, and that too much of my life is filled with emails and other distractions that prevent me from being in the here and now. While I can't pretend that my afternoon wanderings were a radical anti-authoritarian act that could rival 1960s counter-culture, it still felt like a fundamental experience of imaginative liberty.

Certainly we should beware of the dangers of drug abuse and addiction. Yet let's not rule out a chance of returning, if only occasionally, to the hedonistic ecstasy of our childhood whirling on the grass.

On the Pleasures of a Fried Egg Sandwich

In her 1949 classic *An Alphabet for Gourmets*, the revered food writer M.F.K. Fisher makes the following confession in the chapter 'G is for Gluttony':

> As often as possible, when a really beautiful bottle of wine is before me, I drink all I can of it, even when I know I have had more than I want physically. That is gluttonous. But I think to myself, when again will I have this taste upon my tongue? Where else in the world is there just such wine as this, with just this bouquet, at just this heat, in just this crystal cup? And when again will I be alive to it as I am this very minute, sitting here on a green hillside above the sea, or here in this dim, murmuring, richly odorous restaurant, or here in this fisherman's café on the wharf?[48]

There may be no more eloquent defence of carpe diem hedonism: this very moment and everything it contains is set to disappear into oblivion – a little death never to be revived – so pour another glass. Yet there is the hint of elitism lurking beneath her words. How many people can really afford to drink such glorious wines in crystal cups? Isn't there something inherently exclusionary in the seize-the-day philosophy of the refined gourmand, just as there was in the dining habits of wealthy ancient Romans?

Thankfully Fisher is aware of this dilemma, which is why her books not only contain recipes for fancy dishes like quails *à la financière* but are also abundant with more down-to-earth delicacies. One of the most delicious is her recipe for Aunt Gwen's Fried Egg Sandwiches: cook the eggs so they are as tough as leather, add plenty of dripping, wrap the sandwiches in grease-proof paper, then pop them into your pocket until they are nice and soggy, ready to be eaten at the top of a hill at sundown.[49] Another concerns her discovery, while living in Strasbourg in the 1930s, of how to eat tangerines. 'My pleasure in them,' she wrote, 'is subtle and voluptuous and quite inexplicable.' The trick is to peel the tangerine in the morning, separate out each segment, tear off the white strings, then place the segments on newspaper on top of a hot radiator, where they should be forgotten about until the afternoon. They should then be eaten slowly, one by one, your teeth cracking through their little shells, 'thin as one layer of enamel on a Chinese bowl'.[50]

Such recipes are an ode to modesty rather than moderation. Fisher is not an advocate of restraint and self-control like the Stoics: her credo is to indulge yourself in the full-blown pleasures of the senses. Yet we can choose to do so, she believes, with a modesty that does not break the bank. Nearly everyone – at least in the West – can fry an egg or get their hands on a fresh tangerine. She is a culinary apostle of what I think of as 'democratic hedonism', a worthy ambition to spread hedonistic pleasures such as food and sex in an unequal world.

There is one further step we can take to deepen the democratic potential of carpe diem gourmandism: to share the tangerine segments instead of hoarding them for ourselves. Sharing food, cooking it for others and extending hospitality are ancient forms of gift-giving that transcend the hyperindividualism of our market societies. When I was living for a short time in a refugee settlement in Guatemala, where food was scarce, I was invited one day to a community feast. Having eaten virtually nothing but corn tortillas with black beans for three weeks, I was given a small bowl containing some chicken stewed with tomatoes. The whole village ate together amidst the jungle mosquitos and stifling heat, perched on logs in the boggy mud. It was a modest affair. It was generous. It was deliciously hedonistic. And I felt, for the first time, a part of their community. I learned what anthropologists have known for over a century: that food rituals are a form of social exchange with the capacity to create relationships and empathy.

BEYOND THE NEW PURITANISM

Hedonism offers a powerful counter to the growing puritanism of today's happiness industry, which threatens to turn us into self-controlled moderation addicts who rarely express a passionate lust for life. As we have seen, hedonism in its many forms can bring multiple benefits, from helping us explore our imaginations to being an expression of individual freedom. It is an essential ingredient of human wellbeing that should be part of any recipe for the good life.

Like anything, hedonism can be taken too far. Nobody should want to end up like Elvis in his final years: drugged-up, vastly overweight and dead at forty-two. It might be best to cultivate a variety of hedonisms and not become addicted to any one type, helping to spread a healthy diversity of consciousness in society.[51] And a useful rule of thumb would be to do so in short, intense bursts or pulses with plenty of breaks in between (everyone needs recovery time) rather than live for the bland moderation of little and often.

Let's not condemn hedonism as a doctrine worthy only of swine. We need it as a potent elixir of personal and social liberation. Hedonism puts us in touch with an experiential approach to living that goes to the core of what it means to be human. 'Not the fruit of experience, but experience itself, is the end,' wrote the Victorian cultural critic Walter Pater. 'To burn always with this hard, gemlike flame, to maintain this ecstasy, is success in life.'[52]

6

Beyond the Now of Mindfulness

In the final scene of Richard Linklater's coming-of-age film *Boyhood*, two college students are sitting quietly on a rocky outcrop, staring out across a sparse, stony landscape. One of them, Nicole, turns to her companion Mason and remarks thoughtfully, 'You know how everyone's always saying "seize the moment"? I'm kinda thinkin' it's the other way around. Like the moment seizes us.' 'Yeah, I know,' he replies, 'it's constant, the moments... it's like it's always right now.'

This brief exchange marks an important shift: over the past two decades carpe diem has become increasingly associated with being in the here and now. Ask a roomful of people what 'carpe diem' or 'seize the moment' means to them, and you will be surprised by how many bypass the most common interpretation to date – that it's about grasping the fleeting opportunities that life offers – and will instead say it involves being immersed in the present. The database developed for this book shows that this new usage was virtually non-existent in the media and other public sources before the 1990s, and around three-quarters of references to carpe diem as 'presence' have occurred since 2000. While the majority of people still associate seizing the day with taking advantage of windows of opportunity, around one in five today use it to mean experiencing the 'now', a timeless instant where we are unencumbered by memories of the past or thoughts of the future.[1] The day itself no longer matters and has been reduced down to a single moment.

How has this happened? How could such an ancient philosophy of living have gained such a radically new additional meaning in such a short space of time?

There is one overriding explanation: the rise of the mindfulness movement. Since the turn of the millennium, mindfulness – by which I mean the modern, secularised practice rather than the ancient Buddhist tradition of mindfulness meditation on which it is based – has become a major international success story. Hundreds of thousands of people (myself included) have taken mindfulness courses in community centres, hospitals, businesses and schools, learning techniques to calm the mind and focus attention on the present. A flood of scientific studies has inundated the media, proving its impact on tackling multiple maladies from anxiety and depression to violent behaviour and heart disease. It can even help you stop smoking. Mindfulness, says one of its leading researchers, Jon Kabat-Zinn, 'has the potential to ignite a universal or global renaissance… that would put even the European and Italian Renaissance into the shade.' It may, he believes, 'be the only promise the species and the planet have for making it through the next couple of hundred years'.[2]

It sounds almost too good to be true. And it is. Because the very real positive effects of mindfulness have been accompanied by collateral damage that its adherents rarely recognise. Mindfulness has ridden such a wave of popularity that it is seldom subject to critical reflection. It's time to inject more intellectual honesty by exploring three problems. For a start, the popular secularised version of mindfulness – as opposed to the centuries-old Buddhist tradition – has ended up focusing too much on the self, leaving it thin on moral foundations. Second, in placing so much emphasis on attending to the present moment, it overlooks how much human beings thrive on striving for meaningful future goals. Finally, mindfulness as it is typically practised today has increasingly come to overshadow other existentially rewarding ways of being in the now, namely exuberance, flow, wonder and collective ecstasy. There's a difference between the sense of presence that comes from quieting the mind during a meditation session in your local community hall, and the feeling of exhilarating presence you can get while playing a high-energy basketball match or dancing ecstatically with the crowd at a music festival. In other words, mindfulness is just one amongst many varieties of now.

More fundamentally, the modern mindfulness movement has – largely unintentionally – hijacked the carpe diem tradition: opportunity, hedonism, spontaneity and politics are all at risk of being displaced by the power of now. Indeed, many books and courses explicitly equate Horace's ideal with mindfulness itself. According to the website of one university medical clinic that uses mindfulness in its treatment programmes, 'Mindfulness is an innate ability to be present in the moment and seize the day.'[3] While carpe diem can become a richer philosophy by including mindfulness as one of its approaches, we should ensure that this approach does not come to dominate over all the rest.

Many people I have talked to about these ideas have been taken aback or even outraged by my critiques of mindfulness. It is clearly a topic that arouses strong emotions. Nevertheless, while I recognise that mindfulness is valuable and valued by many people, I believe it is crowding out other equally important approaches to carpe diem.

Beware the Mindful Sniper

A fascination with living in the present moment has been part of Western culture since at least the 1950s, when the import of

Eastern spiritual and religious thought popularised practices such as Zen Buddhism and Transcendental Meditation. One devoted fan was Aldous Huxley, whose 1962 utopian novel *Island* is set in a jungle paradise where specially trained mynah birds loudly screech out 'Here and now! Here and now!' and 'Attention! Attention!' at random intervals, as a reminder to its inhabitants to focus on the present. Soon a whole generation was searching for the sacred now, including The Beatles, who spent hours in cross-legged meditation with their Rolls-Royce-loving guru Maharishi Yogi. 'I think you can reach a certain state of consciousness, a state where you are not aware of anything… you're just being,' declared John Lennon in 1968. 'The happiest people are those who are being more times a week than anybody else.'[4] Being not doing had become a mantra of the age. A turning point came in 1975, when Vietnamese Zen Buddhist master Thich Nhat Hanh brought the concept of 'mindfulness' into the public eye through his book *The Miracle of Mindfulness*, which associated it with sitting meditation, mindful breathing, and bringing awareness to everyday activities like walking or washing the dishes.[5]

Although Christianity has its own contemplative traditions going back to the Middle Ages, the mindfulness boom of recent times has more clearly grown out of this post-war familiarity with Eastern meditation practices. The two dominant approaches to mindfulness today – Mindfulness-Based Stress Reduction (MBSR) and Mindfulness-Based Cognitive Therapy (MBCT) – both draw explicitly on Buddhist meditation approaches (especially from the Vipassana tradition) as the grounding of their methods, particularly the importance of focusing on the breath.[6] But as MBSR pioneer Jon Kabat-Zinn has repeatedly pointed out, his intention has been to create a scientific and secular version of mindfulness – 'Buddhist meditation without the Buddhism', as he puts it – where people are taught 'present-moment awareness' and the virtues of 'non-judgment' without the trappings of religious doctrines like

Karmic cycles and the Four Noble Truths.[7] This clinical, scientific approach has helped mindfulness extend its reach to everyone from medical practitioners to corporate bosses. Britain can even boast a Mindfulness All-Party Parliamentary Group of MPs who advocate it as a 'cost-effective' route to tackling the country's mental health crisis.[8] Every mindfulness trainer can point to a raft of 'evidence-based' scientific studies that reveal, in statistical terms, how an eight-week course in mindfulness can have measurable benefits for psychological and physical health.

The explosion of mindfulness has also been due to lucky timing. It is the perfect antidote to an historically specific crisis in human wellbeing that has engulfed Europe and North America since the late 1990s: the crisis of distraction.[9] For many people – especially amongst the professional middle classes – life feels like it has become an endless torrent of emails, social media updates and digital news, which has left them constantly running to catch up, permanently stressed and too busy to focus attention on the present. They can't walk down the street or sit on a train for ten minutes without checking their phones. Their minds are constantly flitting from one task to the next, one app to the next, so that being in a state of continuous partial attention has become the norm.

What does this epidemic of distraction look like? Picture this. A few years ago one of the world's great concert violinists, Joshua Bell, took his 1713 Stradivarius down to a Washington DC metro station and spent forty-three minutes playing pieces by Johann Sebastian Bach and other composers during the morning rush hour. Tickets to hear him play normally cost at least $100. Did crowds gather to hear his virtuoso performance? Was his violin case overflowing with dollars from appreciative passers-by? Quite the opposite. Of the 1,097 people who walked past him, only seven bothered to stop and listen for even a moment.[10]

The virtue of mindfulness is that it enables people to stop and listen to the music of their lives. It allows them to be immersed in the moments of their day and be seized by them. To appreciate the benefits of mindfulness myself, I recently went on an MBCT course with a long-experienced teacher at a highly respected UK-based mindfulness centre. The first session, where we were introduced to the idea of sitting, breathing, and letting the flotsam and jetsam of thoughts settle in the mind, was all very familiar, as I had previous experience of attending Buddhist meditation classes, and had long been an admirer of Thich Nhat Hanh.[11] It was helpful to be reminded that we spend so much of the day on automatic pilot, running around trying to get things done, and we should sometimes pause and bring more attention to the present, and really notice what we're thinking, feeling and experiencing.

But as the weeks went on, and we did our body scans and three-minute breathing spaces, I began to notice something. The instructor's emphasis was very 'Me, Me, Me' – how mindfulness would help me deal with *my* stress and anxiety, would boost *my* wellbeing, and enable me to enjoy the pleasures of *my* life, from the taste of a raisin to the song of a blackbird. The sessions were virtually devoid of the ethical component so prevalent in Buddhist meditation traditions, where the focus is not just on relieving personal suffering, but extending compassion beyond the self to relieve the suffering of others. This was brought home to me in the third week, when one participant commented to the teacher that a Buddhist friend of his had described mindfulness courses as 'Buddhism without the ethics'. The class tittered a little uneasily but the teacher refused to engage with the critique, glossing over it by asking him if he had managed to bring his attention back to the present after hearing his friend's opinion. At no point in the tightly scripted course, or any of its handouts, was there any discussion of moral issues and the individualist thrust of mindfulness.

Maybe, I thought, I was being ungenerous in my interpretation, or had an atypical experience.[12] So I decided to ask one of the world's foremost experts on meditation and mindful awareness, the

French Buddhist monk Matthieu Ricard, what he thought about the mindfulness movement. Ricard, who originally trained as a molecular biologist, is renowned not just for his books and TED talks that are known to millions, but for being the subject of brain experiments that led to him being dubbed (much to his annoyance) 'the happiest man in the world'. I fully expected him to be a keen proponent of mindfulness, having spent years in deep meditation in the foothills of the Himalayas. Yet I was wrong. He said:

> There are a lot of people speaking about mindfulness, but the risk is that it's taken too literally – to just 'be mindful'. Well, you could have a very mindful sniper and a mindful psychopath. It's true! A sniper needs to be so focused, never distracted, very calm, always bringing back his attention to the present moment. And non-judgmental – just kill people and no judgment. That could happen! So I talked a lot with Jon Kabat-Zinn and said, 'Please, just add six letters and call it *Caring* Mindfulness'. So simple – you cannot have a caring sniper or a caring psychopath.[13]

He then went on to quote a new study by neuroscientist Tania Singer at the Max Planck Institute in Leipzig showing that taking a mindfulness course can help you deal with stress but has no discernible impact on pro-social behaviour.[14]

Ricard was only half-joking about the sniper. As a growing wave of critics have pointed out, mindfulness courses have become popular in US military training, a somewhat disturbing echo of the mindfulness practices of Kamikaze pilots during World War Two.[15] Others have noted its adoption by the corporate world, a 'McMindfulness' that helps stressed-out Wall Street traders maintain calm and focus in the midst of market turbulence, or gives them the edge in high-stakes deal-making.[16] While the majority of people are not using mindfulness to hone their skills with a Marine Corps M40 sniper rifle or to make a killing in the financial markets, mindfulness is open to the charge of failing to offer adequate guidance to questions like 'What should I be mindful about?' and 'What should I give my attention to?'

There is now an increasing recognition amongst many Buddhist scholars and other critics that in its drive to secularise Buddhist meditation traditions, and to appeal to as wide an audience as possible, the modern 'scientific' approach to mindfulness has ended up creating a morally empty approach to living that risks reinforcing the individualist bias of contemporary self-help culture.[17] What's more, they say, it remains blind to the deep structural problems of society, from child poverty to gender inequality. The central message of mindfulness is to work on the self, not to try changing the world by directly challenging political privilege, power and injustice. As the sociologist Renata Salecl puts it, progressive political change is being held back by a 'New Age ideology that promotes living in the moment and accepting things as they are'.[18] Renowned Buddhist teachers Ronald Purser and Andrew Cooper are even more forthright:

> The rapid mainstreaming of mindfulness has provided a domesticated and tame set of meditation techniques for mainly upper-middle-class and corporate elites so they may become more 'self-accepting' of their anxieties, helping them to 'thrive,' to have it all – money, power and well-being, continuing business-as-usual more efficiently and, of course, more 'mindfully' – while conveniently side-stepping any serious soul searching into the causes of widespread social suffering.[19]

Such critics often contrast today's secular mindfulness with the 'socially engaged Buddhism' promoted by people like Thich Nhat Hanh, who has stressed that mindfulness should be combined with taking action on real world problems such as armed conflict and poverty. During the Vietnam War, Nhat Hanh worked unstintingly for reconciliation between North and South Vietnam, engaged in acts of non-violent civil disobedience, and set up relief organisations to rebuild destroyed villages.[20] Matthieu Ricard has been similarly involved in establishing education and health care projects in poor communities in India, Nepal and Tibet.[21]

The mindfulness movement counters this barrage of attacks with the claim that self-focus does not mean selfishness. Rather, what mindfulness does is raise our levels of self-awareness, which is precisely what we need to open our eyes to a whole range of social problems. Psychologist Daniel Goleman argues that mindful awareness is a prerequisite for empathic action: you are unlikely to stop long enough to notice that someone on the street needs help if you are busily rushing around with your head down texting a friend.[22] Jon Kabat-Zinn has, accordingly, described mindfulness as 'a totally ethical way of being'.[23] Yet his approach to moral issues is unashamedly couched in the language of self-help individualism. 'In the mindful cultivation of generosity, it is not necessary to give everything away, or indeed anything,' he writes. 'Above all, generosity is an inward giving... Perhaps most of all, you need to give to *yourself* first for a while.'[24] That's a pretty generous interpretation of the meaning of generosity. His hope is that being kind to yourself through mindfulness will be a step on the road to giving to others, yet it remains a hope that – at least for now – lacks substantive empirical evidence. A report by Friends of the Earth, for instance, suggests that mindfulness can reduce people's focus on materialistic values, but does not demonstrate clear causal linkages between taking a mindfulness course and making pro-social and pro-environmental choices. Moreover, it notes that the possible benefits of 'mindful consumerism' are limited by the fact that 'mindfulness training is predominantly in the domain of the white middle classes' and its impact 'erodes over time'.[25]

In defence of mindfulness, one could argue that it is able to attract more people by being presented and marketed in an apparently 'neutral', scientific way that focuses on personal benefits. After all, not everyone feels comfortable meditating in the presence of a saffron-robed Buddhist monk and talking about world compassion. And surely it isn't a bad thing to encourage people to stop rushing around like mad, switch off automatic pilot, and instead give a bit more attention to the passing moments of their lives? What's more, mindfulness isn't (usually) setting out to create a social revolution, so it shouldn't be accused of failing to do so: it's just a technique for raising our levels of awareness and capacity to notice life as it streams by us.

I don't think the bar should be set so low. It is too easy for mindfulness to hide behind a cloak of benign moral innocence. Matthieu Ricard is right: until mindfulness becomes more explicit in stressing an ethical vision it will serve to sustain our culture of self-interest, or at least fail to mount any serious challenge to it. Buddhism manages to integrate a moral outlook into its teachings, so why not mindfulness courses too? Of course, it is also true that any approach to carpe diem – whether mindful presence or others such as opportunity or hedonism – should take ethics seriously, which is precisely why, later in this book, I will be exploring what a morally robust version of carpe diem might look like. For the moment, however, we need to recognise that mindfulness – as typically taught in its secular, scientific form – does not make the grade.

There is another challenge for mindfulness to which we must now turn. It concerns nothing less than the ultimate question of the human journey. Can mindfulness satisfy our existential hunger for a life of meaning?

WHY BEING PRESENT IS NEVER ENOUGH

A curious feature of mindfulness techniques, whether of the new scientific or the older Buddhist variety, is that they set us a task – focusing on the present – that our brains are not well designed to perform. It's no surprise that so many people get frustrated when they take up meditation, with their thoughts jumping about like crazy, worrying if they embarrassed themselves at work that day or wondering what to make the kids for dinner. That's because thinking about the past and future is a natural trait of a healthy human mind: it's essential for both our sense of identity and how we navigate the world. Just consider what it's really like to live completely in the present – and I mean all of the time. If you find this scenario difficult to imagine, let me introduce you to Henry Gustav Molaison, one of the most studied individuals in the history of neuroscience research.

Henry, known in the scientific literature as 'HM', was born in Connecticut in 1926. In 1953, aged twenty-seven, he underwent an experimental form of lobotomy to relieve his debilitating epilepsy. But something went wrong. Although the frequency of Henry's seizures went down, from that day until his death in 2008, he suffered from almost complete amnesia. Henry's memory lasted around thirty seconds, and after that he forgot nearly everything. At the same time, his botched brain surgery deprived him of the ability to imagine future experiences – he couldn't plan anything for the next day, month or year. This left Henry in a state of what neuroscientist Suzanne Corkin called 'permanent present tense', where he was 'trapped in the here and now'.[26] Corkin ran tests on Henry for forty-six years, but right to the end he still failed to recognise her whenever they met, even if she popped out of the lab for just ten minutes.

Could Henry function in day to day life? Only just. He could talk, read, do basic arithmetic and play bingo, but that was about it.

When he went to a restaurant, he found it hard to order food as he had no idea what he liked. He couldn't hold down a job because the moment he was taught to do something, he forgot it. He read and re-read the same magazines. He needed round-the-clock carers to remind him to wash himself and make sure he didn't get lost walking in the local neighbourhood. He was pleasant and mild-mannered but he couldn't make real friendships as he couldn't recall anybody's name or anything about them. He couldn't remember his own age – and was often out by decades when he guessed. He had some memories of the time before his operation, but these were highly limited. 'Being unable to establish new memories,' said Corkin, 'Henry could not construct an autobiography as his life unfolded'.[27] Permanent immersion in the now left him with only the vaguest sense of personal identity, and unable to live independently.

We can read Henry's story almost as an allegory about how much we need the past in our lives. It's something we all know from meeting people with dementia, where acute memory loss (first short-term then later long-term) can leave them unable to recognise family members, socially isolated and disoriented. Their unwilled capacity to live in the present is hardly enviable. Who we are cannot be separated from the memories that give us a sense of continuity through time and connection to others.

Neurological research reveals that the future is just as important to us as the past. Human beings are prediction machines. Our brains are constantly looking to what is about to happen next, and whether some action or event will bring us pleasure or pain. 'One of the most important goals of any animal,' writes neuroscientist Morten Kringelbach, 'is to become sufficiently skilled at predicting the influence of future events on their levels of pleasure and reward'.[28] Will I enjoy that third piece of chocolate cake? Should I prepare for tomorrow's meeting right now, or spend the time playing with my kids? Our lives are permeated by decision-making that requires projecting our minds forward in time and considering the consequences of our actions. Of course, we are good at developing rules of thumb so we don't have to constantly make calculations on the spot about future outcomes: we know that if we see a tiger in the wild, it's time to run. In general, however, thinking about the future is a necessary survival mechanism, a compass that helps us navigate the often unpredictable challenges that life throws at us.

The danger of mindfulness is that by drawing our attention to the present moment, the past and future may get relegated too far into the background. What lies behind and before us matters: as with riding a bike, while it can be refreshing to focus on feeling the breeze on your face, it's useful to know if there is a double-decker bus just behind you or if there's a traffic light up ahead. Mindfulness might encourage us to notice our current thoughts and feelings more clearly, and produce space for reflection, but we will always need guideposts based on our past experiences, and future goals or desires, to help us make choices and live a life of meaning.

This is one of the major discoveries of the Viennese psychiatrist Viktor Frankl, many of whose insights came from his experiences in Auschwitz and other concentration camps. It is worth exploring his work in some detail, as it raises serious questions about the priority that mindfulness gives to the present.

Frankl, who died in 1997, invented a therapeutic approach known as 'logotherapy' – a name based on the Greek *logos* or meaning. In contrast to Freud's belief that we are motivated by the 'pleasure principle', Frankl argued that human beings are ultimately seekers of meaning rather than pleasure. A person finds meaning, he says, when 'he commits himself to something beyond himself, to a cause greater than himself'. He quotes the psychiatrist and philosopher Karl Jaspers who wrote, 'What man is, he ultimately becomes through the cause which he has made his own.'[29] Frankl referred to this cause as a 'concrete assignment', a task or project that directs our minds forward in time toward something that matters deeply to us. It might be designing a new kind of space telescope, campaigning against biodiversity loss, running a semi-professional choir or caring for an ailing parent. Whatever the cause, its purpose is to act as an existential compass, orienting the direction of our future choices and actions – helping us decide what to seize when we seize the day.

Frankl's theory has a long intellectual pedigree. Aristotle, for instance, recognised that each of us should have 'some object for the good life to aim at… since not to have one's life organized in view of some end is a mark of much folly'.[30] Frankl's originality was to discover this first-hand in what he called the 'living laboratory' of the death camps.[31] He noticed that dedication to a cause or project not only ensured that people stayed in good mental health, but that it literally kept them alive. He gave the example of a scientist who wanted to commit suicide: Frankl helped him see that it was worth staying alive to finish writing the series of books he had started before the war – a task that could not be completed by anybody but himself. Having that future goal gave the scientist an inner strength that became a means of survival. In the camps, those without such a 'will to meaning' frequently killed themselves, or succumbed more quickly to disease. It wasn't so much being physically robust that determined whether people would live or die, but whether they had identified a cause that allowed them 'to retreat from their terrible surroundings to a life of inner riches and spiritual freedom'.[32]

He offered other powerful examples outside the extreme context of the war. Frankl pointed out that even when Goethe was extremely ill and close to death, sheer force of will kept him alive for seven years until he finished writing the second part of *Faust*. Two months after completing the manuscript, aged eighty-two, he died. Goethe's mission kept his heart beating, and once he had achieved it he was able to let go of life.[33] We often observe a similar phenomenon when an elderly person dies soon after their husband or wife has passed away: once their most meaningful relationship disappears, so does their will to live.

Frankl also believed that we should endeavour to find meaning in our suffering. He cites the case of a woman who attended one of his group therapy sessions in Vienna after trying to kill herself. One of her sons was confined to a wheelchair, and her other son had just died, aged only eleven. Frankl first asked a different, thirty-year-old woman in the group, to imagine being on her deathbed at eighty, having lived a childless life full of financial success and social prestige. This young woman described how her life had been replete with luxury living and amusing flirtation but was ultimately lacking in substance. 'My life was a failure,' she concluded. He then asked the mother of the disabled boy to imagine herself looking back aged eighty. Through tears she described how she had done her best to look after her son and made a fuller life possible for him. 'My life was no failure!' she declared. Frankl's observation was this: 'Anticipating a review of her life as if from her death bed, she suddenly was able to see a meaning to her life, a meaning which even included all of her suffering'.[34] For Frankl, this kind of example revealed that while we can't always change our circumstances or eradicate our suffering, we have the power to choose the attitude that we take to them.[35] That's what freedom and responsibility are really all about.

I am convinced that Frankl, were he alive today, would have been a vocal critic of mindfulness. Why? Because it orients the mind toward the present and away from future goals that can contribute to and enhance meaning.[36] 'Logotherapy focuses rather on the future,' he wrote, 'that is to say, on the assignments and meanings to be fulfilled'.[37] Frankl would also have been wary of the way mindfulness puts emphasis on bringing us into a state of peaceful inner calm, where our anxieties about the past and future float away. He was a firm believer that we absolutely need tension, challenge and a certain amount of anxiety and suffering in our lives. It is the struggle to close the gap between where we are today

137

and future objectives beyond the self that we wish to achieve that can give life its meaning. A concrete assignment provides a reason to get out of bed in the morning, even if pursuing it isn't always pleasurable in any obvious sense. Without such tensions we might find ourselves in what he called an 'existential vacuum'.[38] A state of serene calm can actually become a void where we have nothing to strive and struggle for, and so we become starved of meaning.

Proponents of mindful presence might reasonably counter that they are not completely dismissive of the past and future, but rather believe we should simply put more emphasis on living in the moment, especially in our high-speed world of digital distraction.[39] 'Make the Now the primary focus of your life,' suggests spiritual thinker Eckhart Tolle, 'have your dwelling place in the Now and pay brief visits to the past and future when required to deal with the practical aspects of your life situation'. In other words, we might need the past to remember what to buy from the supermarket, and the future to plan when to go shopping, but beyond their use for such everyday functions, neither should be considered a route to spiritual sustenance. In fact, as Tolle explains, they should be primarily seen as a source of 'pain, dysfunction and sorrow'. It is only in the present that we can realise our 'true nature'.[40] I consider such a view to verge on extremism. Frankl, for instance, shows us just how powerful the future can be as a wellspring of meaning in our lives. We need to find a healthy mix between dwelling in the past, present and future, not make any one of them our singular object of adulation.

Am I saying that we should refrain from practising mindfulness and bringing ourselves into the present? Not at all. Mindfulness has plenty going for it: it can be good for our mental health, offer us the headspace to clarify a concrete assignment that can give our life direction and meaning, and bring an awareness and attention to the way we make carpe diem choices in our lives. But it is not the answer – or at least not the only answer – to the great question of life, the universe and everything.

The Lost Varieties of Now

Exuberance: Unleashing a Lust for Life

Who can forget the opening of *The Sound of Music*? Even if you find the film sentimental and saccharine, you can probably recall Maria, the postulant nun, swirling with exuberant delight in the Austrian Alps, singing her heart out about the hills being alive with the sound of music. Lost in song, she eventually hears the distant ringing of convent bells and rushes back late for mass. Her superiors are not amused, and she is hauled in for an audience before the boss, the Reverend Mother. Maria explains how she just couldn't help climbing up the Untersberg, lured by the fragrant green slopes and blue sky, and singing as she went.

What's Maria's problem – at least from the perspective of the nuns? It's her natural and almost uncontrollable exuberance. Rather than adhering to the convent rules and immersing herself in a mindful state of Christian prayer, she is bursting with energy and excitement, and can't help losing herself in the moment, in the beauty of the mountains, the sky, the birds, in life and laughter. Maria's joie de vivre gives her an extraordinary capacity for being in the now, but it's a version of being present that is very different from the poised calm of mindful breathing or a composed and contemplative session of what is known as 'walking meditation'.

What, exactly, is exuberance? According to clinical psychologist Kay Redfield Jamison, 'exuberance is an abounding, ebullient, effervescent emotion… certainly it is no lulling sense of contentment: exuberance leaps, bubbles and overflows'.[41] It is an aliveness and passion for life that is more energetic than joy but less intense than ecstasy. The exuberant amongst us are the embodiment of enthusiasm, in the original Greek sense of *en theos*, having a god within. Not that this is always a good thing, notes Jamison. If everyone was continually exuberant all of the time, 'the world would be an exhausting and chaotic place, driven to incoherence by competing enthusiasms'.[42] You can't have too many Marias on the scene.

For Jamison, exuberant individuals represent a particular personality type, making up an estimated 6 to 10% of the general population.[43] It's a mostly innate trait or disposition, closely related to extraversion (and in some cases bipolar disorder). You can't take a course in exuberance as you can with mindfulness: either you've got it or you haven't. She cites many character examples, from the naturalist John Muir to the physicist Richard Feynman, from Toad of Toad Hall to Snoopy. One of her favourites is US President Theodore Roosevelt. He had an irrepressible zest for life and was always speaking with great animation, bursting into roars of laughter every five minutes. He could often be found racing around the White House with his children, chasing them and their ponies up and down the marble stairs. 'You must always remember,' said one British diplomat, 'the President is about six'.[44] Like Maria von Trapp, Roosevelt had a carpe diem lust for life, a capacity to squeeze everything he could out of each moment.

Too often today the idea of being present is simplistically equated with the stillness of mindful awareness. Exuberance is a reminder that mindfulness has no monopoly on bringing us into the here and now. Yet there are further varieties of now we should learn to appreciate, which tap into other parts of the human psyche and may leave different traces of meaning on our lives. So what alternatives are available, especially if we don't happen to have an excitable inner Maria ready to surge out of us? The surfing fraternity might offer some help.

Flow: Stepping into the Zone

Surfers have a deeply attuned sense of being in the now. Their descriptions of what it feels like to ride a wave – especially a tough one – typically overflow with the language of presence:

When you surf the best, you are in the zone. You are there alone. It is you, the wind, the waves, the salt in your mouth and the vision of the bumps and the chops and the sucking phase. There is nothing else there. There is nothing else in your mind. There is nothing else that matters. For a moment in time, time stands still.[45]

When you're on a wave, time ceases to exist, and you're in such an intense combined state of euphoria, peace, presence and excitement that it's something you have to return to over and over again... If there's anything that surfing teaches you, it's how to be present.[46]

These surfers, perhaps without realising it, are describing a phenomenon that psychologists call 'flow'. This is when you

Laird Hamilton, one of the greatest 'big wave' surfers of all time. This doesn't look like any meditation class that I've ever been to.

become so absorbed in an activity that neither past nor future seem to matter, and you are completely and unselfconsciously immersed in the present. All sense of time disappears and whatever it is, you are just doing it. We have a colloquial term for this state: being 'in the zone'. You might experience it when involved in an intense and energetic football game, or playing guitar in the pub, solving a Sudoku, or conjuring up a five-course dinner for friends. For more than four decades the psychologist Mihaly Csikszentmihalyi has studied flow amongst a wide range of people, including basketball players, surgeons, rock climbers, chess players and concert pianists (though not, to my knowledge, surfers). He noticed that there is a trick to getting into flow: you need to be engaged in an activity that is not so easy that it makes you bored, but not so difficult that you become anxious about failure. An element of challenge or risk is part of the mix. In other words, you've got to be a bit out of your comfort zone to get into the zone.

Csikszentmihalyi believes that flow is as good a proxy as any for 'happiness' or what he prefers to call 'optimal experience'. Apart from being engrossed in the moment, those in flow report that it has other tell-tale signs: you feel in control of your own actions, experience a sense of exhilaration and also of transcendence, you are displaying mastery of a skill, and the activity is done for its own sake rather than as a means to an end. Alas, I cannot claim familiarity with this checklist as a result of my surfing prowess, which unfortunately failed to appear during the surfing lesson I had as research for this book. But as an addict of the obscure medieval game of real tennis – an indoor sport played with bent racquets that is a combination of regular tennis, squash and chess – I know just what it's like to be in flow.[47] I enter the now not through quiet meditation but by diving through the air reaching for a backhand volley. I feel not so much that I am living in the moment, but that the moment is an impulse surging through me, fusing mind and body into a single instant of time. Being and doing collapse into one another. Of course, I can only write this description after the fact. While I'm in the middle of a rally (which real tennis players perversely call a 'rest') I'm not consciously thinking or feeling anything at all. I'm just hitting the ball.

How does this help us understand the varieties of now? One of Csikszentmihalyi's key points is that, contrary to popular opinion, these moments of optimal experience 'are not the passive, receptive, relaxing times'. In fact, 'the best moments usually occur when a person's body or mind is stretched to its limits in a voluntary effort to accomplish something difficult or worthwhile.'[48] As with Viktor Frankl's idea of the concrete assignment, the actual experience itself will not always be pleasurable: your body might be aching or your brain twisted in knots. But you will nevertheless have a profound feeling of carpe diem aliveness. Don't worry, be happy? Csikszentmihalyi would beg to differ. Enjoying an engaged and fulfilling life is not a matter of getting rid of worries or entering a state of inner stillness. Rather, it is about riding a challenging wave that requires every ounce of attention and focus you have to avoid a wipeout, while still being able to enjoy the thrill. That's what it takes to get the high that surfers call being 'stoked'.

Wonder: Being Stirred by the Universe

Alongside exuberance and flow is a more primordial route to the now: wonder. The word 'wonder' goes back to Old Norse, but its precise etymology is unknown. Its elusive origin is appropriate, for wonder itself often seems somehow beyond our grasp. We associate it with being in a state of awe or astonishment. There is something that arrests us, that seizes us, that holds us in the present with its immensity, beauty or mystery. I've felt wonder gazing into the vast silent chasm of the Grand Canyon, when surrounded by a fever of stingrays undulating past me in the Great Barrier Reef, staring up at the Eiffel Tower as a stupefied six-year-old, and studying the tiny, perfectly formed hands of my daughter just a few seconds after she emerged from the womb.

We know wonder when we experience it, but putting it into words is another matter. I could try to describe a profound moment of wonder when I was seventeen, standing alone on a mountainside in the Himalayas: I felt so tiny and insignificant in relation to the endless huge peaks before me, and I suddenly understood that my own problems were petty and insignificant compared with those of the world. Yet this does not come close to capturing that instant of awareness and the lasting effect it has had on me. Conveying wonder requires a poetic sensibility, which may be why the Romantics were amongst its most fervent and successful early apostles.

One of them was Samuel Taylor Coleridge. Especially in his twenties – before he was consumed by opium – Coleridge's greatest addiction was the natural world of mountains and valleys, woods and seas, or as he once wrote, a 'sycamore, oft musical with bees'. He embarked on gigantic walks (often with William Wordsworth) that sparked his poetic imagination and filled him with the awe and wonder of creation. During a solo tour of the Lake District in August 1802, as he strode across the fells he was confronted by scenes that were 'heart-raising' and 'wild as a dream'. His descent from the peak of Scafell Pike produced an effect of 'almost religious intensity', according to one biographer.[49] To make his way down, Coleridge ignored the careful pathways and picked his own near-vertical route, dropping down seven-foot ledges at full stretch. He soon landed on a narrow ledge that was too high and dangerous to descend, but from where he could no longer climb back up. He was trapped on the cliff-face. While most people would have panicked, for Coleridge it turned into a moment of ecstatic union with the raw majesty of nature. 'My limbs were all in tremble,' he recalled. 'I lay upon my back to rest myself, and was beginning according to my custom to laugh at myself for a madman, when the sight of the crags above me on each side, and the impetuous clouds just over them, posting so luridly and so rapidly northward, overawed me. I lay in a state of almost prophetic trance and delight, and blessed God aloud.'[50] He eventually managed to escape by wedging himself between two rock-faces and descending to safety. The Lake District's Fell & Rock Climbing Club now celebrates Coleridge's adventure as England's first ever recreational rock climb.

Writers such as Coleridge and Goethe not only created poetry out of the awe-inspiring sublime in nature; both of them also had a strong scientific bent. Indeed, it is the poet-scientist, possessing a capacity to observe the world and a curiosity to understand it, who may be best placed to speak the language of wonder. I will always remember the opening words of Carl Sagan's television documentary series *Cosmos*, first broadcast in 1980 and now seen by over 500 million people. Sagan was an astronomer who knew the power of poetry. To launch his epic, he deliberately eschewed statistics and attempted to convey the wonder of the universe in almost biblical cadences:

> The Cosmos is all that is or ever was or ever will be. Our contemplations of the Cosmos stir us – there is a tingling in the spine, a catch in the voice, a faint sensation, as if a distant memory, of falling from a great height. We know we are approaching the grandest of mysteries. The size and age of the Cosmos are beyond ordinary human understanding. Lost somewhere between immensity and eternity is our tiny planetary home, the Earth... I believe our future depends powerfully on how well we understand this Cosmos in which we float like a mote of dust in the morning sky.

Sagan was a champion of wonder. 'My parents were not scientists,' he wrote, 'but in introducing me simultaneously to scepticism and to wonder, they taught me the two uneasily cohabiting modes of thought that are central to the scientific method.'[51] His reflections raise a question: can we really learn to wonder, like we can learn to ride a bike? A natural capacity for wonder is a deeply human quality, and is reflected in the way that most creation stories express wonder at the very existence of the earth, the sky and the starry firmament above us. Yet how often, in our world which worships speed as much as gods, do we pause long enough to feel that tingling in the spine, the stir of the Cosmos? This is where mindfulness comes into its own as a tool for wonder, a key to unlocking its possibilities. It can slow us down and open our eyes to objects of wonder in everyday life, from the changing seasons to the laughter of a child. An iPhone app might help you name the stars, but a state of mindful awareness can provide the attention you need to gaze at them in awe. Even when packaged as a method for solving our personal problems, mindfulness has a capacity to give us a vista beyond the self.

Collective Ecstasy: Dancing with the Crowd

While mindfulness and wonder are close cousins amongst the varieties of now, there is a final form with a distinct personality: collective ecstasy. Perhaps our most common experience of ecstasy in daily life comes from sex, which can embody not just a sense of presence, but also other forms of carpe diem such as hedonism and spontaneity. But here I want to focus specifically on ecstasy as a collective or group phenomenon. Some of the earliest accounts of this come from European explorers who witnessed communal rituals on far-flung shores, which they usually viewed with horror and revulsion. The 'savages', wearing strange masks or headdresses, would dance, sing and chant, often for hours on end, and frequently enter a state of trance or frenzied possession, shouting and groaning amongst the blazing fires. Charles Darwin was a typical observer, writing with unbridled disgust about a corroborree dance of the

White Cockatoo Aboriginal people he encountered in Western Australia in 1836:

> Their heavy footsteps were accompanied with a kind of grunt, by beating their clubs and spears together, and by various other gesticulations, such as extending their arms and wriggling their bodies. It was a most rude, barbarous scene, and, to our ideas, without any sort of meaning.[52]

What Darwin failed to remember was that Europe had its own tradition of ecstatic rituals, ranging from the Eleusinian Mysteries of the ancient Greeks and Rome's Bacchanalian cult through to the masked revelry of Venice's annual pre-Lent Carnival. Perhaps at heart the Europeans were not quite so different from the natives as he liked to think.

In his 1912 book *The Elementary Forms of Religious Life*, the French sociologist Emile Durkheim pointed out that such indigenous ceremonies and festivities were actually abundant with meaning. These rituals produced what he called 'collective effervescence', an ecstasy that created social bonds and formed the ultimate basis of religion.[53] There was a stepping outside the self – what the Greeks termed *ekstasis* – which melted away individuality into a larger unity, something like a group consciousness. It was a process that brought participants utterly into the now, dispossessed of their personal pasts and futures, and suspended in time in the social body.

Where can we find such collective ecstasy today? You might come across it in Pentecostal churches such as the Assemblies of God, where charismatic preachers excite their congregations into collective effervescence with rousing cries of 'Hallelujah!'. If you are lucky you will see someone entering a trance state like being 'Slain by the Spirit', a kind of sensory override where people feel so filled with the Holy Spirit that they collapse backwards (into the arms of 'catchers') and may find themselves speaking in tongues, or laughing or weeping uncontrollably.[54]

Stepping away from the pulpit, you may also find communal ecstasy at your nearest rave, the mass dance phenomenon that emerged with electronic dance music and drugs such as Ecstasy in the 1980s. Those attending raves frequently describe how they can lose their sense of self, feel a strong communal bond with their fellow ravers, and may enter a trance-like state where they can dance for hours on end, seemingly oblivious of the passage of time (similar to being in flow). While certain drugs can help generate such experiences, they can also occur without any artificial stimulants, possibly due to the effects of the musical rhythms on modifying brain activity, or as a result of the psychological phenomenon of 'emotional contagion', where an emotion such as joy can spread and lead to an ecstatic merger with the group. Anthropologists have pointed out that modern 'trance' music – a genre characterised by repeated melodic phrases that build up to a mid-song climax, followed by a soft breakdown – can have a particularly mind-altering effect, and have noted that the mesmerising rhythmic beat resembles the ritual drumming found in indigenous communities around the world.[55] If you have absolutely no idea what I'm talking about, go online and have a listen to Tobias 'TB' Bassline's classic 'Supernova' psytrance mix. And make sure you turn it up loud.

While dancing at a rave can be a blissful experience, there is no doubt that collective ecstasy also has dark sides. From the ecstatic atmosphere generated by the Nazis in their annual Nuremberg Rallies, to the violence that can quickly spread amongst rival supporters at a football match, there is a possibility that a mass immersion in the now can erupt into what Elias Canetti referred to as 'the destructiveness of the crowd'.[56] In this sense, mindfulness could provide a less volatile route to entering the present, avoiding the potential formation of a toxic 'us' versus 'them' mentality.

On the other hand, in our highly individualised and atomised world, where social trust is in freefall, long-term neighbours often hardly know each other, and one in four people say they are chronically lonely, collective ecstasy may play an important role in creating new kinds of social bonds and communal values.[57] This is clearly what Evangelical church movements are doing, generating a collective effervescence that provides a sense of community to their followers. But it is also the case with dance, which the neurobiologist Walter Freeman has described as 'the biotechnology of group formation'. He argues that the rhythmic beats and movements in unison in many forms of dance 'can lead to altered states of consciousness, through which mutual trust among members of societies is engendered'.[58] So in the interest of communal bonding, it might be time to get yourself to a festival like Burning Man or Glastonbury, head for a tent playing trance music, and dance the night away.

Some admirers of mindfulness might wish to claim that all four ways of entering the now that I've been describing – exuberance, flow, wonder and collective ecstasy – are really just different forms of mindfulness. You can dance mindfully, gaze at the stars mindfully, surf mindfully and sing mindfully on a mountaintop too. But if mindfulness simply becomes a catch-all term for every kind of living in the moment, it begins to lose meaning and coherence. The conscious practice of MBCT mindfulness techniques – such as a three-minute breathing space done with your eyes closed – offers a very different mental and physical experience than being immersed in the flow of a high-speed ice hockey match. Mindfulness is best thought of as one amongst several varieties of being in the now, all of which share a common feature, which is to absorb us in a timeless present.

Confronting the Digital Now

In May 1844 a breathless article published in the *New York Herald* celebrated an astonishing new invention that, in an instant, appeared to annihilate both space and time: Professor Morse's telegraph. Suddenly, thanks to the tapping down the telegraph line, you could be aware not just of the 'now' in your immediate surroundings at 11am in a town like Baltimore, but simultaneously aware of another 'now', such as the words of a legislator being spoken in Washington DC at that very same moment. As the article put it, 'it requires no small intellectual effort to realise that this is a fact that *now* is, and not one that *has been*.'[59]

The internet and other digital technologies have taken this transformation to a new level. Courtesy of instant messaging, Facebook, rolling Twitter feeds and streaming electronic news, our own present moments have been invaded by the present moments of potentially millions of other people from around the planet, which are all competing for our limited stock of attention. While we can attempt to filter them out, the space in which we experience our personal present can feel difficult to protect. The multiple nows of humanity have been crammed into our own, often leaving us bedazzled and bewildered.

This electronic multiplication of the now ranks as one of the most momentous changes in the history of presence. How should we negotiate it? Which of these nows should we seize, or let ourselves be seized by? A good case can be made that mindfulness may be one of the most effective tools at our disposal. It can offer calm in the digital storm, allowing us to attend to specific presents – whether it's a text from a friend or a video report about an earthquake in Japan – with sufficient focus that they don't just add to the glut of information but can touch us and even change us. Mindfulness might also encourage us to step away from the screen and immerse ourselves in a more tangible now, where we can hear the live tweet of a songbird rather than the 140-character variety. 'Where can we live but days?' wrote the poet Philip Larkin. Mindfulness allows us to be in our days, and immunises us against a constant distraction of digital nows.

It also raises the possibility of turning carpe diem into an everyday way of living instead of an occasional act that punctuates our existence. Some forms of seizing the day, such as grasping windows of opportunity, may not present themselves with great regularity: true opportunities in work, love, travel and other realms can be few and far between. Mindfulness is different; no matter where we are and what we are doing, we can almost always seize the moment by bringing more attention to the present. And if you've got good at it, you can probably maintain your focus for more than the twenty seconds that most competent surfers manage to ride a wave.

This does not mean, however, that we should allow mindfulness to be a 'big now' that dominates our routes to the present tense. Exuberance, flow, wonder and collective ecstasy all offer alternative and valuable ways to be in the moment. The carpe diem tradition will be richer for incorporating this diversity of nows. Yet it will be diminished if seizing the day is reduced to the single dimension of living in the present. We will always need to draw on a range of approaches to Horace's ideal to help us live full and vibrant lives, and ensure that we do not become consumed by regret as our mortal clocks tick by. We need many stars to help us navigate the course of our personal journey. Having explored opportunity, hedonism and presence, we must now turn our gaze toward another of them: spontaneity.

7

Recovering Our Spontaneous Selves

I am not, as a rule, a particularly spontaneous person. I'm organised. I like to plan. I've got plenty of inhibitions. But occasionally I break the mould. For me, spontaneity is the moment when my daughter sees a steep grassy slope in the park, throws herself to the ground, and starts rolling down it – and I join in with her too. It's the moment when I'm running a workshop in a prison and I realise that the inmates are taking the discussion away from my planned topic – and I suddenly decide (despite some trepidation) to abandon my plan and do an improvised session around what *they* want to talk about. It's the moment when a friend of mine hears some fireworks outside while we're having dinner, and immediately gets us all to scramble up onto the rooftop to watch them, leaving our rhubarb crumble half-eaten. It's the moment at the end of the film *Zorba the Greek* when the repressed, bookish Basil turns to the life-loving Zorba and says, totally out of character and out of the blue, 'Teach me to dance' – and they dance the sirtaki together on the beach.

What do these instances of spontaneity share? For a start, they involve taking immediate action and not procrastinating, an echo of Horace's advice in Ode XI to 'leave as little as possible for tomorrow'. They are about acting freely and being unconstrained, reflecting the Latin origin of spontaneity, which comes from *sponte*, meaning 'of one's own accord, freely, willingly'. Spontaneity is also often associated with abandoning plans and timetables, and breaking social norms and conventions, so we act in ways that are out of the ordinary. When was the last time you rolled down a grassy hillside?

Some people appear to be naturally spontaneous and possess an effervescent seize-the-moment personality. They are ready and willing to 'play things by ear' – a metaphor calling for an unrehearsed and unscripted approach to life. Others are more like the philosopher Immanuel Kant, who was known as 'the Königsberg clock' for his unwavering habit of taking his daily walk at precisely 5pm, and always along the same route. Most of us are somewhere in between.

Yet as I have discussed in an earlier chapter, in historical terms spontaneity is in long-term decline. Western societies have, over the centuries, become increasingly scheduled: we have, for instance, inherited a regimented attitude to time as a legacy of the Industrial Revolution. We are now in an era in which we plot out our lives weeks in advance in our diaries, and focus on ways to efficiently manage our time as we battle against a barrage of emails and information overload, while trying to meet work deadlines and get the kids to swimming class. Spontaneity has been subject to a devastating cultural hijack: instead of 'just do it', we 'just plan it'.

There may be no greater symbol of this hijacking than an electronic time management system used by over 100,000 lawyers worldwide that logs every six-minute chunk of their time, as a way of increasing productivity and ensuring clients are charged for every possible moment. The software's name? *Carpe Diem*. You couldn't make it up.[1]

Spontaneity ranks – alongside presence, hedonism, opportunity and politics – as one of the core approaches to seizing the day that have emerged in Western society.[2] In an effort to preserve and revive the spirit of carpe diem, this chapter explores how we should respond to the decline of spontaneity. One reaction has been the rise of impulsive action in digital spheres such as online shopping and instant messaging. Yet this amounts to little more than a superficial compensation for what has been lost, and it is vital to distinguish this tech-led impulsivity from more profound forms of spontaneity. To recover our spontaneous selves we can look for inspiration in realms ranging from traditional Persian music and theatre improvisation to sensory travel and Brazilian football strategy. Spontaneity, we will discover, is far more than an impromptu burst of action: it is – counterintuitively – a skill that can be practised and cultivated.

On this journey we should travel with the words of the nineteenth-century poet and essayist Ralph Waldo Emerson in our pockets. Emerson was a firm believer in the carpe diem ideal: 'Write it on your heart that every day is the best day in the year. No man has learned anything rightly until he knows that every day is Doomsday.'[3] At the same time, he saw spontaneity as a wise route to making the most of our precious days. Spontaneity, he wrote, is 'the essence of genius, the essence of virtue, and the essence of life'.[4] Let it be our guide and our aspiration.

THE RISE OF LAST-MINUTE LIVING

A recent newspaper article titled 'How Britons Learned the Art of Last-Minute Living' notes how 'mobile technology is erasing the rhythms of life,' because it enables people to be more spontaneous in their shopping habits. We no longer visit travel agencies and plan our holidays months in advance. Thanks to smartphones and travel websites full of late-booking deals, more than half of people booking short holiday breaks now do so in the week they depart, and around 44% say they have booked a trip on the spur of the moment. 'These days it's easier than ever to be spontaneous,' says Matthew Crummack, CEO of leading British travel firm lastminute.com. 'The rapid and continuous evolution of technology has given us a wealth of consumer choice, whenever and wherever we need it.'[5]

This outbreak of spontaneity extends to a whole culture of instant, one-click shopping online. Suddenly moved to take up yoga? Then take out your phone and buy yourself a yoga mat, pants and top. Fancy watching a film after dinner? Simply stream it from Netflix or Amazon. It can be exciting to book an eleventh-hour holiday or order some yoga gear with next-day delivery, but there is a danger that we are mistaking impulsive consumerism for spontaneity. Last-minute shopping is not just convenient for ourselves, but also remarkably convenient for retailers who are experts at tapping into our impulsive instincts, selling us a narrow form of spontaneity for the benefit of their bottom line. A key by-product of the digital, just-in-time economy is that it enables products and services to be easily sold at the last moment – whether it's a cheap holiday flight or a discount TV in a pop-up January Sale advertisement. Buying such items on the spur of the moment can give us the *feeling* of acting spontaneously, making purposeful choices and really living in the now. We click the 'buy now' button and are rewarded with a heady rush of dopamine – the brain chemical that gives us a pleasure kick. But do we really want to reduce spontaneity to filling up an electronic shopping basket?

It is not only impulsive consumerism that is hijacking the spirit of carpe diem spontaneity: the innocent text message is just as responsible. You might, for instance, invite a friend out to see a band playing in a bar on a Friday night, and suggest meeting at 9pm. But rather than commit to a firm arrangement, your friend says, 'I'll text you later if I can make it'. Particularly in the world of Generation Y – those born in the 1980s and 1990s – people tend not to make definite arrangements when it comes to social life: decisions are made 'spontaneously' at the last moment. Maybe they'll come. But maybe they won't, especially if a better offer comes along. The instant text message has created an epidemic of non-commitment that masquerades as spontaneity.

What underlies this phenomenon? The answer, to use its social media hashtag, is #FOMO – fear of missing out. Behavioural psychologists define it as 'a pervasive apprehension that others might be having rewarding experiences from which one is absent'.[6] As cultural critic Steve Poole puts it, FOMO is 'a generalised attitude of always looking over the shoulder of the person you are talking to in case there is someone more interesting or attractive at the party'.[7]

Surveys reveal that 56% of social media users suffer from this new cultural disorder, and that it is most common amongst young adults, especially men.[8] Its pervasiveness is unsurprising, with everyone's 'friends' constantly posting messages about the great film they've just seen or the wild party they're at. Jane Austen's heroines may have worried about missing a dance where they might find a potential suitor, but this is nothing compared to the scores of social events that people today discover they are missing out on when they check their social media feeds, and see lost opportunities cascade down the screen in front of their eyes in a waterfall of unfulfilled possibilities. Suddenly there are simply too many moments to seize.

Yet the plague of FOMO is not spread by the surfeit of digital information alone. It also arises in a culture that increasingly values 'being connected' with others – a desire that social media both satisfies and exacerbates.[9] The cost of trying to be connected with everybody at once is to promote superficial relationships both online and offline. In the quest for perfect experiences with as many people as possible we may end up satisfying nobody, not even ourselves, as we flit from one social engagement to another, permanently thinking that there might be a better option. We are losing touch with the ancient Greek ideal of *philia* – deep friendships based on loyalty and comradeship where we are willing to make sacrifices for others.[10] In the pursuit of hyperconnection, what looks like spontaneous action is in fact a failure of commitment that results in our relationships being built on a foundation of sand. 'Only connect', wrote the novelist E.M. Forster. Today, we need something more: 'Only commit.'

Shouldn't we ask more of spontaneity than believing it can be satisfied through impulsive consumerism and last-minute commitment? Emerson, were he alive today, would surely set the bar higher. So how can we reclaim it to satisfy deeper existential needs? For a start, by turning the ideal of spontaneous action on its head by recognising that it can be born from practice and persistence.

IF YOU WANT TO BE SPONTANEOUS, PRACTISE, PRACTISE, PRACTISE

'Freedom,' wrote the psychoanalyst Erich Fromm in his 1942 book *Fear of Freedom*, 'consists in the spontaneous activity of the total, integrated personality.' He argues that we are most likely to experience the sense of freedom that lies at the root of genuine wellbeing when we are being spontaneous in our reactions to the people and landscape around us, and also in our own thoughts. This is when we truly exercise free will, and escape from social conventions and being ruled by fear and inhibition. Spontaneity is thus a key to self-realisation. In modern society, according to Fromm, we can most readily observe this trait in truly creative people: 'the artist can be defined as an individual who can express himself spontaneously'.[11]

So what could we learn from artists and other highly creative types about unleashing our spontaneous selves? An initial thought might be that we should take inspiration from creative geniuses like Jackson Pollock, whose innovative method of splattering paint on the canvas with rapid flicks and drips embodied a spontaneous approach to artistic expression. Following his lead, we ought to take chances, break rules, and express ourselves freely on the canvas of our lives.

The problem with this view, however, is that if you look closely at the life and work of most great artists – Jackson Pollock amongst them – you will find that their capacity for spontaneous expression has usually grown out of years of practice and honing their skills. It has been born from persistent effort and training in traditional techniques that serve as a rite of passage from which they can emerge with creative freedom. Take, for example, a celebrated photograph called 'Picasso draws a centaur in the air', one of the best-known depictions of spontaneity in twentieth-century art.

It shows the bare-chested artist crouching behind what looks like the doodled form of a centaur, drawn with a single white line and seemingly floating in the air before him. The photo was taken in 1949 by *Life* magazine's Gjon Mili when he visited Picasso, then in his late sixties, in the South of France. Mili convinced Picasso to conduct a fifteen-minute experiment: Picasso was given a 'pen' containing a small electric light, and then asked to use it to 'sketch' pictures in the air. Mili photographed the action in a darkened room using two cameras, keeping the shutters open to catch the light streaks swirling through space. Picasso was so thrilled with the experience of drawing with light that he did five sessions, swiftly making around thirty drawings of centaurs, bulls and Greek profiles. Each image was a spontaneous creation that vanished the moment he drew it. It was the ultimate in instantaneous, ephemeral art. Picasso was unable to see the forms he had created – which became known as his 'light drawings' – until after the photographs were developed.

Now pause for a moment and consider a much more conventional work of art, a portrait titled *The Old Fisherman*, dated 1895. As the art critic John Berger has pointed out, it clearly displays advanced technical skill.[12] The shining skin is extraordinarily realistic and the coarse shirt is perfectly rendered. The broad brush strokes help to juxtapose the light and shadow, giving a fleeting quality to the figure, as if his image has been photographically captured at a single instant of time. The fisherman looks down with a serious expression – we can practically see him thinking. In its subtle detail and specificity, the painting is reminiscent of works by Velázquez and other masters.

Who painted the fisherman? Picasso – when he was just fourteen years old.

Wander through an exhibition of Picasso's later works – full of almost childlike sketches of doves, dachshunds and flowers – and you will invariably overhear someone exclaim, 'My five-year-old could have done that!' But could she have painted the fisherman? What those spectators cannot see is that Picasso had to pass through years of training and artistic practice to arrive at the moment when he could draw and paint with spontaneity and freedom, using just a few lines to bring a dove, a centaur or a sleeping woman to life. As an art student in Barcelona and Madrid, he took classes in classical academic draftsmanship, working with live models and plaster casts of Greek and Roman sculptures, giving him a foundation for his later experiments with the human form. Although chafing against formal instruction, he spent days roaming the Prado, studying the works of Velázquez, Goya and El Greco – all of whom had a major influence

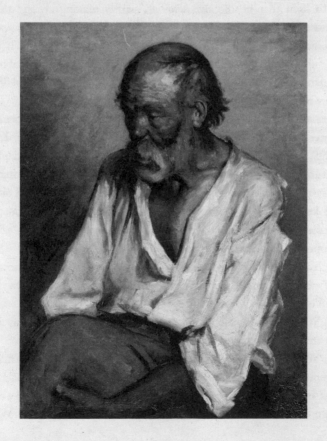

on his early style. He had to immerse himself in tradition and convention in order to break free from it. As the Picasso scholar Natasha Staller notes, Picasso became a 'self-consciously radical artist' who rejected his early academic education while at the same time remaining deeply influenced by it, in terms of 'his technical virtuosity, his knowledge of fine materials, his belief in the importance of drawing and the utility of preparatory drawings, his fascination with geometry and perspective.'[13]

The point is that Picasso was not born a miraculous unconventional artist filled with the fire of creative spontaneity. He had to become Picasso, and that took practice, application and education. He *had* to paint the fisherman before he could draw the centaur in the air forty-four years later.

Spontaneity in art, then, can be understood as an emergent property of practice. We learn it, like any craft or skill. This may be even more obviously the case in music than in the visual arts. The primary musical form embodying spontaneity is improvisation – the creation of a musical work as it is being performed. Improvisation appears, to a greater or lesser extent, in virtually every musical culture, from the Western classical tradition and jazz to Middle Eastern and classical Indian music. It is not only a learned skill, but also rests on conventions or implicit rules. In other words, the freeform nature of improvised musicianship typically takes place within a well-defined structure.

Amongst Western musicians, budding organists understand the challenges of learning improvisation. 'You have to study the whole history of music,' says Daniel Roth, organist at Saint-Sulpice in Paris, and 'have a thorough knowledge of harmony and music theory even to be able to start.'[14] Similarly, in the Karnatak music of southern India, where the skill of improvisation is highly revered, young musicians are taught the rules of improvising by practising a series of exercises to help them juxtapose rhythmic and melodic structures with the melodic grammar of a *rāga*. Amongst the formal rules is always to return to the point of departure. Such learned spontaneity is equally apparent in Iran, where improvisation techniques are based on memorising a repertoire of 250 to 300 short pieces known as the *radif*. Developing a true mastery of the *radif* – which may be sung or played on traditional Persian instruments such as the guitar-like tar – can take literally years of practice, so any part of it can be performed at any given moment.

What about jazz? Most jazz styles – apart from tightly scored big bands – put improvisation at their core. But for all the spontaneity that one can hear in a jazz performance, there are tacit rules when it comes to improvising. The cornerstone is a collection of popular songs known as 'Standards', which provide not just the melodic material but also the chord changes, the underlying harmonic progressions over which musicians improvise. My partner, an accomplished jazz singer and saxophonist, has initiated me (an utterly unaccomplished musician) into the secret language of jazz improvisation. The band starts by playing the 'head' or melody together, then each musician takes a solo, improvising over the chord changes. Soloists sometimes 'trade fours' with each other, taking it in turns to play four-bar solos with a call and response that bounces off the other. Many jazz musicians develop a repertoire of favourite phrases or 'licks' – musical fragments that are woven into their improvisations. Saxophonist Charlie Parker had at least 100 licks up his sleeve that he would artfully work and rework into his solos. Improvisation at its best becomes an exchange between the musicians resembling a conversation, such as the almost comic back and forth between Charles Mingus's double bass and Eric Dolphy's bass clarinet in their 1960 recording 'What Love' (based on the popular tune 'What Is This Thing Called Love').

When it comes to art and music, it is clear that spontaneity arises from practice and application – which is hardly what most people believe spontaneity is all about. We can think of it as 'prepared spontaneity'.[15] So too in life more generally we might think about applying the idea of prepared spontaneity. There are certain realms where it might be difficult: when it comes to big decisions like choosing a career or if we should have children, we have rarely had much opportunity to practice. But there are other areas where we may have developed particular skills, which lend themselves to expressing deeply learned spontaneity, whether it's cooking a meal, throwing a pot or telling a story. When I play tennis, and instinctively and unexpectedly volley the ball cross court for a winner, my free and spontaneous action occurs within the strictures of the rules of the game, and it's the fact that I have been practising and playing competitively for three decades that gives me the confidence and skill to occasionally wing it and do something unpredictable.

When we look at Picasso drawing with light, or listen to Charlie Parker, what we really need to ask ourselves is this: are there areas in my life where I can further nurture and practise a particular craft or skill, so that I then feel liberated enough to improvise and be spontaneous? Just as scientists realised that there is no such thing as spontaneous generation, let's not mythologise spontaneity in daily life as a realm of completely unrestrained and instinctive action that somehow comes out of nowhere. So if you are hankering after some carpe diem spontaneity, here's a clear lesson: practise, practise, practise.

EVERYTHING'S AN OFFER

We might be prepared to practise a skill to the extent that we can eventually break free and act with Picasso-like spontaneity. But there's a danger: what happens if all that practice – the proverbial 10,000 hours – turns us into an automaton enslaved by perfect technique and convention? We could find ourselves forever mechanically following the methods taught in a life drawing class, or never deviating from the recipe in the cookbook, or the strategic plan devised by the marketing department. How can we ensure that the spark of seize-the-day spontaneity remains alive in us, and that we maintain a creative approach to life?

For hundreds of years creativity itself was thought to be a gift from God. In the sixteenth century, Giorgio Vasari wrote about the 'Divine Michelangelo', who in all the major arts possesses 'a perfect mastery that God has granted no other person, in the ancient or modern world, in all the years that the sun has been spinning round the world'.[16] God began losing his monopoly on creative genius in the 1960s, when the first books on creativity techniques began to be published, such as Edward de Bono's classic *Lateral Thinking: A Textbook for Creativity*. Today you can find shelves of books offering methods to cultivate creative potential, all of them based on the premise that creativity is as much a learned skill as a divine (or genetic) gift.[17]

I believe in that premise but, in my view, if you are interested in nurturing your creativity and spontaneity, the best place to look for inspiration is neither in God nor a creativity guidebook, but in the theatre; specifically, in the improvisation techniques practised by actors. And even more specifically in a singular, electrifying idea: *accept the offer*. If there is an alchemical formula for spontaneous living, this may be it.

I first discovered the idea of the offer in an improv class run by a friend of mine, the writer, activist and creativity coach John-Paul Flintoff. There were fifteen people in the workshop, none of us professional actors. Most said they were there in the hope that improv might free them from fears, or make them more spontaneous, or just because it looked fun. It was a completely exhilarating – and often confronting – experience. We began with a hilarious exercise where we paired up with someone who spoke a language we didn't know. Person A started speaking in the language B was unfamiliar with, and B had to copy exactly what A was saying, speaking their words at precisely the same time. My partner talked to me in Mandarin. He began slowly while I tried to mirror the unfamiliar vowel sounds and tone inflections, my words clumsily overlapping his. After a few minutes I got into it, and found myself reciting an ancient Chinese poem in the original language (though not understanding a word of it, of course). For the next exercise, we split into teams where our task was to speak to each other without using the letter S. At first this activity seemed to freeze our brains and made it impossible to say anything at all, but it eventually led to engaging conversations marked, admittedly, by some unusual turns of phrase ('How old might your male child be?' or 'Would your abode happen to be near the park where Diana the female prince once lived?'). It was like tapping into an unused and rather rusty part of your linguistic intelligence.

All this was really a warm-up to shake us out of shyness and self-consciousness. The turning point was when John-Paul introduced the idea of the offer with the help of a deceptively simple game called 'Presents'. Again we split into pairs. Person A held out both hands and gave B an imaginary gift. B's role was to accept the gift offered to them, interpret what it was and respond to it. It was fun once we got the hang of it. So A might hold their arms out wide, and B would take the present with complete joy. B might then put it on, pretending it was a clown suit. B would then offer a present to A, perhaps cupped in her hands. Person A unpacks it, winds it up and follows it around the floor – it's a mechanical mouse. What made Presents work was not just accepting the gift with enthusiasm, but also making the gift we received as interesting as possible.

This exercise, as John-Paul explained, was originally devised by one of the gurus of theatrical improvisation, Keith Johnstone, when he was teaching at the Royal Court Theatre in London in the 1950s. What's really going on in Presents? Anything an actor does, Johnstone calls an 'offer'. Each offer can be either accepted or blocked. Scenes spontaneously generate themselves, according to Johnstone, if both actors offer and accept alternately. The game Presents is about encouraging us to accept an offer and work with it. In his book *Impro*, Johnstone gives an example of a failed improvised scene from one of his acting classes:

A: I'm having trouble with my leg.
B: I'm afraid I'll have to amputate.
A: You can't do that, Doctor.
B: Why not?
A: Because I'm rather attached to it.
B: *(Losing heart)* Come, man.
A: I've got this growth on my arm too, Doctor.

The scene fizzles out because A blocks B when he says, 'You can't do that, Doctor'. The action is unable to develop in a free and spontaneous way. Johnstone then had the same actors replay the scene, but this time making sure to accept rather than block the offers:

A: Augh!
B: Whatever is it, man?
A: It's my leg, Doctor.
B: This looks nasty. I shall have to amputate.
A: It's the one you amputated last time, Doctor.
B: You mean you've got a pain in your wooden leg?
A: Yes, Doctor.
B: You know what this means?
A: Not woodworm, Doctor!
B: Yes. We'll have to remove it before it spreads to the rest of you.
(A's chair collapses)
B: My God! It's spreading to the furniture![18]

Here the scene works because the actors have discovered the art of accepting the offer. It's dynamic, it's spontaneous, it's funny, it flows. The actors are responding to and embracing what's alive in the other person.

For Johnstone, learning to accept the offer is a lesson that extends far beyond the acting workshop. 'In life, most of us are highly skilled at suppressing action,' he writes. 'There are people who prefer to say "Yes", and there are people who prefer to say "No". Those who say "Yes" are rewarded by the adventures they have, and those who say "No" are rewarded by the safety they attain. There are far more "No" sayers around than "Yes" sayers.'[19] So most of us spend much of our lives blocking rather than accepting the offers that come our way. Johnstone's ideas ask us to identify the parts of our lives where we tend to block, and to consider accepting the offers instead.

How might we put this all into practice? A compelling response comes from Robert Poynton, an innovative thinker about creativity and communication in organisations who has spent fifteen years working with Johnstone's improvisation approach.

Poynton's key idea is this: Everything's an Offer.

This foundational principle contains three components: Notice More, Let Go, and Use Everything.[20] Notice More is about heightening our levels of awareness so we don't spend so much time on automatic pilot, letting potential offers pass us by. If you're listening to someone speak, what can you pick up from their intonation or the pauses in their speech? Are the walls of the room really white or – if you look closely – actually grey or tinged with blue? Can you hear a musical note in the humming of the office photocopier (and maybe sing along)? This kind of mindful attention primes us for creativity. We need to notice more of our immediate environment by opening up our senses, or as Poynton puts it, 'Can you learn to love the corner of your eye?'[21]

Next comes letting go. This is about jettisoning our assumptions, inhibitions and fear of judgment from others. Typically it requires making ourselves vulnerable. When I did the first activity at the improv workshop I felt self-conscious and it held me back. But once I sat down, I realised that nobody was judging me or really cared whether I was 'good' at speaking mock Chinese. We have to let go of those people who we imagine might be looking over our shoulder. They're probably not even there.

The third element – and this is the part I find most liberating – is the advice to Use Everything. We should recognise that everything we notice around us, and everything that happens to us, is a potential spark we can use for spontaneous living and thinking. We are surrounded by an abundance of offers. Here's an example. I was recently walking around Sydney Harbour, thinking about the structure of this book. Then I remembered to Use Everything. Looking around me, I noticed the long single-curved span of the Sydney Harbour Bridge, which made me wonder if the book had a sufficiently strong single narrative arc running through it. I then turned toward the nearby Opera House, which prompted a different thought: each chapter could be viewed as the sail of a boat, but it was no problem if those sails were of different shapes

and sizes – they could work together harmoniously to help the boat sail forward. And I suddenly realised that I wanted the book to be more like the Opera House than the Harbour Bridge.

Once we become adept at using everything, it also becomes possible to reinterpret negative events as potential offers, transforming them into possibilities for new kinds of action. It could be the budget that's just been cut, or the rainy day that stops you going to the park with your kids but turns into an opportunity for an indoor craft fest. When the director Robert Rodriguez made *El Mariachi*, he was short of proper lighting equipment. But he turned this obstacle to his advantage, using it to give the film its trademark moody feel.[22] Groucho Marx, who was famously skilled at using everything, was once faced with a contestant in a quiz show who 'froze', so he took the man's pulse and remarked, 'Either this man's dead or my watch has stopped.'[23]

Put together Notice More, Let Go, and Use Everything and you get improv: a spontaneous approach to life based on an attitude that Everything's An Offer. For me, it's epitomised by the time I was giving a workshop in a prison and suddenly abandoned my plan. I *noticed* the inmates drawing the discussion away from my planned topic, I decided to *let go* of my desire to control the structure of the session, and I *used everything* in the sense that I created an improvised workshop led by the ideas and energy of the prisoners. The difficult moment when I realised that they were talking with great enthusiasm about issues that were not on my agenda (such as the psychology of trust) was an offer there for the taking. Was I going to block it or embrace it? I chose the latter and it turned out to be one of the most interesting, rewarding and thought-provoking workshops I've ever done. One of the inmates came up to me afterwards and said, 'That was the most intelligent conversation I've had in the last three years.' Sure, it was a little chaotic at times, but this was a small price to pay for the freedom it unleashed.

This improv approach to living is, on one level, rather naïve. Everything is *not* an offer. A miscarriage is not an offer, it's a tragedy. Being sacked from your job is not an offer, except in rare circumstances. And it would be unwise, even reckless, to say 'Yes' to every possibility that comes our way. When I'm at the final stages of writing a book, I choose to say 'No' to nearly everything – I go into lockdown and rarely leave the house. But we need not reduce the idea of the offer to a cult of positive thinking that considers every occurrence a magical opportunity that must be grasped. We don't need to seize *every* offer. What we can do, however, is to notice those parts of our lives where we receive lots of offers and usually block them. Is it at work or home or with friends? Are we doing it more often as we get older? What underlies our kneejerk blocking? And then we might experiment with embracing a few more offers.

Improv encourages us, like Shakespeare, to see the world as a stage on which we act out our lives, while challenging the idea that our roles are fixed. Do we always want to stick to the lines we've rehearsed and the stories about ourselves we know so well? Or might it be time to throw away the script?

THE PLAN IS THERE IS NO PLAN

Opening ourselves to the offers around us might sound good in theory, but in practice we could still feel hemmed in by schedules, deadlines and routines. How can we seize the day when the diary is so full and the To Do list unending? Perhaps there's a simple solution to it all: move to Spain, or even better to Brazil.

When I lived in Madrid, I had a much more effervescent spur-of-the-moment existence than when I lived in north London. My Spanish flatmates would suddenly decide at midnight to go out to a flamenco bar, or on Friday afternoon suggest that we all head off to the mountains for the weekend. Even conversation felt charged with spontaneity: meals were invariably accompanied by heated and passionate arguments about the merits of Almodóvar's films, the ethics of bullfighting, or whose turn it was to clean the bathroom. I've never lived so intensely or had such little sleep. It was as if I was in Hemingway's novel *Fiesta: The Sun Also Rises*, where the characters continually throw themselves into impulsive drinking sessions, wild parties and reckless love affairs in an effort to live their lives 'all the way up'.[24]

Brazil is even better known for spontaneous living than Spain.[25] There's the dancing and music everywhere you go, the vibrant street life and the carnival tradition. It's a culture that extends from the spontaneous emotion with which people greet each other to the improvised housing of the urban poor in the favelas of the big cities, where DIY dwellings are swiftly constructed with any material to hand. Spontaneity is most clearly visible in the way people change their social plans at the last minute, and defy scheduled living by being late for almost everything (a trait that can be rather frustrating for clock-watching foreigners). 'Hey, stay for a drink,' someone once said to me in Rio. I replied that unfortunately I had to leave as I had to give a lecture. 'It doesn't matter if you start a bit late,' he countered, 'relax, everything will be fine!' Time feels different in Brazil, somehow slower and more malleable. The lack of hold that timetables and deadlines have on daily life is evident from a survey of thirty-one countries revealing that Brazil ranks twenty-sixth for the accuracy of its public clocks (Switzerland comes first and El Salvador last).[26]

Some of this spontaneity may be a myth, an idealised picture painted by those living in less vibrant and more strictured societies who are yearning for a sense of freedom and escape. Not every Brazilian is a carpe diem virtuoso: people from the south of Brazil are known for being much less carefree and more focused on turning up to meetings on time than their northern counterparts.[27] And the young bankers I've met in São Paolo are as stressed and trapped by routine as any I've met in New York or London. Still, it is worth exploring whether there are any clear lessons we might draw from Brazilian culture for escaping the constraints of hyper-scheduled living.

It is difficult to dissect a culture as a whole, so I want to examine one specific element of Brazilian society that is renowned for exhibiting spontaneity, and which has been subject to detailed study by sociologists and anthropologists. I'm talking, of course, about football.

Brazilian football has long had a reputation for its spontaneity, flamboyance and flair. As early as 1945, the Brazilian sociologist Gilberto Freyre noted that the national football style was distinct from the European approach 'through a conjunction of qualities of surprise, guile, astuteness, swiftness, and at the same time the brilliance of individual spontaneity'.[28] It was not so much a sport as an art, characterised by sublime feints and improbable acrobatic shots for goal. In the 1960s and 1970s, the individual genius of players like Pelé stood in stark contrast to the machine-like efficiency of the German national team or the dour English who dropped their most exciting and talented player, striker Jimmy Greaves, from the 1966 World Cup final team in favour of the much more dependable and workmanlike Geoff Hurst. England may have won the cup that year, but Brazil's World Cup wins in 1958, 1962 and 1970 seemed to confirm the triumph of Dionysian spontaneity over the technocratic approach of European sides with their clever offside traps and tactical negativity. As the Uruguayan intellectual Eduardo Galeano wrote, in the 1970 World Cup, 'Brazil played football worthy of her people's yearning for celebration and craving for beauty'.[29]

So what was the secret of Brazilian football? The general consensus amongst the experts is that its spontaneous energy was due not so much to the style promoted by particular coaches and managers, as to the place of the game in Brazilian society. Football became a popular pastime in the early twentieth century, mainly played by blacks (Afro-Brazilians), people of mixed race and the poor. In a country riven by racism and inequality, and where employment prospects were determined more by social contacts than ability or qualifications, it was seen as a rare oasis of democracy and equality of opportunity. Through the sheer demonstration of individual talent on the field, it was possible to make your way in the world – at least more so than in many other realms of life. This is what drove the style of Brazilian football, where players made an effort for their individuality to shine.[30]

In other words, the character of Brazilian football is rooted in historically specific factors related to the country's economic and social heritage, which cannot be easily replicated. The 'Brazilian way', such that there is a way (and some would dispute this today, noting that in the last two decades Brazilian teams have played defensive, even boring football), is much more a matter of circumstance and context than deliberate design.[31] And this goes for other aspects of spontaneity in Brazilian culture, such as the carnival tradition, the centrality of music and dance, and the relatively freewheeling attitude to time. Social scientists argue that these are rooted in myriad factors ranging from the legacy of colonial slavery to the adoption of African musical forms, from the impact of Catholicism and indigenous culture to the highly stratified nature of wealth inequality based on centuries of unequal land distribution. The tropical climate plays a role in it too.[32]

So I'm sorry to say it, but it might be difficult for Westerners to grab some Brazilian spontaneity for themselves: this melange of social and historical forces cannot be invented out of thin air. You could try living in Brazil for a while and see if it starts rubbing off on you, but you will probably be hard-pushed to import it to your high-velocity, über-planned homeland. This might all sound rather disheartening. Yet there is a message of hope in it all. On an individual level we can make an effort to defy our own social traditions and develop new habits that bring more improvisation into our lives. Having spent more than a decade teaching workshops on creative living, I think there are two practical steps we can take to encourage our spontaneous selves and become, in our own ways, just a little bit Brazilian. They are captured by a single slogan: The Plan Is There Is No Plan.

The first thing to do is take out your diary or calendar and schedule in regular time for spontaneous living. So you might block out from 2pm to 6pm every Sunday afternoon, where you resolutely make no plans at all. When 2pm on Sunday arrives, that's when you decide what to do. It could be anything from baking a cake with your kids for a new neighbour or taking a sketch pad to the park, to turning up at the cinema and seeing whatever is on. The key is to do something a little out of your ordinary routine. This is an opportunity to nurture your inner Brazilian. Scheduling in spontaneity might appear artificial, but it's an effective strategy in a world where endless commitments can easily leave us gasping for free time that may never arrive. I consider it deliciously subversive: it's using the scheduled structure of a diary against the culture of scheduling itself.

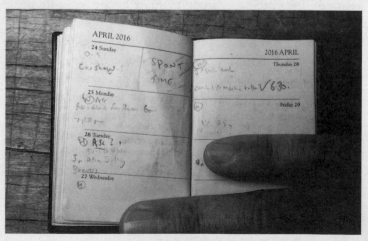

The author's Tiny Diary, an unlikely source of spontaneous living.

I take it a step further by having a diary that is so tiny – less than half a little finger allocated to each day – that I can barely write in more than one or two daily activities or meetings. It sounds ridiculous but I swear it means my week doesn't get cluttered and I have more time for impromptu living.

A second approach is to engage in experimental travel. Ever since Karl Baedeker invented the travel guide in the 1830s, many people have allowed the standard guides to determine their holiday itineraries.[33] It is common to arrive in a new city and immediately bring out a Lonely Planet or log on to TripAdvisor in search of the Top Ten Things To Do, and then to follow the maps and take in the requisite sites, views, cathedrals and museums. Yet there is a growing trend of taking a more experimental, spontaneous approach to travel, similar to that favoured by the character of Eleanor Lavish in the Edwardian-era film *A Room with a View*. When Miss Lavish and her friend are lost in the back streets of Florence, she admonishes her companion who starts bringing out her guidebook: 'No, Miss Bartlett, you will not look into your Baedeker. Two lone females in an unknown city, that's what I call an adventure. We will simply drift.' A moment later, as they pass by a group of young men, she suddenly stops, closes her eyes and inhales deeply. 'The smell! A true Florentine smell – inhale, my dear,' she says in a kind of ecstasy. 'Every city, let me tell you, has its own smell.'[34]

Today's carpe diem travellers take their cue from Miss Lavish and do things like devising sensory itineraries, where they might spend a whole day following smells or sounds, and seeing where they end up. Or they may jump on random buses to unknown destinations, or talk to strangers wearing hats, or take every second turn, or draw a love heart on a map and walk its route. The point of doing so is not simply to break with the Baedeker tradition; it is to start developing the habit of improvised, unplanned living. Once you try it on a holiday, you might start bringing it into your regular life, from the way you walk to work or manage meetings at the office, to the way you choose food on a menu.

Experimental travel is a stepping stone to a more seize-the-day existence. Ultimately we may not need to visit Brazil. We can simply kindle our spontaneity by experimenting with how we travel through our daily lives.

PUT YOUR LIFE TO MUSIC

We now have three tools at our disposal to take spontaneity beyond impulsive shopping sprees and last-minute socialising that acts as a veil for non-commitment. We can practise (and practise and practise) crafts or skills – like art, music or sport – as a route to releasing spontaneous invention. We can strive to use everything and accept the offers, so we become more open, aware and ready to be creatively sparked by the world around us. And we can directly stand up to the tyranny of the timetable by consciously planning freedom into our lives.

In doing so, we are honouring Horace by reclaiming the spirit of carpe diem that has been hijacked over the centuries. We should, however, approach spontaneity with a touch of moderation. This is not only because impulsive responses might be morally reprehensible or inappropriate, for instance an outburst of spontaneous anger or a snap cutting putdown of a colleague. It is also because order has its place in human affairs. Gustave Flaubert advised, 'be regular and orderly in your life, so that you may be violent and original in your work'. We all need a dose of planning and organisation to steady our lives and keep them grounded. Continuous spontaneity would be both exhausting and also unwise: in both a literal and metaphorical sense, I wouldn't recommend buying a house on a whim without first getting a surveyor to check the foundations.

Last night I watched my seven-year-old son perform as a worker bee in a contemporary dance show. He buzzed around the stage with twenty other little bees dressed in black with yellow stripes on their shirts and homemade wings on their backs. He looked completely absorbed and utterly unselfconscious. He was free. He was spontaneous. It was beautiful. I was envious of the children, and also of the parents who took part in it too. Afterwards, I watched an online talk by his inspiring dance teacher, Cecilia Macfarlane, founder of Oxford Youth Dance, whose philosophy is based on encouraging spontaneity and creativity amongst everyone she works with, from schoolchildren to prisoners and people in hospices. 'I believe my last dance will be my last blink, because any movement is a dance,' she told the audience. She continued:

> If you think dance is the thing that you do if you can
> do splits or if your hair is in a bun, I have spent my
> life rule-breaking and changing those stereotypes.
> Most of you in this room have probably said 'I'm no
> good at dance, I can't dance'. But you're all dancers

because you just got up for coffee and sat down again. If you'd done that in silence, with a lovely piece of music, we'd have seen the whole room dancing... I'm passionate about dance. If you can find a passion, and ownership of your passion, break rules please, and celebrate your individuality and uniqueness.[35]

I'm one of those people who say, 'I'm no good at dance, I can't dance.' My son's performance was an offer. I think it's time I joined him on the dance floor and got some spontaneous freedom buzzing through my body.

8

Just Doing It Together

June 18th, 1999. I was sitting quietly in the British Library in London, dutifully working on my politics doctoral thesis, when a friend approached with a flyer calling me to a different kind of politics. It was an invitation to a 'Carnival Against Capitalism' at noon that day at Liverpool Street Station, promising a 'global street party' to protest against the corporate-fuelled neoliberal economics championed by the wealthy G8 nations, whose 25th Annual Summit was opening the same day in Germany. How could we resist such as opportunity? It was nearly noon, so we spontaneously decided to abandon our books and jumped on the Tube.

We emerged into a completely transformed station. The concourse was packed with thousands of young people bopping to the beat of a Brazilian samba band. A gigantic blow-up Planet Earth was being tossed around above this human sea, with whoops and shouts as it landed on a new part of the crowd. People wearing Venetian-style carnival masks were handing out copies of a mock edition of the *Evening Standard* newspaper called *Evading Standards*, announcing a 'Global Market Meltdown' on the front page. They then started giving out masks in four different colours.

We were instructed to 'follow your colour', and surged out of the station in four different directions, each group dominated by red, green, black or gold masked revellers. Soon we were dancing down the streets of the city's financial heartland, banners waving, the masks offering both a sense of freedom and anonymity from CCTV cameras and the police. We were immersed in the rhythmic pulse of the drums and exuberant festival spirit, while bemused office workers watched us pass by, clearly wondering what the party was all about. Each of the four groups snaked past the banks and insurance companies, dodging and weaving through the streets to avoid the police cordons.

By around 2pm we'd finally reassembled on the wide avenue of Lower Thames Street. While some protesters converged on the nearby London International Financial Futures Exchange, where they attempted (but failed) to occupy the trading floor, my friend and I joined the thousands who were sitting in the middle of the road having impromptu picnics and dancing to the bands that had suddenly appeared on a makeshift stage. Cyclists from the Critical Mass movement were riding about amongst an array of huge walking puppets and the occasional naked eco-activist or intrepid pinstriped financier. All work had stopped, the clocks seemed to stand still, and the carnival continued into the long summer evening. I spotted a banner that read 'The Earth Is a Common Treasury For All' – a quote from the seventeenth-century radical Gerrard Winstanley. For those few hours, as we reclaimed the streets, it really did feel like the celebration of a common treasury.

J18, as it has come to be known, didn't just happen in London: there were protests that day in forty countries. Ten thousand people marched in Port Harcourt in Nigeria. South Korean activists dressed up as Zapatista rebel Subcomandante Marcos. In Barcelona they playfully revived the slogan used by Paris students in 1968, *'Sous les paves, la plage'* ('Under the pavement, the beach'), by wearing swimsuits and sunbathing on the roads.

It was the birth of the Global Justice Movement, a wave of protests targeting the behemoths of transnational capitalism – the IMF, the World Bank, the WTO and G8 – which captured the streets of cities such as Seattle, Genoa and Prague over the following four years, frequently in the face of club-wielding riot police.[1]

THE POLITICS OF SEIZING THE DAY

The Global Justice Movement was a powerful example of what I call 'carpe diem politics', a term that cannot be found in any political science textbook, but I believe deserves to be there. What exactly is it? I define it as a strategy for political change based on mass popular mobilisation, which harnesses the four forms of seizing the day – opportunity, hedonism, presence and spontaneity – to achieve political influence. Each of these four types of carpe diem was evident at J18, which was not just a street protest brimming with spontaneity, but embodied hedonistic revelry, brought its participants into the present moment, and was an effort to grasp a window of political opportunity. Of course, politics has always involved people trying to seize opportunities – think of Boris Johnson deciding at the last minute to back the 'leave' campaign in the 2016 referendum on UK membership of the European Union, and his accomplice Michael Gove then stabbing him in the back in a (failed) effort to become leader of the Conservative Party. The difference with carpe diem politics is that all four modes of seizing the day are brought together on a mass scale to create change. As such, it constitutes a distinct, fifth approach to Horace's original ideal, where we don't 'just do it' but 'just do it together'.

Carpe diem politics is a strategy most often used by social movements that engage in large-scale collective action, rather than political parties that focus more on electoral politics – although traditional parties will sometimes employ it when mobilising their popular support base. So it is much more about seizing the people's streets than the political seats. It is also a politically neutral concept, in the sense that movements across the political spectrum might conceivably draw on its potential: while carpe diem politics was evident in the anti-capitalist Global Justice Movement and the pro-democracy Hong Kong 'Umbrella Revolution', it has also been visible in the strategies of the conservative Tea Party movement in the US and the far-right Golden Dawn organisation in Greece.

Social movement protest is not the only way that political change happens. Political parties, electoral alliances, interest-group lobbying, media strategies, ideological shifts and many other factors all play a role. We should, however, remember a well-known lesson of history: pressure from mass movements on the ground has often been a fundamental force in creating substantive political transformation.[2] The New Deal in the 1930s, for instance, was not the gift of benign US politicians: it was forced on them by a groundswell of public protests by unemployed workers, war veterans and even street marches by starving children, who were rebelling in the face of the destitution created by the Depression.[3] As the social anthropologist James Scott reminds us, 'the great emancipatory gains for human freedom have not been the result of orderly, institutional procedures but of disorderly, unpredictable, spontaneous action cracking open the social order from below.'[4]

This is precisely what we are starting to witness today. As we are about to discover, over the past decade there has been a dramatic upsurge of social movement action on a global scale that has tapped into the power of carpe diem to shift the political landscape, and has engaged a new generation in public life. Although facing challenges – including a reliance on digitally generated mobilisation that may be short-lived – it has been remarkably effective in many countries. And if you have any doubts about the potential of such movements to shake up politics, recall a wall that stood as the symbolic dividing line of the Cold War for nearly thirty years.

182

1989: A CARNIVAL OF REVOLUTION

Around 8pm on Thursday, November 9th, 1989, crowds began gathering at the Bornholmer Street border crossing in East Berlin. There was a rumour, based on a press conference announcement earlier that evening, that the East German government would allow its citizens to freely cross into the West. More and more people started pouring out of their homes and local bars, and headed for the border. By 11pm, the crowd had grown into the tens of thousands, despite frantic government TV and police announcements that visas would still be required to cross. The border guards at Bornholmer Street, completely unprepared, looked on in horror as people began to chant, 'Open the gate! Open the gate!' Finally, just before 11.30pm, the head guard, Harald Jäger, realised they could no longer contain the increasingly agitated assemblage, and the main gate was opened.[5]

Juggling on the Berlin Wall, November 16th, 1989.

Jubilant East Berliners began streaming across. Video footage soon sped around the world showing them cheering, crying and embracing as they reached the other side. Champagne seemed to appear from nowhere and there was dancing in the streets. There were similar scenes at other border posts throughout the city. With the breaching of the Berlin Wall, suddenly one of the most repressive regimes of the Eastern Bloc, notorious for its secret police – the Stasi – which seemed to infiltrate every aspect of people's lives, had effectively crumbled. It was the emblematic moment when the dreams of the revolutionaries of October 1917 were finally shattered and the Cold War was over.

In an unplanned, spontaneous moment of mass action and collective exuberance, East Berliners had grasped the opportunity to secure their freedom. The street parties that erupted across the city had all the hallmarks of a raucous and hedonistic medieval carnival. The events that night were infused with the spirit of carpe diem.

Yet the apparent spontaneity of the crowd was something of an illusion. In fact, it was a deeply prepared spontaneity, rooted in years of organising by opposition movements going back at least to the early 1980s. This was not just the case in Berlin, but in other cities where protest erupted in 1989, such as Prague and Budapest. Their carpe diem energy didn't suddenly come out of nowhere – they had been primed for such a moment. 'The throngs that appeared on the streets,' writes historian Padraic Kenney, 'emerged onto a stage already prepared for them and by them.'[6] It is only when we take this longer-term perspective that we can truly recognise how much carpe diem politics shaped the downfall of the East German regime, and others across Eastern and Central Europe between 1989 and 1991.

The East German opposition movement, mainly based in the city of Leipzig, organised at least thirty-five anti-regime public protests in the two years prior to the events at Bornholmer Street.

In June 1989, inspired by street demonstrations in Poland and Czechoslovakia, and sensing that the government leadership was in disarray, they did something new, holding an illegal music festival with bands, dancers and street theatre, which led to eighty-four arrests.[7] Then a demonstration organised for October 9th drew an unexpectedly massive crowd of nearly 100,000 people and was too big for the police to stop. This was the tipping point: the opposition had taken the initiative and the ruling elite was on the back foot. In response to the Leipzig events, a wave of colossal protests swept across the country. In East Berlin, rock musicians held a public concert calling for democracy while the Stasi looked on in dismay. On November 4th a theatre group called for another mass street protest.[8] By the night of November 9th, public opposition to the regime was already supercharged. The breach of the wall was not a freak occurrence; East Berliners were ready and waiting to seize the moment.[9]

The carpe diem flavour of public protest was even more pronounced in other countries than in East Germany. In the Polish city of Wrocław, the opposition movement – led by the guerrilla street-theatre collective Orange Alternative – explicitly drew on the spontaneity and hedonism of the carnival tradition to taunt the ruling regime. One typical event that took place on Tuesday, February 16th, 1988 – Mardi Gras or 'Fat Tuesday', the eve of Lent – was a 'ProletaRIO Carnival' (*Karnawal RIObotniczy*), described by its organisers as 'socialist surrealism' and attended by thousands of people. The crowds were entertained with children's ditties and Stalinist songs. A parade of playful characters caroused around the streets, including people dressed as skeletons, Smurfs, a Red Riding Hood arm-in-arm with a wolf, a bear carrying a machine gun, and a group of Ku Klux Klansmen waving a sign reading 'Open the borders, we'll run to Calgary!' The crowd chanted 'Hocus pocus!' and 'The police party with us!' When the police grabbed a reveller, the boisterous crowd immediately rushed in to free them: the authorities had never been properly trained to deal with Smurfs. In a similarly surreal event in Prague in August 1989, The Society for a Merrier Present held a silent march called 'A Fruitless Action', where they paraded up and down the Charles Bridge wearing helmets made from watermelons and holding up blank banners.[10]

These kinds of left-field cultural events – frequently organised by theatre groups, musicians, peace activists and ecological campaigners – which took place throughout the region between 1986 and 1989, might have looked frivolous, but were far from being so. They kept ruling regimes off balance, and created new social spaces for the expression of public dissent. Gradually they grew into larger opposition movements – the very movements that took to the streets in Prague, East Berlin, Krakow, Budapest and other cities in the crucial year of 1989. As Padraic Kenney concludes, 'What started as just a carnival became a revolution.'[11]

Looking at the big picture, the demise of state socialism in East Germany and elsewhere is revealing about the potency of carpe diem politics. It is certainly true that other factors played a critical role in events, including Mikhail Gorbachev's reforms that encouraged political dissent, the economic failures of the communist system itself, and a catalogue of miscalculations by state socialist leaders.[12] But there is no doubt that seize-the-day movements were a vital and necessary element of what turned out to be one of the major political transformations of the twentieth century. The story of 1989 cannot be told without them. In the absence of carpe diem activism, the political possibilities would have remained small cracks rather than the grand openings they became, and the opportunities they offered may never have been seized with such vigour. Seizing the day is not just a philosophy of everyday life; it is the stuff of history itself.

We also learn an important lesson about one specific carpe diem trait, namely spontaneity. Although a potentially powerful ingredient of effective mass mobilisation, it is not a magical one that can be conjured out of nowhere. It might take years of nurturing before it is ready to erupt on the political scene. Just as spontaneity in the creative arts may be a matter of practise, practise, practise, so spontaneity in the political arts may be a product of organise, organise, organise. Social movements looking to draw on the energy and force of carpe diem must recognise that spontaneity is like a cherry tree: its blossom may burst open in a day, but its buds are the fruit of a year.

How Horace Inspired a New Age of Dissent

The events in Eastern and Central Europe were not a one-off, flash-in-the-pan instance of carpe diem taking centre stage in politics. The wave of social movements that emerged in the West in the 1960s and 1970s – including the movements for gay rights, women's rights and the peace movement – were equally suffused with Horace's spirit, as were the carnivalesque demonstrations of the Global Justice Movement. Now I can report that his spirit is back: over the past decade an extraordinary upsurge of popular mobilisation has emerged across dozens of countries, much of it fuelled by the fire of carpe diem politics. So where does it come from, and what does it look like?

The recent outbreak of grass-roots rebellion has its origins in a growing dissatisfaction with governments that have failed to deal successfully with a series of major global crises, ranging from the influx of refugees and international terrorism, to climate change and – perhaps most importantly – a worldwide economic recession since 2008 that has had a devastating effect on jobs, housing and the provision of public services. It is also because of a growing sense that governments no longer represent their citizens, and are much more effective at representing the corporate interests to which they are beholden, from big banks to Big Oil. Trust and confidence in governments has plummeted as a result.[13]

In such circumstances, it is no surprise that 'anti-system' political candidates are on the rise, offering to break with the traditional party politics of the past: witness the election of Donald Trump. But just as important has been the arrival of a new generation of social movements attempting to change politics from the ground up. Most – but by no means all – of them are broadly on the political left, or anti-authoritarian in character. I'm thinking, for example, of the anti-austerity Indignados movement that ignited the streets of Spain in May 2011, whose main slogans were 'They Do Not Represent Us' and 'Real Democracy Now'.[14] A few months later came the Occupy Movement – inspired by the Indignados and the Arab Spring – which rapidly spread from Wall Street to 951 cities in eighty-two countries, prompting *Time* magazine to declare 'The Protester' as its Person of the Year in 2011.[15] Since then waves of mass protest have erupted everywhere from Rio and Istanbul to Kuala Lumpur and Hong Kong.

There has simultaneously been the rise of new global issue-based movements that bear little resemblance to conventional political parties, such as the climate change campaigning organisation 350.org. We have also seen the emergence of web movements like Avaaz, which mobilises its international brigade of 40 million members to protest on matters ranging from human rights and ecological destruction to animal welfare and wealth inequality, focusing its efforts on 'tipping point moments of crisis and opportunity'.[16] While such organisations often concentrate on online campaigning, they are also active offline: if you had been at the 50,000-strong London march to pressure the Paris Climate Change talks in November 2015, you might have seen the Avaaz truck pumping out disco classics from its loudspeakers – and my seven-year-old daughter holding a homemade placard and dancing down the streets next to it.

Put all these movements together and it becomes clear that we are experiencing one of the most dynamic periods of public protest action ever recorded, on a par with momentous periods such as the 1960s. Although we may not necessarily detect it as we go about our daily lives, the evidence is overwhelming. A recent study of over 800 protests in more than eighty countries revealed a steady rise in the number of mass demonstrations and other forms of protest since 2006, with the majority focusing on economic justice and anti-austerity issues, and failures of democratic representation and corporate influence in politics. Some have been amongst the largest protests ever known: thirty-seven of them – in countries such as France, India and Chile – gathered crowds of over a million people.[17] Another study showed that the frequency of public protest in the UK has been escalating since 2008, reaching a peak of 206 recorded protest events such as marches and strikes in 2015 – the highest level since the 1970s.[18] One of the most important developments is the changing profile of who turns out on the streets: along with traditional protesters from the labour movement, there are an increasing number of students, middle-class professionals, housing activists and minority groups. We are witnessing a new age of dissent, and it's happening on a global scale.

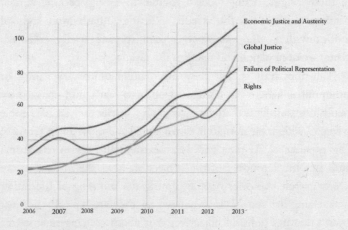

Number of protests worldwide by main grievance/demand, 2006–2013.[19]

But the really fascinating part of it all – at least for anyone with Horace on their mind – is that these movements are hotbeds of carpe diem activism. One of the world's most influential thinkers on this new wave of protest, the sociologist Manuel Castells, calls them 'networked social movements'. Like all social movements through history – such as the anti-nuclear and feminist movements in the 1970s – they primarily aim to influence politics from outside the formal sphere of elections and political parties. So what makes the latest wave so novel?

For a start, the movements operate in 'hybrid public space': you will find them not only occupying physical urban spaces like the Puerta del Sol in Madrid or Tahrir Square in Cairo, but digital public space created by networking platforms such as Twitter, Facebook and Tumblr, which authorities find difficult to control. They are relatively 'horizontalist' in their organisation, favouring democratic consensus decision-making over more hierarchical structures with easily identifiable leaders. This, according to Castells, is a reflection of the horizontal and leaderless nature of internet networks themselves. They are also 'largely spontaneous in their origin', using social media to bring people almost instantaneously onto the streets, creating a flash-mob style of politics with a viral quality that can spread rapidly and take advantage of new political openings.

A further trait is that they often build temporary camps or communities where supporters sleep, eat, learn and make new friendships and alliances. In doing so, says Castells, they enable people to step outside their normal lives to 'live in the moment in terms of their experience'. At their core is an existentialist vision to create a 'utopia of the autonomy of the subject vis-à-vis the institutions of society', where the priority is 'exploring the meaning of life rather than seizing the state'.[20] In other words, they are typically not just about achieving political objectives, but about creating new spaces for the expression of personal freedom and agency.

This all sounds to me remarkably close to a recipe for carpe diem politics. What Castells is really telling us – without quite realising it – is that we are seeing the rise of a new generation of social movements whose chief characteristics are not simply their digital flavour or egalitarian ethic, but that they embody features of the centuries-old carpe diem tradition. It's as if Horace has been their secret political advisor, whispering into their ears.

The majority of movements identified by Castells and other analysts tend to have progressive, social justice agendas that we might associate with the left. What about movements on the right? Are they too listening to the wisdom of Horace? While there has been a significant surge in right-wing populism in many countries, especially in Europe and the United States, Castells points out that it is generally expressed in the form of political parties that operate mostly within the sphere of conventional electoral politics. Examples include Britain's anti-European UKIP, Marine Le Pen's Front National in France, and the quasi-Nazi True Finns party in Finland. These parties do hold rallies and other mass gatherings, but it is not their primary operational mode. There are, however, some exceptions, such as the explicitly Neo-Nazi Golden Dawn organisation in Greece, which styles itself as a social movement as much as a political party.[21] There is another exception that deserves special mention, since it has so clearly brought a carpe diem quality to its campaigning: the Tea Party movement in the United States.

The Tea Party emerged in early 2009, just weeks into the Obama presidency. Its agenda, which the political scientists Theda Skocpol and Vanessa Williamson describe as 'right-wing conservatism', has included issues such as radical cuts in public spending, lower taxes, gun rights and tougher immigration rules, summed up in patriotic slogans like 'I Want My Country Back!'[22] Backed by plutocratic financiers such as the Koch brothers and conservative news channels like Fox News, it quickly developed into a social movement that could mobilise thousands of people onto the streets.[23]

The Tea Party's larger demonstrations have had a distinct carpe diem character. In April 2009 it organised 'Tax Day' protests in more than 750 locations across the country as a response to the Obama administration's $800 billion stimulus package. Amongst the crowds were people dressed up in colonial garb – a reference to the 1773 Boston Tea Party – and others wearing hats with tea bags hanging off them, waving the Stars and Stripes. In September that year, at least 60,000 Tea Party activists marched on Washington DC in the biggest public protest since Obama had taken office. Again there were the flags and costumes, the defamatory banners, the singing of patriotic hymns, folk music and pipe bands, all alongside rousing political speeches denouncing Obama's health care plan as 'socialism'. As the *New York Times* reported, 'While there was no shortage of vitriol amongst protesters, there was also an air of festivity.'[24] This was seize-the-day politics in action, bringing elements of the carnival tradition together with the ideology of the Republican far-right. Whether the Tea Party will continue to use carpe diem strategies, and indeed how long it will manage to survive in the post-Obama era (especially given the rise of the 'alt-right'), are open questions. But it is evident that seizing the day, in its various forms, has contributed to the story of its success.[25]

While some organisations on the right have drawn on the power of carpe diem politics, they have not hijacked it for themselves. Its real heartland is the new landscape of networked social movements fired by the ideals of social justice, democratic values and progressive change. They recognise that if you want to mobilise people, excite them, and maintain their allegiance and involvement, then you could do with a little help from Horace. To really understand how seizing the day functions in modern politics, and assess its prospects for bringing about substantive change, we now need to put one of these movements under the microscope.

The most obvious contender, which more than any other captures the carpe diem spirit, is the Occupy Movement.

The Ballerina on the Bull

The Occupy Movement was born online. On July 13th, 2011, the Vancouver-based anti-consumer magazine *Adbusters* issued a call to #OCCUPYWALLSTREET on its blog and Facebook page. The instructions were simple: 'Are you ready for a Tahrir moment? On Sept 17, flood into lower Manhattan, set up tents, kitchens, peaceful barricades and occupy Wall Street.' The poster showed a dancer poised calmly in an arabesque pose on the Charging Bull statue near Wall Street, surrounded by riot police. It was a serious image, but also a creative one that represented a supreme depiction of carpe diem freedom – opportunity, spontaneity, presence and hedonism all wrapped into one.

The timing of the action was all about seizing a perfect political opportunity. It wasn't just that September 17th was the anniversary of the signing of the US constitution. It also built on the momentum of public protests in Spain and Egypt, and a brewing summer of discontent, with growing public rage about the inequalities and corporate greed at the heart of American society, especially in the wake of the financial crisis. This anger could be found amongst people who had lost their homes and jobs, pensioners whose retirement savings had been decimated, and especially amongst an army of young graduates who were fed up with using their expensive educations to become baristas and draw love hearts on cappuccinos, with little prospect of paying off their student debts with a decent job (or any job at all). The 99% were becoming indignant, and *Adbusters* knew it.

Then came the spontaneity. By 'spontaneity' I don't mean that Occupy Wall Street was unplanned. In reality, a committed group of New York anarchists and other direct action radicals worked hard

at strategic planning leading up to September 17th, some of them drawing on what they had learned through taking part in the Global Justice Movement ten years earlier. The spontaneity that occurred was much more in the form of the agile nature of the movement and its unexpectedly rapid expansion. On the day itself people started gathering at the bull statue in Bowling Green Park. The original intention was to head for Chase Plaza, but the police had received word and fenced it off overnight. As the crowd reached around 1,000 people, a snap decision had to be made. Out of the five alternative destinations up their sleeve, the organisers chose Zuccotti Park.[26]

Nobody could have predicted what happened next: a potentially one-off protest turned into a global movement for non-violent change. Thousands of people turned up to Zuccotti Park over the following weeks to pitch their tents and take part in Occupy's trademark General Assemblies, as well as to participate in mass demonstrations against the rampant police bullying and arrests. But the real surprise was that within a month Occupy had expanded from Wall Street to over 600 US communities and dozens of countries. There were Occupies taking place not only in politically vibrant cities like Seattle and Oakland, but in tiny towns in North Dakota and Oregon. At the same time, Occupy tents were popping up everywhere from Dublin and Brussels to Buenos Aires and Seoul. The 'We Are the 99%' slogan was a cultural meme that spread virally with the help of social media. During November there was an average of around 120,000 Occupy-related tweets per day, peaking at over 500,000 during the police raid on Zuccotti Park on November 15th.[27]

While there was plenty of spontaneity and grasping of opportunities, the Occupy Movement had another seize-the-day trait woven into it: presence. A strong sense of being in the here and now emerged because many Occupy zones were, as one participant described them, 'twenty-four-hour-a-day experiments in egalitarian living'.[28] Along with the daily assemblies, there was communally organised food distribution, sleeping arrangements, laundry and education facilities. It would be wrong to say that the camps were utopian idylls: there were frequent internal disagreements, and problems with those who didn't pull their weight. Still, camp culture embodied a temporary lifestyle shift with a novelty and freshness that gave people a feeling of being immersed in a different present, allowing them to step out of the daily grind of dead-end jobs and paying the rent. As Castells puts it, they entered a kind of 'timeless time', where they refused 'the subservient clock time imposed by the chronometers of their existence'.[29]

And what about the final carpe diem element of hedonism? According to the anthropologist David Graeber, one of the organisers behind Occupy Wall Street, the great mobilisations of the Global Justice Movement between 1999 and 2003 'were essentially parties', full of bands, radical clowns and 'Pink Blocs' of protesters in tutus armed with feather dusters to tickle the police. Occupy, in contrast, 'is not a party, it's a community. And it's less about fun, or not so much primarily about fun, as it is about caring'.[30] When I turned up to the Occupy encampment near St Paul's Cathedral in London, there was hardly an atmosphere of Bacchanalian carnival: everyone was on edge, ready for a police raid.

Yet many Occupies around the world made an effort to generate a festive feeling, with mass singalongs, street musicians and dancing flashmobs, which all helped to create a strong sense of community.[31] It seems that even when the stakes are high, carpe diem activists want to bring a little hedonism into their lives. As Barbara Ehrenreich notes, 'Almost every demonstration I have been on over the years – anti-war, feminist, or for economic justice – has featured some element of the carnivalesque: costumes, music, impromptu dancing, the sharing of food and drink… the urge to transform one's appearance, to dance outdoors, to mock the powerful and embrace perfect strangers is not easy to suppress.'[32] Moreover, an element of carnival can be a smart tactic, as a troop of riot police brandishing tasers doesn't usually know how to react to a bunch of activists in tutus taunting them with feather dusters – just as Eastern European police in the 1980s didn't know how to deal with protesting Smurfs.[33]

Looking back at the emergence of the Occupy Movement, it seemed almost too good to be true: carpe diem politics was making waves on a planetary scale that – at least in terms of sheer numbers and geographical spread – rivalled the global revolts of 1968.[34]

When the anarchist band Seize the Day played for the Occupy protesters in the English town of Sheffield, they were, in effect, also celebrating the hidden power of that old line from Horace, *carpe diem, quam minimum credula postero*. Seize the day, and leave as little as possible for tomorrow.

Yet within a few months it looked like it was all over: the music was no longer playing and the ballerina had fallen from the Charging Bull. Most of the Occupy camps had been shut down by the police, over 7,000 people had been arrested in the US alone, and the energy that marked the beginning of the protests had disappeared. Wall Street was still standing, capitalism hadn't collapsed, and the mainstream media was declaring Occupy a dead and buried force that had failed to achieve any significant results. While East Berliners had managed to tear down their wall in 1989, what had the Occupiers of 2011 to show for all their efforts? Yes, it was undoubtedly a fine example of carpe diem politics in action, but doesn't it ultimately show that seizing the day – even on a global scale and powered by digital technology – has no serious future as a force for political change?

The Hidden Power of Carpe Diem Politics

I have to admit that I was initially on the side of the sceptics, doubting the practical impact of Occupy and similar seize-the-day movements. But after considering the main critiques – discussed below – I have gradually come to a different conclusion, or at least a more nuanced one: for all their drawbacks, these movements are not just playing an increasingly prominent role on the political stage, but are more effective than at first meets the eye. Horace is making a serious mark on contemporary political life.

The major criticism levelled at Occupy is that it failed to achieve anything substantial because it refused to issue any concrete demands, for example radical tax reforms or new rules limiting corporate funding in politics, a position captured in the slogan 'Occupy Everything, Demand Nothing'.[35] Yet from another angle, Occupy was a resounding success as it catapulted the issue of economic inequality onto the public agenda and changed the terms of political debate. Largely as a result of the protests, media coverage of inequality issues in the US increased five-fold, even more than a year after Occupy Wall Street was shut down.[36] The movement also played a vital role in creating the space for the emergence of radical anti-austerity politicians, such as Bernie Sanders running for the Democratic Presidential nomination in the US and Jeremy Corbyn's surprise victory to become leader of the UK's Labour Party. Moreover, without Occupy, powerful books on inequality like Thomas Piketty's *Capital in the Twenty-First Century*, published in 2013, would never have had such global resonance. In the language of the cognitive linguist George Lakoff, Occupy changed the 'frame' of economic discourse, using the 'We Are the 99%' slogan to help erode the dominance of neoliberal ideology.[37] And that's no small achievement.[38]

A second critique of movements like Occupy is that too much of their activism is taking place in the digital sphere. It is now relatively easy to get tens of thousands of people to support your cause online through 'liking' your Facebook page, following you on Twitter or signing an electronic petition: within just a month Occupy Wall Street was the proud recipient of 400,000 Facebook 'likes'.[39] But this might be best termed 'slacktivism' – political action that requires little thought, effort or sacrifice beyond clicking a mouse or sharing a video, and which generates only weak ties between supporters and similarly weak levels of commitment.[40]

It is true that slacktivism will not be a panacea for our social and political ills. But what is notable about the movements I have been discussing, such as Occupy, the Indignados, Hong Kong's 'Umbrella Revolution', and earlier examples like the Global Justice Movement, is that they have been incredibly successful at getting their online supporters to step away from their screens and onto the streets. Technology has been used mainly as a means, not as an end in itself. When *Adbusters* issued the call to #OCCUPYWALLSTREET it was not asking people to click on a 'donate' button or sign a petition: it was urging them to take part in face-to-face carpe diem activism. And they did, not just turning up for a few hours of banner waving, but marching in the face of riot police, getting arrested and braving all weathers to set up camps where they lived for days and sometimes weeks. People have been drawn to these movements by the very fact that they offer an embodied, social experience rather than just another shallow virtual encounter. If the slacktivist contingent are right, we should have seen a decline in active social protests on the streets since the dawn of the internet age. But just the opposite has occurred. They are more vibrant and prevalent than ever, and are helping to challenge our culture of digital distraction.

A final criticism is that the most striking carpe diem feature of the new wave of social movements – their capacity for spontaneous mobilisation – is in fact one of their fatal weaknesses. Movements such as Occupy may be extremely adept at using social media to bring huge crowds onto the streets with little notice, but this burst of energy might be short-lived and serve little purpose if there is no clear planning behind it. As the journalist Paul Mason observes, 'horizontalism can stage a great demo, but does not know what it wants'.[41] The problem, any worldly-wise activist will tell you, is that spontaneous action is not enough: you also need a highly strategic vanguard group to provide direction, unity and leadership, and to organise the movement's support base. Angela Davis, a veteran of the US civil rights movement, is worried about where political activism is currently heading:

> It seems to me that mobilization has displaced organization, so that in the contemporary moment, when we think about organizing movements, we

think about bringing masses of people onto the
street... The Internet is an incredible tool, but it
may also encourage us to think that we can produce
instantaneous movements, movements modelled
after fast food delivery.[42]

So have we succumbed to fast food politics? I agree with
the critics that if we understand 'spontaneity' as unplanned
mass action, then this in and of itself will rarely be sufficient for
achieving fundamental change. But the spontaneity of many new
social movements is less ephemeral and undirected than at first
appears, and more clearly resembles the 'prepared spontaneity' of
artists and musicians I have discussed earlier, which is based on
extensive practice and dedicated training. The most prominent
movements have often been highly organised, with deep historical
roots. Spain's Indignados (also known as the 15-M Movement)
may have brought massive crowds into the plazas, but its ability
to manage deliberative assemblies of up to 5,000 people was based
on three decades of autonomous neighbourhood organising in
Madrid and other cities, as well as what had been learned during
the Global Justice Movement. Similarly, Occupy Wall Street didn't
simply spring from an *Adbusters* post on Facebook: organisers spent
the summer of 2011 planning the action at the 16 Beaver Street art
space in Manhattan.[43] Amongst their ranks were many experienced
activists who were schooled in the art of prepared spontaneity.
That's why, for instance, when the numbers that turned up were
larger than expected, making the assembly proceedings hard to
manage, they began using a 'people's mic' method where the crowd
passed back each speaker's words to people behind them, sentence
by sentence, so everyone could hear what was happening and feel
involved.[44] It was precisely this kind of practised spontaneity that
was so much in evidence in Eastern and Central Europe in 1989:
in Leipzig, the opposition movement was able to respond swiftly

and deftly to new political openings by organising a succession of street protests at short notice (and back then they didn't have any help from Twitter).

Prepared spontaneity is an essential prerequisite of successful social movements today, which must learn to harness the energy of the impromptu public protests that have become increasingly frequent due to the rise of digital mass communications. The trick is to develop an organisational nimbleness and dexterity to take advantage of sudden outbreaks of mobilisation before the fire dies or chaos breaks out. When a political opportunity arises, they must be ready to pounce and seize it, being spontaneous in the sense of agile. As any Scout who knows their Horace will tell you: Be Prepared, or You'll Miss the Chance to Seize the Day.

'Gather ye rosebuds while ye may,' proclaimed Robert Herrick in his seventeenth-century carpe diem poem. Fine advice. But this does not mean we should wear rose-tinted spectacles when assessing the impact of social movement action that has taken place worldwide over the past decade. Many of the movements of the Arab Spring were failures, beset by internal divisions and unable to bring down authoritarian leaders backed by powerful militaries. In my personal view, Occupy could have been more successful if it had adopted a few clear policy aims like the feminist movement that arose in the 1970s, which campaigned on specific issues such as equal pay and reproductive rights. Maybe it should even have transformed itself into a progressive political party with a strong grass-roots support base, similar to Podemos in Spain or Syriza in Greece: although electoral politics hasn't always been easy for them, both have made a difference by engaging more directly with the state.[45]

These are, however, speculations. What we do know is that despite possessing weaknesses, many social movements such as Occupy have been extremely influential, especially in putting issues like inequality onto the public agenda. Moreover, much of their success has been due to drawing on the power of carpe diem politics. By combining opportunism, presence, hedonism and spontaneity they have been able to create an explosive cocktail of social action and political transformation.

SEIZING THE *VITA ACTIVA*

This new wave of social movement action rarely dominates the mainstream political news, which tends to get caught up in the immediacy of upcoming elections, political scandals and party infighting. But in a world where governments are struggling to deal with endemic problems such as economic recession, immigration, terrorism and global warming, and where traditional parties are losing public trust, these movements are unlikely to go away soon. Indeed, there is a strong possibility that mass protest on the ground – from both the left and right – will play a significant role in shaping the political future and be an important forum for citizen engagement in public life, together with more conventional participation at the ballot box.[46] As I write these words, 50,000 people are on the streets of London protesting against the recent EU referendum result and proclaiming 'We Are The 48%!' – an echo of the slogan that galvanised the Occupy Movement.[47] Such protests may well transform themselves into a broad-based citizens' movement for progressive change.

In her recent book *This Changes Everything*, Naomi Klein argues that tackling one of the greatest issues of our day – climate change – cannot be done without forging these kinds of mass movements.[48] I agree. Technological fixes will not be enough. Vague global agreements between political leaders will not be enough. Market solutions will not be enough. There is no doubt that we will need the power and pressure of social movements like 350.org and Rising Tide to shake the politicians and fossil fuel companies out of complacency, and to help create the cultural change and economic alternatives that a sustainable, thriving, clean energy future requires.

But here's the real point: the examples of Eastern Europe in 1989 and Occupy in 2011 tell us that such movements will boost their possibilities of success if they can tap into the potential of carpe diem activism. They will need to be strategically savvy about seizing opportunities, they must learn to harness the spontaneity created by digital contagion and cultivate their own 'prepared spontaneity', they should strive to build communities that immerse people in the present, and they would be wise to inject some carnivalesque hedonism that keeps everyone's spirits high in the face of the daunting challenge. It's time they placed their hope in Horace.

Apart from its role as a strategy for social movements, why does carpe diem politics matter? Because it helps expand our conception of the good life. It enriches Horace's Ode XI, suggesting that the adventure of being fully human and grasping the most from life goes beyond 'just do it' to 'just do it together'. Alongside the singular injunction 'carpe diem' we need the plural 'carpamus diem' – the idea of seizing the day with others – as a way of overcoming the excessive individualism of contemporary life and expressing our collective selves.[49] As I learned at the J18 protest that drew me out of the British Library back in the summer of 1999, it is about valuing what the philosopher Hannah Arendt called the *vita activa*, by which she meant a life where we actively engage as citizens in the public arena, as opposed to the *vita contemplativa*, a much more introspective, self-oriented and private mode of living.[50] It calls on us to embrace the existential challenge to nurture both 'me' and 'we'.

9

I Choose, Therefore I Am

Carpe diem, as a philosophy of life, is not simply composed of the five ways to seize the day: it is also a fundamental route to human happiness in and of itself. By 'happiness' I don't mean a buoyant state of joyfulness and good cheer, but something closer to what the ancient Greeks called *eudaimonia* or 'the good life' – a life of deep wellbeing and flourishing that offers a sense of meaning or purpose. Certainly carpe diem cannot claim to be *the* route to this ideal of happiness. As John Locke noted in the seventeenth century, 'all men seek happiness, but not of the same sort... you will as fruitlessly endeavour to delight all men with riches or glory as you would to satisfy all men's hunger with cheese or lobsters; which, though very agreeable and delicious fare to some, are to others extremely nauseous and offensive.'[1] Rather, more modestly, carpe diem is *a* route to happiness that deserves to sit together with other major approaches, but one that for too long has been captured by its cultural hijackers such as the 'just buy it' messaging of rampant consumerism.

So where does it fit into the pantheon of philosophies of happiness? First we need some historical perspective. In most ancient Western cultures, happiness was considered to be largely out of our control and in the hands of the Gods. This view found its way into language itself. In almost every Indo-European language, the word 'happiness' was originally associated with luck, fortune or fate. In Middle English and Old Norse 'happiness' is rooted in *happ*, which means chance or fortune, or what happens. That's where we get words like 'happenstance', 'hapless', 'haphazard' and 'perhaps'. In German the words for happiness and luck are the same – *Glück*. The French *bonheur* comes from *bon* (good) and *heur* (fortune, luck), and the Italian *felicità* and Spanish *felicidad* are based on the Latin *felix*, meaning luck or fate. In other words, happiness is what happens to us. Our wellbeing is not subject to our own will or agency.[2] This attitude reflected the realities of pre-modern life: you might be born into slavery, you could be struck down by a deadly disease or killed in war, and would in all likelihood be condemned to a life of poverty. Under such circumstances creating your own happiness – for instance, through freely choosing your career path – was wishful thinking.

It was not until the Age of Enlightenment, in the eighteenth century, that happiness came to be seen as a matter of choice and a viable life aspiration for those outside wealthy elites. This was due to several momentous cultural shifts, such as rising standards of living which meant that for many people the struggle for mere survival could start giving way to the loftier pursuit of happiness, and the erosion of Church doctrines peddling the view that happiness was to be enjoyed in a heavenly afterlife rather than in mortal life on earth.[3]

Over the last two centuries, a range of approaches to happiness have emerged as dominant in Western culture. While often rooted in the writings of pre-Enlightenment thinkers, and visible in human behaviour since ancient times, it has only been in the modern age that most of them have become subject to explicit and widespread discussion as philosophies of happiness. They include utilitarianism, a 'scientific' theory of happiness from the eighteenth century focusing on maximising pleasure and minimising pain, and the pursuit of a 'transcendent cause', which involves striving for meaningful goals beyond the realm of self-interest, such as creating a more equal society or living by the commandments of a particular religion. The Romantic movement championed the idea of deriving happiness from personal relationships, especially romantic love, family life and friendship. The more recent 'emotional state theory' of happiness extols the view that it is essentially about experiencing positive feelings – it's about feeling joyful and 'up' rather than sad and 'down'.[4]

Yet amongst such commonly recognised paths to happiness, one is typically left out: carpe diem. At its core lies a very simple and powerful idea, which is that we forge meaning in our lives by making choices and acting upon them. What matters is not so much *what* we choose, but *that* we choose. We create ourselves through the exercise of freedom itself, seizing the day by taking decisions. The common thread running through the various forms of carpe diem, from grasping a fleeting opportunity to turning our attention to the present moment, is that they usually involve making a conscious choice. The life projects that shape our identities – supporting a cause, starting a family, building a business, training for a marathon – emerge from these instants of commitment. It's an idea that I like to sum up in a single maxim: I choose, therefore I am.

The task at hand is to understand what 'I choose, therefore I am' looks like in our everyday lives, and what it can contribute to our search for the good life. Before delving into it directly we need to address two fundamental challenges to the carpe diem tradition that have reared their heads at various points in earlier chapters, both of which raise dilemmas for making seize-the-day choices. First, that it is a philosophy that celebrates the value of freedom while failing to place sufficient moral boundaries on it – are we really free to choose *anything*? Second, that there are formidable psychological barriers to putting carpe diem into practice, namely procrastination, overload, risk and apathy. The deeper our understanding of these challenges, the more robust – and compelling – carpe diem will become as a paradigm for living.

Does Carpe Diem Pass the Morality Test?

There is one word you will rarely find in the index of those self-help books on 'how to be happy': ethics. Tricky moral questions are generally glossed over, while the focus remains firmly on *my* happiness with little consideration for anybody else's. Advocates of the different types of carpe diem tend to suffer from the same myopia. Ethics is a taboo topic in most of the 'feel the fear and do it anyway' guides that encourage seizing opportunities and making daring choices. Similarly, as we have seen, the modern mindfulness movement extols the virtues of living in the present moment without putting any substantive limits on what we should be mindful about – hence the awkward problem of the mindful sniper.

Some people might believe that a philosophy of carpe diem should be kept distinct from moral considerations, perhaps on the grounds that 'my morals are mine, and yours are yours, so you can't go around telling people what they should seize and what they shouldn't'. I take a different view. Human beings are social animals and we must learn to live alongside one another. We cannot retreat into a naïve individualism that assumes our actions miraculously have no effects beyond our own lives and never impinge on others. If we truly wish to reclaim carpe diem, we should explore some of its moral challenges.

The place to begin is by recognising that carpe diem has a powerful ethical foundation built into it, through advocating a supreme value: freedom. The whole idea of 'seizing' the day, or 'harvesting' it or 'plucking' it, is about taking action, and places absolute importance on individual choice and agency. This regard for freedom is what gives it such strong resonance with existentialism, which I consider to be a modern philosophical expression of the ancient carpe diem ideal (the former has been around for about a century, the latter for two millennia).[5] During the heyday of existentialism in the years after World War Two, the movement's stress on 'freedom as the foundation of all values', as Sartre put it, seemed apt for the times.[6] It was a rejection of the heavy-handed totalitarianism of Nazism and Stalinism that scuppered individual freedom of expression. It made a radical call for liberty in every sphere of life, for instance sexual relations: Sartre and Simone de Beauvoir – the other half of existentialism's very own dynamic duo – not only had an open relationship in defiance of the bourgeois institution of marriage, they were also advocates of LGBT rights half a century before their time.[7]

Today, don't we still value the freedom to choose? Is it not an essential human right – the right to join a trade union or faith of your choice, to blog against the government or engage in public protest without fear of imprisonment? Or to marry someone of the same sex? In this sense, carpe diem may be *more* ethical than other routes to happiness, since it builds freedom of choice into its very essence, embodied in its defining motto, 'I choose, therefore I am'.

So what is the ethical case against carpe diem? It can be accused of what philosophers call 'moral subjectivism', which means that it offers no criteria with which to distinguish right from wrong actions. There is nothing, it seems, to stop us from doing as we please. A playground bully who intimidates a puny new kid and steals her lunch could simply claim that he was seizing the day. So could a sweatshop factory owner who decides to seize the opportunity to double his profits by paying his workers slave wages, while also exploiting legal loopholes to avoid taxes. How do we know when we are taking our enthusiasm for seizing the day too far? De Beauvoir was well aware that the same criticism could be made of existentialism. 'If man is free to define for himself the conditions of a life which is valid in his own eyes,' she wrote, 'can he not choose whatever he likes and act however he likes?'[8]

No matter how much we celebrate individual freedom as a moral good, there will always be a case for putting limits on it in some circumstances. And that's where carpe diem falls short: it has no inbuilt mechanism to constrain the way we seize the day. What is to stop it, say, from being expressed as violence? Horace's Ode XI unfortunately offered no answer to this question. Sartre's view was that violence was sometimes necessary for the greater cause of freedom. In his 1961 preface to Frantz Fanon's *The Wretched of the Earth*, he argued that Algeria's independence fighters were perfectly justified in seizing the day and using force to oust their colonial French oppressors. 'Violence, like Achilles' lance, can heal the wounds that it has inflicted,' he wrote. 'The rebel's weapon is the proof of his humanity. For in the first days of revolt you must kill… shoot down a European'.[9] Somehow it had escaped him that Gandhi had led India to independence without resorting to arms. If the fighting had come anywhere near his beloved Café de Flore, perhaps he would have thought again.

Sartre's position was undoubtedly controversial and for many repugnant. Still, it raises larger issues. What is the relation between my own freedom and the freedom of other people? Does mine trump yours when they come into conflict? What obligation should I have to uphold your freedom? A useful way to think about these questions is to consider adopting three rough moral rules of thumb that we can pop into our mental back pocket and consult whenever faced with tricky choices.

The first of them, which serves as something of a foundation for the other two, is this: *Those who believe in the carpe diem ideal should uphold it for all people, not just for themselves.* That is to say, it cannot be only for you, or your family, or people of your religion or nation – it's for everyone and should possess a universal quality. Sartre took a similar view when he said, 'I am obliged to will the liberty of others at the same time as my own'. So did de Beauvoir, who wrote, 'to will oneself free is also to will others free'.[10] For the philosophically minded, this tenet resembles Immanuel Kant's categorical imperative: 'act only according to a maxim by which you can at the same time will that it shall become a general law'.[11]

Now for the second rule of thumb: *Do not act in such a way that you deprive other people of their carpe diem freedoms.* That reins in the bully because stealing the new kid's lunch is depriving her of her freedom to sit in the playground and enjoy her sandwich without fear of intimidation. It's a clear encroachment on her choices. Likewise, the bankers who helped to create the subprime mortgage crisis, which led to millions of people losing their jobs and homes, were responsible for diminishing the capacity of people to make free choices about their lives: you don't have a lot of options if you are unemployed and up to your neck in debt. This ethical guidepost echoes a long tradition of liberal thought, going back to philosophers such as John Locke and John Stuart Mill, arguing that we should be free to act however we wish except insofar as we encroach on the liberty of others.

A final rule of thumb is: *Act in such a way that you enhance the capabilities of others to exercise their carpe diem freedoms.* So an advocate of seizing the day should not only ensure that they don't deprive other people of choices, but wherever possible take positive action to expand their capacity for making choices. I have unashamedly borrowed this perspective on freedom from the Nobel Prize-winning development economist Amartya Sen. Sen's 'capabilities approach' to human development puts an emphasis on our capacity to make meaningful choices in our lives, and so has close affinities with carpe diem thinking.[12] He argues that the aim of development should not be reduced to purely economic goals like increasing GDP or eliminating income poverty, but should rather focus on 'expanding the freedoms that we have reason to value' and 'creating more opportunities for choice and for substantive decisions for individuals'. Above all it is about increasing 'individual agency'.[13] For example, we should ensure that all children have access to education, so that they are then free to make choices later in life such as taking up employment opportunities or starting a small enterprise. In doing so, writes Sen, we would be upholding the ideal of 'individual freedom as a social commitment'.[14]

Translating this perspective to the realm of carpe diem, we should aim to create a world that enables people to make seize-the-day choices. Certain essentials are needed to establish a society where carpe diem can thrive, such as good medical care and education, freedom from material deprivation and discrimination, personal safety and freedom of expression.[15] It is only when these are in place that we have the capability of making genuine choices and exercising our agency to full effect. There are many ways we might advance this cause, for instance by publicly advocating for universal health care, gay marriage or a living wage. By doing so, we become activists in a carpe diem revolution.

Indigenous Guatemalan children at school. What are their carpe diem prospects?

Like all ethical principles, these three moral rules of thumb are not always easy to apply, and might sometimes conflict with each other. In the contentious case of Algerian independence, shooting a French official living in Algiers would plainly violate the second rule (he can't make a lot of choices when he's dead), but might serve to uphold the third one of promoting the seize-the-day choices of native Algerians by contributing toward their struggle for independence. To adjudicate between them, it might be necessary to appeal to a higher-level ethical principle outside the carpe diem framework, such as a commitment to non-violence or the right to national self-determination. A second challenge concerns the relation between present and future generations. My parents have just made the carpe diem decision to fly from Australia to England to visit their grandchildren while they're still physically able to do so. But the carbon emissions from their flight contribute to global warming, and may create a world of fewer life choices for future generations, including their own grandchildren. Do their seize-the-day holiday plans contradict the carpe diem ethic? There may be no clear answer to this conundrum.

So does carpe diem pass the morality test? Can we give it a social conscience? The three rules of thumb, based on a rather unorthodox fusion of existentialism, liberal thought and development economics, might serve as a beginning. Their purpose is less to be precise guidelines than act as mental prompts to raise our levels of self-awareness. They can help us pause for thought so we consider the consequences of our individual seize-the-day actions, and how they might affect the world beyond ourselves.

That is easily said. But if we're constantly checking the morality of our choices, doesn't this conflict with the whole action-oriented ethos of carpe diem? I'm not saying we should immerse ourselves in days of angst-filled moral deliberation every time we are thinking of seizing the day – by the time we have made a decision, the day may well have passed. Rather, I'm saying that we should aim to develop a discerning 'double awareness': to become aware of the moments of choice that emerge in our daily lives, and to be just as aware of the wider impact they may have. Only then will we be doing justice both to our own sense of freedom and the freedom of others.

If Seizing the Day Is So Good for Us, Why Don't We Do It More?

It's not hard to see the value of carpe diem: life is short and the clock is ticking, so let's take action now and grasp the possibilities before us, otherwise we might end our days looking back with regret at all the paths not taken. But if seizing the day is so obviously good for us, why don't we do it more? Even if we judge some particular action as worthwhile, and are morally comfortable with it, why do we so often find ourselves failing to live up to the Nike slogan by just *not* doing it?

There are clearly different kinds of barriers at work. De Beauvoir was especially sensitive to one form of obstacle: the structures of power and inequality in society that place limits on our choices. In *The Second Sex* she argued that the patriarchal system that women are born into – the expectations they grow up with about what they should look like, how they should behave, and the roles they play as mothers, wives and sexual objects – comprises a web of constraints that stand in the way of making free choices. Women are historically gendered beings who must continually struggle to escape from this web or situation.[16] In the contemporary world there are many such factors that constrain carpe diem living, such as poverty, racism, and religious and age discrimination. If, like an old neighbour of mine, you work double shifts as a forklift truck driver to support your family and elderly parents, and can barely make ends meet, then the idea of following your dream of opening a beach café in Thailand is going to seem hopelessly utopian.

Alongside such socioeconomic obstacles, which can be extremely difficult to overcome, is a set of four psychological barriers that are certainly formidable but may be easier to surmount: procrastination, overload, risk and apathy.

Procrastination is the arch-enemy of carpe diem. This is evident in its etymology: *pro* is the Latin for 'forward', while *crastinus* means 'belonging to tomorrow'. Put them together and we get 'forward it to tomorrow', or more colloquially, 'I'll do it later'. This sentiment is the precise opposite of Horace's ode, which urges us to 'leave as little as possible for tomorrow'. Procrastination has always been with us. Horace's near contemporary, Seneca, believed that 'postponement is the greatest waste of life'.[17] Even earlier, the ancient Greek poet Hesiod warned, 'Do not put your work off till tomorrow or the day after, for a sluggish worker does not fill his barn'.[18] Today, most of us are experts at failing to fill our barns, in one way or another. We put off doing our tax return, writing a college essay or finishing off the DIY. We never get around to signing up for that course or making that phone call. And it can be damaging: one US study revealed that procrastinating on doing taxes resulted in more than $450 million of overpayments in a single year because people rushed and made mistakes, while delaying medical check-ups – for instance, having a prostate or breast cancer test – can be deadly.[19]

There are undoubtedly times when postponement is a wise move: you might defer making a decision to buy a house because you're waiting for the surveyor's report, or because house prices are predicted to fall in the coming months. In a strict psychological sense this doesn't count as procrastination, as true procrastination is not functional, being defined as 'to voluntarily delay an intended course of action despite expecting to be worse off for the delay'. It's a phenomenally widespread affliction, chronically affecting 15–20% of adults, 95% of whom wish they could reduce it.[20]

Why delay something if we think doing so will make us worse

off? The most extensive academic investigation of procrastination, based on an analysis of 691 separate studies, concluded – unsurprisingly – that a whole range of factors come into play.[21] For a start, twin studies show that 22% of procrastination is genetically determined, so there's not much you can do about that. What about the remaining 78%? There are certain tasks we delay, like filing our taxes, because we simply don't take pleasure in doing them, or the deadline is so far off that it doesn't feel urgent, so we leave it until the last moment. But there are other actions – which tend to be less time-bound, and often relate to bigger life decisions – that we generally postpone due to fear of failure or a lack of self-confidence. We don't ask someone out on a date because we fear rejection, or we perpetually postpone handing in our notice at work since we're worried we won't find another job.

The most important research finding may be that procrastination is on the increase. We all know the main reason: the temptations of digital technology. There is probably no better way to delay getting on with something than checking our phone, having a quick look at some emails, and peeking at our social media feeds. Doing so this morning led me to start writing forty-three minutes later than I had planned. Taking this figure as typical of my daily working pattern, I have already spent at least 21,500 minutes *not* writing this book.

A close cousin of procrastination, which scuppers our carpe diem intentions, is choice overload. Its most obvious manifestation is in consumer culture: you want to buy a pair of jeans, and even in a single shop are faced not just with multiple colours and fabrics, but options for straight leg, stretch, slim fit, skinny and flared. The human brain, which is not designed to deal effectively with such an abundance of options, freezes up into indecision, and you walk out frustrated and empty-handed. Psychologist Barry Schwartz calls it the 'paradox of choice': more choices can lead to decision paralysis. He believes the problem extends far beyond shopping, pervading areas ranging from sex and friendship to religious observance and career choice.[22] How are you supposed to make a career change when there are websites listing thousands of job categories? And if you do eventually decide to retrain as a psychotherapist, which type will you go for – humanistic, psychodynamic, integrative, existential or some other brand? In the end you may make no decision because you don't want to regret making the 'wrong' decision. The diem remains uncarped.

Schwartz offers two main strategies for confronting choice overload. First, voluntarily constrain your choices: don't spend all afternoon shopping for jeans, just let yourself visit two shops and set a time limit of one hour. Second, become a satisficer rather than a maximiser, lowering your expectations by making 'good enough' choices.[23] You don't need the perfect jeans – just buy a pair that are good enough and get on with your life. That seems fine when you're thinking about your wardrobe. But what about when it comes to the more profound issues of existence? Here, too, there might be good reasons to embrace imperfection. The idea of being a 'good enough parent' saves many new parents from worrying that they are failing in their task and feeling guilty for not being a 'better' parent. And if you wait too long for the perfect job to turn up, you may never make a change. Yet I'm not sure, when I'm a crumbling old man, that I want to look back and think that my life – my relationship with my family, my career, my political commitment – had been merely 'good enough'. I aspire to something more, a sense that I had made the most of the possibilities and grasped what I could from the human adventure before I end up six feet underground. And that may require taking risks.

What do we know about risk, the third barrier to seizing the day? The scientific study of risk has been a booming industry over the past three decades, producing a star-studded cast of Nobel laureates and stock market prophets. Amongst its major findings is that we are far from being rational creatures and display numerous 'cognitive biases' that skew the way we assess risk. One of these, known as 'loss aversion', is that when faced with uncertainty, we tend to exaggerate potential losses relative to gains. In fact, experimental studies reveal that we hate losing about twice as much as we like winning. So imagine you are offered a gamble on the toss of a coin. If the coin falls tails you will lose $100. For you to accept the gamble, you would probably need to be offered a win of at least $200 if the coin falls heads – $100 or even $150 wouldn't be enough to entice most people.[24] The practical impact of loss aversion is that it breeds an inherent caution in our decision-making and a bias toward seeking security. This may have been a useful evolutionary trait when our early ancestors encountered a succulent new berry that could potentially poison them, but is of less use in the current day when it might serve to focus our attention on everything that could possibly go wrong if we decided to move to Berlin. When faced with a seize-the-day choice, it's worth remembering that your brain might be pulling you toward taking the safe option.

Another important cognitive bias, first described by Daniel Kahneman and Amos Tversky as the 'availability' bias, states that we make decisions based on more recent and accessible information that is easily retrievable from our memories. If you've just read about a plane crash in the newspaper, then you are likely to be more cautious about flying for a time until memory of the incident fades from your mind.[25] Similarly, if you are thinking of going freelance and know several people who recently did so but severely struggled, this is likely to have an exaggerated impact on your decision-making. This doesn't mean we should ignore their experiences: talking to them about how they ended up working 80-hour weeks is probably more informative than getting sage advice from a career counsellor. Yet we should still ask ourselves how factors like 'availability' might be deterring us from (or sometimes luring us toward) carpe diem choices.

It is easy to be seduced by the neat experimental findings of behavioural psychologists like Kahneman and forget that our attitudes toward risk are shaped just as much by waves of cultural change as by the biases built into our brains. Since the 1990s sociologists have been pointing out that Western societies are becoming increasingly risk-averse and seem to have elevated safety and caution into sacred ideals. It's not just all the traffic rules that tell us how fast to drive or when we can walk across the road. The media stokes our fear of paedophiles who might snatch away our children, or creates panics that we might all be swept away by a global epidemic of Ebola. Then there is the insurance industry constantly urging us to protect ourselves from missed flights and heart disease, and a litigious culture that scares schools into cutting playtime in case children get injuries that might bring on an expensive lawsuit. As we get bombarded by all this 'play it safe' messaging, we begin to lose touch with *Homo aleatorius*, the part of our natures that craves the excitement of taking some gambles in life.[26]

Perhaps, most fundamentally, we should consider what I think of as our personal risk story. Here's an example. A couple of nights ago in the pub a friend told me about an epiphany she experienced. She had been working as an arts producer in London for about ten years. But when running one project, where she met a number of self-employed producers, she suddenly had a startling revelation: that the reason she had stayed with her organisation for so long was due to an aversion to risk that was a product of her upbringing. She discovered that many of the freelance producers had parents with relatively high-risk, entrepreneurial jobs. Her own parents, by contrast, had steady careers – her father was in the army and her mother a teacher – and had essentially brought her up to avoid risk and stick with the secure option. It was a liberating moment, as she realised she was afraid of risk because her parents were, and the people she was working with were not because their parents were not. Everyone's attitudes were shaped by their specific family history. The result? She left her job and went freelance, then later decided to move out of London to live with her boyfriend on a farm with 800 sheep. There is a lesson here that escapes the much-lauded science of risk: exploring our personal histories and narratives of risk may be an enlightening way of bringing more carpe diem into our lives. If you drew out your own risk story on a sheet of paper, what shape would it take and what patterns would you see?

Apathy, the final barrier to carpe diem action, has a bad reputation, a legacy of its association with the Christian deadly sin of sloth. We typically associate it with laziness and indifference. It's the guy lying on the sofa in front of the telly who can't even be bothered to pick up the remote control and switch channel even though he's bored of what he's watching. It's the person who might think climate change is a problem but that it's up to other people to do something about it, or maybe there's no point anyway. It's a kind of numbness to the world, reflected in the ancient Greek origin of apathy, meaning 'without feeling'.

Psychologists often attribute apathy to stress, depression or a lack of meaning in life. I think the roots of apathy lie, most significantly, in a feeling of powerlessness. It's a sense that our actions will make no difference, whether to our own lives, or to the wider world around us. This seems especially prevalent in politics, where we often remain passive spectators while corporations infiltrate the upper echelons of power, the biosphere is ravaged and politicians rule in their self-interest.

'How did we acquire this superhuman passivity?' asks the writer and activist George Monbiot.[27] He and other critics have argued that the source of our apathetic response is that we are all too busy shopping and glued to home entertainment, and I think they're generally right. But our failures to seize the day also reflect a sense of powerlessness – that the system is too big to change and that any actions of our own will be pathetically insignificant, the merest drop in the ocean. At this point, one might invoke the notion of solidarity. We can overcome apathy when we act together with others, whether locally with people we know, or as part of a larger group. That's why people join running clubs: it's the incentive of being part of a community of runners that helps get them out of bed on a Sunday morning. This goes for politics as well: we are far more likely to take to the streets if we think thousands of others are doing the same.

What most people don't recognise, however, is that there may be an even more obvious cure for apathy: choice itself. Simply making a decision to act. Even if our actions might not make a huge difference to the wider world, making a choice by its nature changes us. It is an assertion of personal power. But how does choice actually transform and redefine us? And how do we put it into practice to overcome not only apathy but procrastination, risk and overload?

WE ARE WHAT WE CHOOSE

The characters in Samuel Beckett's play *Waiting for Godot* are masters of indecision. They plan and resolve, but a decisive choice is never made. It is an unmistakable theme in the final lines:

> Vladimir: Well? Shall we go?
> Estragon: Yes, let's go.
> [Stage directions:] They do not move.[28]

Waiting for Godot is a window on our lives. So often we fail to move. We know there are choices to make but somehow we are paralysed, inert or forever wavering in the sea of indecision. We might know that a relationship isn't working, that a career is unfulfilling, or that we should visit our parents more often. The choices are there waiting to be taken, yet we frequently fail to seize the day and the possibilities drift away.

We can see our lives as a series of choices extending through time, each with the potential to shape not just what we do but who we are. I'm not talking about the trivial choices of which brand of chocolate biscuits to buy or what jacket to wear on a night out, but the significant decisions that go to the core of our being. It is no surprise that life-defining moments of choice are a recurring theme in novels, plays and films. Think of Oskar Schindler in *Schindler's List*, who must decide whether or not to save his Jewish factory workers, at risk to his own life. Or Neo choosing between the red pill and the blue pill in *The Matrix*. Or Amélie, who angsts over telling Nino that she loves him. 'If you let this chance go by,' an old man says to her, 'eventually your heart will become as dry and brittle as my skeleton.' And then there's that masterpiece of existential anomie, *The Graduate*. Elaine stands in the chapel aisle having just married a characterless jock, while staring at Ben who is screaming her name. She must make a carpe diem choice: to stay with her new husband, or to run away with Ben into a different life. She pauses, looks at the wedding guests around her – and then she runs.

The importance of choice as a route to a life of meaning was central to the thought of Viktor Frankl, one of the founders of existential psychotherapy in the 1940s. 'What is a man?' he asked. 'He is a being who continually decides what he is.'[29]

Frankl's simple statement is one of the most profound distillations of the carpe diem ideal I have ever encountered. The act of choosing reveals what we care about – it is a reflection of our worldviews, desires, priorities and fears. It is a mirror in which we can judge ourselves not just by our beliefs but by our actions, and which shows us the shifting contours of our identity. When you decide to train as an actor, rather than follow your parents' advice to go into accountancy, you are saying something about who you are and what you value. In effect, you are asserting, 'I am *for* acting,' and 'I value creativity'.[30] Similarly, when you decide to go on your first political march, you add a new layer to your identity and reshape your personal narrative: you become an activist. The choice is now part of you. We are what we choose to do, or as Jean-Paul Sartre pithily proclaimed, 'To be is to do.'[31]

Look over your own life, and its course will have been determined in part by factors outside your control (Did you lose your job through no fault of your own? Were you born into poverty? Or with a genetic predisposition to depression?). But it will also have been shaped by decisions for which you are responsible, where you were at a crossroads and selected a path. Either this road, or that one. These are the decisions through which we invent ourselves. They express and give form to the fundamental projects that provide our lives with meaning and direction.[32] Such projects – what Frankl called 'concrete assignments' – are different for everyone, and might include anything from promoting theatre for children or making scientific discoveries to caring for stray animals or keeping the family business going. We affirm their importance to us through our choices.

Despite all the upbeat self-help manuals that confidently urge us to get out there and make bold decisions, there is nothing easy about making choices. In his 1946 essay *Existentialism Is a Humanism*, Sartre tells the story of a pupil of his who sought his advice during the war. The young man was torn between looking after his mother, or joining the Free French Forces to fight the Germans and avenge his brother's death. He was sure that remaining with his mother would have a beneficial effect on her life, but wasn't certain if volunteering to fight would make much difference: he could end up stuck in a training camp and never see action. What should he do in the face of this excruciating dilemma? Should he choose the love of his mother or the love of his country?

Sartre's answer was probably the most annoying response in the history of modern philosophy, but undoubtedly profound: 'You are free, therefore choose.' That was it. The young man could weigh up the reasons for and against on either side for as long as he liked, and seek advice from many quarters, but in the end it was up to him to make a decision. There was no escape: he must stare into the abyss of possibilities and simply make a choice. The final decision had to come from within himself. 'Man is condemned to be free,' wrote Sartre.[33] The reality of freedom is that there are no excuses and we must take responsibility for our actions, knowing that for every path we choose others must be rejected. If this causes anguish, so be it. That is the nature of the human predicament. That's the trouble with freedom.

This story, which is central to the existentialist canon, makes freedom of choice sound rather melodramatic. It isn't always so. Sometimes the choices before us are not impossible ethical conundrums that leave us writhing in anguish no matter what we do. They could be relatively small but still significant decisions: how we treat colleagues in a meeting or someone needing help on the street, whether to make time to join a choir or play with our children. These are all instances of carpe diem possibility. There are bigger decisions too that are not about facing profound moral dilemmas like Sartre's pupil, but simply involve confronting a difficult choice and finding the courage to act. Let me give a personal example.

I once had a job running a community project collecting stories of personal change. Although great to start with, after a few years my enthusiasm began ebbing away. I felt I wasn't learning much any more, and that I had become an administrator spending most of my time answering emails. I was turning up and going through the motions, but became increasingly desperate to leave. Meanwhile, I had been cooking up a one-day, some-day, alternative plan: to start teaching my own courses on the art of living. But I just couldn't see how to make it happen. It was financially risky and, having never done it, I had no idea whether I'd be any good at it. My partner encouraged me to leave my job but I kept up coming with excuses, for instance that even if I did leave, I had nowhere to hold the workshops I was planning. After three months of my complaining and procrastinating, she said, 'You don't need to resign yet. Why don't you just start teaching your courses in our kitchen on the weekends?'

Her suggestion jolted me into action. That night, in a moment of carpe diem enthusiasm, I sent out an email to a few friends, and friends of friends, inviting them to a course on rethinking our attitudes to love and time, although I had only the vaguest idea of what I'd actually teach. Two Saturdays later, they turned up and we sat in our kitchen, eight people squeezed around the table. It was a great success, so I repeated the experiment with different topics, like work and empathy. As the kitchen workshops grew, people heard about them and I was soon invited to hold them for the wider public at a cultural centre. Within a few months the courses were going so well that I plucked up the courage to leave my day job and embark on a new career running workshops and writing about the challenges of how to live. It later led to me being a founding faculty member of The School of Life, an organisation

My first kitchen workshop in 2007. I didn't really know what I was doing.

that began in London and now has branches around the world.

The decision to run that first workshop was a turning point in my life, taking it in a radically new direction. But just as important was how I felt about it. I remember the excitement and exhilaration I felt after sending out that very first email invitation. It was a sense of absolute freedom – along with a feeling of relief, and a little anxiety too. Finally I had made a choice and become the author of my own life. Even though I had fears about whether I could pull it off, I felt released from the shackles of my indecision. I experienced what I can only describe as an internal glow of aliveness. It was a feeling that returned the evening after my inaugural workshop. I sat alone at the kitchen table, surrounded by leftover coffee mugs and Post-it notes, consumed by a heady lightness of being.

'In every action,' wrote Dante, 'what is primarily intended by the doer, whether he acts from natural necessity or out of free will, is the disclosure of his own image… in action the being of the doer is somehow intensified.'[34] Dante understood the philosophy of 'I choose, therefore I am'. When we make a meaningful choice we experience an intensification of our being. Some call it the thrill of choosing. Even when accompanied by trepidation, it can fill us with a sense of vitality in body and mind. It is the process through which we discover that existence lies in agency. The fact that a choice might be difficult shouldn't be a deterrent. Imagine if all our decisions were as easy as choosing whether to have strawberry or vanilla ice cream, or worse if all the significant decisions were made for us. Life would lose its lustre. Our humanity would be diminished. We should embrace hard choices as a creative space where we are given an opportunity to write the script of our own lives.[35]

Staying true to the carpe diem ideal requires developing a heightened consciousness of the choices before us, rather than sleepwalking our way through life. Camus may have put it best: 'Being aware of one's life, one's revolt, one's freedom, and to the maximum, is living, and to the maximum.'[36] It's easy to put an iconic quote like this on your screensaver, so how might we follow Camus' advice in practice? I think it is about making a habit of noticing the possibilities for making choices in our daily lives, both large and small, instead of letting them pass by through inattention, denial or blissful ignorance. At the end of each day we might look back and ask ourselves: Was I fully aware of the choices I made – at home, at work, as a parent, as a friend, as a citizen? We can then reflect on what these choices tell us about our values and priorities. Eventually we may come to recognise that carpe diem calls on us not to live each day as if it were our last, but to live each day as if we are what we choose, and as if each of our choices were a matter of consequence.

DISCIPLES OF EXPERIENCE

The choices that we make do more than shape our identities and give meaning to our lives; they are also a route to experiential insight. And it is when we become disciples of experience that the barriers to seizing the day really begin to crumble.

If you visit the personal development shelves in bookshops, you will encounter hundreds of bullet-point tips and tricks for surmounting the barriers to taking action. One bestselling anti-procrastination guide suggests the following classic method: 'break your goal into small, specific minigoals'. So instead of saying, 'I'm going to write the report,' you say, 'I'll spend thirty minutes working on a plan for my spreadsheet tonight. Tomorrow I'll spend another thirty minutes filling in the data, and then the next day, I'll spend an hour writing a report based on the data'.[37] And Hey Presto, it's done.

Such behavioural strategies might work if your carpe diem ambitions are limited to writing data reports and other checklist, self-contained tasks. But what about when it comes to more emotionally charged, socially complex or personally challenging issues like whether to have IVF treatment, or set up a charity, or attend Alcoholics Anonymous, or move in with your partner, or abandon your legal career, or come out as gay?

In such cases, where the existential stakes may be higher and the uncertainties greater, we need a different approach. But what? It's a question I have been grappling with for years, both in my own life, and as a writer and teacher on the art of living. How do we make the big decisions? After we've read books, attended courses and talked about it endlessly, how do we overcome the barriers and seize the day?

I am sceptical of simplistic, one-shot solutions to life's struggles, but if I were to build a temple in honour of carpe diem, I would have this motto carved over the entrance: Act First, Think Later.

This piece of guidance may be worth more than all those other tips and tricks put together. I first grasped its importance when writing a previous book about career change.[38] It turns out that if you are searching for fulfilling and meaningful work that does more than just pay the bills, you are most likely to find it by rejecting what careers counsellors usually advise, which is to do lots of research and planning to pinpoint the right career, then start sending out your résumé. This might get you a job, but it's unlikely to be fulfilling in the long term. In fact, you should do the opposite of this 'plan then implement' model. Instead of thinking then doing, we need to do first and reflect afterwards. In practice this means getting out into the real world and trying out different jobs for yourself, for instance by shadowing, volunteering or experimenting. That's what I did with my first kitchen class – it was an Act First, Think Later experiment that I did on the side of my existing job. And that's how we best find out what is likely (or not likely) to give us fulfilment – through being immersed in the white heat of experience. As the organisational change expert Herminia Ibarra observes, 'The only way to create change is to put our possible identities into practice, working and crafting them until they are

sufficiently grounded in experience to guide more decisive steps...
We learn who we are by testing reality, not by looking inside.'[39]

What goes for career change goes for life more generally.
We should move beyond the old Enlightenment attitude that
treats life decisions as a rational process where we think through
the options and arguments, weigh them up on a set of perfectly
calibrated existential scales, then make a decision. The truth is that
there are no scales – or at least none that we should fully trust.[40]
You can draw up a list of carefully defined criteria for the perfect
lover – their physical appearance, educational background, sense of
humour – and yet when you finally meet someone who ticks all
the boxes they may do absolutely nothing for you. But then you
stumble across someone who seems a total mismatch and they
completely blow you away. Life isn't always about logical planning
– it's about lived experiences that challenge our assumptions and
offer a route to insight and self-discovery.[41]

This does not mean we should jettison rational deliberation
completely. It's just that there can come a point when thinking
about it more doesn't help. Stepping into experience gives us useful
new information – not just about what a particular experience is
really like, but also how it makes us feel.

We might find inspiration in Leonardo da Vinci, who signed
his name with the added flourish, 'disciple of experience'.[42] Yet
beware, for experience can be a cruel master. The word 'experience'
is rooted in the Latin *experimentia*, meaning 'experiment', and is
also related to *periculum*, the Latin for 'danger'.[43] The implications
are clear: there is an inherent peril or risk in following a more
experiential path in life. Just as Leonardo's brilliant career was
full of failed experiments, our own seize-the-day experiments will
sometimes fail too. But what of it? Ralph Waldo Emerson, one
of the nineteenth century's greatest proponents of carpe diem,
entreated us to embrace this reality:

Do not be too timid and squeamish about your actions. All life is an experiment. The more experiments you make the better. What if they are a little coarse, and you may get your coat soiled or torn? What if you do fail, and get fairly rolled in the dirt once or twice? Up again, you shall never be so afraid of a tumble.[44]

Sculpting the Self

All the sculptures of today, like those of the past, will end one day in pieces... So it is important to fashion one's work carefully in its smallest recess and charge every particle of matter with life.

Alberto Giacometti[45]

Carpe diem living is ultimately an act of profound self-creation. We can imagine ourselves as a sculptor who builds up a figure by adding small pieces of clay, layer upon layer – a little like the works of the Swiss artist Alberto Giacometti. Each choice we make is like one of these wads of clay, giving shape to our self-portrait. Over time, with the accumulated additions, we continually refashion ourselves.

Occasionally we make a major decision and our sculpted self takes on a new form. Sometimes we make mistakes and struggle to scrape off the ill-placed clay, but we can always add more layers over and around it, re-adjusting the figure by making wiser, more experienced choices. There may be times when our choices begin to follow social conventions, and so the sculpture starts to resemble others we know and loses its uniqueness. We might procrastinate, circling round and round our work in progress, unsure where to add the next layer.

Periodically, we stand back and look at the figure before us, created by an accretion of choices over the years. Are we satisfied with what we see? Can we detect meaning in its features and purpose in its gaze?

The sculpture will, inevitably, end in pieces and be crushed back into the earth. Until that day, we possess a creative power to give it such energy and vitality that it might almost come to life and start moving of its own accord. That is the promise of carpe diem.

Epilogue:
A Carpe Diem Mandala

Horace is not known for his humility. 'I have built a monument more lasting than bronze and set higher than the pyramids of kings,' he proclaims in the final poem of his third book of *Odes*. 'I shall not wholly die. A great part of me will escape Libitina.'[1] He was talking about his poems, and the Libitina in question was the Roman goddess of funerals. As the son of a freed slave who rose to become a famous lyricist and confidant of the Emperor, perhaps he had some grounds to be boastful. His apparently smug declaration might also have been a way of saying that his verse explored the universal themes of everyday life – from love and friendship to mortality – and would therefore stand the test of time.

Whatever his intention, he was right. Horace is still read today, and he may have no greater legacy than the fragment of Ode XI that has inspired this book: carpe diem. Over the last three years it has been my guide and companion, taking me on an exhilarating journey into myriad realms, including the history of sexuality, Renaissance poetry, moral philosophy, theatrical improvisation, and the lives of surfing fanatics, drug addicts and political activists. I find it extraordinary that a mere two words from an ancient poem have touched on so many aspects of human culture, and generated such a rich tapestry of associations.

Given this diversity inherent in the carpe diem ideal, it is difficult to draw any single conclusion about its meaning or message. There is no supreme life lesson that it offers the world, no definitive set of principles or commandments. What I have done, however, is bring together the main elements and arguments of this book into a single picture – a Carpe Diem Mandala. The word 'mandala' comes from the Sanskrit for 'circle', and typically refers to a symbolic representation of the universe that focuses the mind and offers spiritual guidance. I am using the term more loosely. The mandala I have created functions as a mental *aide-mémoire* for thinking about seize-the-day choices. It is not a prescriptive device that directs us to making particular decisions but rather represents an attitude we can take in our lives, where we keep the

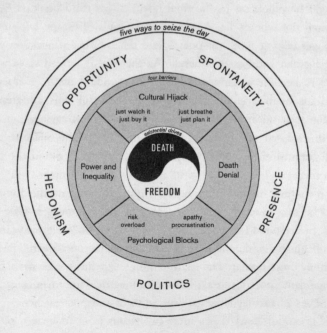

possibility of seizing the day at the forefront of our minds. It is less about *what* to do and more about *how* to do it, reminding us of the different ways of putting Horace's advice into practice, and the challenges of doing so.[2]

At the mandala's centre lie the core existential drives of freedom and death, which have an interdependent, yin-yang relationship with one another.[3] Our carpe diem instinct partly emerges from the deep human desire for freedom, to feel that we have agency and the capacity to shape the course of our own lives rather than have our fate chosen for us. But it is also a product of knowing that the time we have for expressing this freedom is limited by the prospect of death, and that we ought to make the best of it before the clock strikes, or risk being consumed by regret. Like the Venerable Bede's sparrow flying into the warmth and light of the king's hall, we only have the briefest moment to spread our wings before flitting out again into the dark night. What path should our flight take as we sweep through the fire-lit room? With whom should we fly? To what purpose? Freedom and death compel us to make the choices that determine the course of our journey.

The mandala is encircled by the five ways to seize the day that humankind has discovered over the centuries. Between them and the core drives are four kinds of barriers to putting Horace's ideal into practice. There are the cultural hijackers that threaten to co-opt carpe diem and narrow its scope, such as the Just Watch It enticements of the home entertainment industry and the Just Breathe mantra of the mindfulness movement. These are accompanied by the psychological blocks of procrastination, risk, overload and apathy, the socioeconomic barriers of power and inequality, and the pervasive influence of death denial, which prevents us from tasting the elixir of our mortality. They are formidable obstacles, but not impossible to surmount. The challenge is to overcome them and get back in touch with the accumulated carpe diem wisdom of humanity.

I would like to see this Carpe Diem Mandala become a tattoo as popular as the current vogue for having the words 'carpe diem' etched in Gothic script on your skin. It might be a little wordy and complicated, requiring extra painful pricks, but it would offer a deeper and more nuanced depiction of what the carpe diem ideal is all about. Personally, though, I'm happy to keep it on the lock screen of my phone, a portal I have to pass through every time I want to send a text or check my email.

Although carpe diem is a philosophy with roots going back centuries, it is not an ideal frozen in time. How might it evolve in the future? It will no doubt be influenced by factors such as our increasing lifespans and growing wealth inequality. But perhaps the most powerful – and least predictable – dynamic shaping its destiny will be the impact of digital technologies. An electronically networked society is rushing toward us at breakneck speed, with the potential to alter almost every aspect of seizing the day. As we have seen, this is already happening. Impulsive one-click shopping has helped consumer culture to hijack carpe diem, and our efforts to manage a flood of digital information lock many of us into a 'just plan it' mentality of hyper-scheduling.

Where it will go next is uncertain. Back in the 1990s many technology theorists were hopeful that the internet would release an explosion of individuality and free expression. But since those heady days, it has become a place of increasing conformity, passivity and social control. Instead of building their own websites, full of creativity and personal quirks, millions of people express their digital selves in the ready-made formats of social networking sites such as Facebook, fitting themselves into the narrow categories offered on the profile page, and have become experts at boiling their thoughts down to 140-character tweets.[4] The end result could be what the novelist Zadie Smith has called a 'flattening' of the human personality, where social media erodes our capacity to express our individuality and uniqueness.[5] We can also become trapped in the echo-chamber of digital networks, surrounded by like-minded voices that cut us off from fresh ways of looking at ourselves and the world.

Yet there is room for optimism that can counter such dystopian visions. There are digital designers, artists, software programmers and social entrepreneurs who are adept at using technology to express their creative selves and personal values, and most of us have now had experiences of falling in love, finding community or discovering new aspects of our political selves online. Moreover, technologies such as video gaming and virtual reality, as well as chat rooms and messaging, are generally more interactive than that paragon of passivity known as television, which has done so much to sap our carpe diem energies. The problem is that most technologies still place a filter between us and analogue reality, expanding the dominion of mediated, secondary experience. It might be fun to play virtual football for your favourite team, but it is very different from the intense cut and thrust of a real game.

Although we spend an increasing proportion of our waking hours online, I also know that Horace's words have retained their cultural power for more than two millennia, and his call to seize the day will not be easily silenced by the incessant electronic texts and tweets invading our minds. I am as addicted as anyone to digital media, yet in the course of writing this book have still been able to hear Horace's voice, and have become more inspired than ever by the philosophy of carpe diem. I have found myself doing things I have never done before, from attending an acting workshop to kayaking with basking sharks, and am engaging in political activism for the first time in more than a decade. I have taken my kids on crazy camping adventures and let them frolic in the rain, and – yes – have even become a little more mindful along the way. After years of procrastinating, I finally found the courage to establish the world's first Empathy Museum, an international travelling exhibition dedicated to helping us look through other people's eyes – and I have Horace to thank for it. I admit that these are not earth-shattering examples of carpe diem living. I haven't done a parachute jump or moved with my family to Timbuktu, and I probably still spend too much time reading biographies of people like Patrick Leigh Fermor. But with the mandala in my mind, I feel my life opening up to new possibilities.

In our age of individualism, we are too easily drawn toward seeking such possibilities for ourselves alone, focusing narrowly on the question, 'What's in it for me?' But their full richness arises when our gaze shifts beyond the self. We are social creatures who thrive in and depend upon community. The real future of seizing the day is in striving to 'just do it' not only for ourselves, but for others, and with others. That is how we can transform carpe diem into a common treasury to be shared by all.

Appendix:
Films, Songs and Poems

Here is a select list of crowd-sourced films, songs and poems on the theme of carpe diem. I've also thrown in a few of my own favourites. In honour of Horace's Ode XI, there are eleven items in each category.

FILMS

Ikiru (Akira Kurosawa, 1952)
Harold and Maude (Hal Ashby, 1971)
McCullin (David Morris and Jacqui Morris, 2012)
Zorba the Greek (Mihalis Kakogiannis, 1964)
The Brand New Testament (Jaco Van Dormael, 2015)
Ways of Seeing (John Berger/Michael Dibb, 1972)
About Time (Richard Curtis, 2013)
After Life (Hirokazu Koreeda, 1998)
Trainspotting (Danny Boyle, 1996)
Dead Poets Society (Peter Weir, 1989)
Man on Wire (James Marsh, 2008)

SONGS

Lou Reed, 'Perfect Day'
Eminem, 'Lose Yourself'
Nils Frahm, 'Says'
Metallica, 'Carpe Diem Baby'
Henry Purcell, 'When I Am Laid in Earth (Dido's Lament)'
Seize the Day, 'With My Hammer'
Iggy Pop, 'Lust for Life'
Guy Lombardo, 'Enjoy Yourself'
Bob Marley, 'Wake Up and Live'
Prince, '1999'
Pink Floyd, 'Time'

POEMS

Horace, Ode XI, Book 1 ('Tu ne quaesieris')
Edward FitzGerald, *Rubáiyát of Omar Khayyám*
Emily Dickinson, 'A Death blow is a Life blow to Some'
Tony Harrison, 'Polygons'
Robert Frost, 'Carpe Diem'
Andrew Marvell, 'To His Coy Mistress'
Walt Whitman, 'I Sing the Body Electric'
A.E. Housman, 'XVI: How Clear, How Lovely Bright'
Robert Herrick, 'To the Virgins, to Make Much of Time'
Philip Larkin, 'Days'
Dylan Thomas, 'Do Not Go Gentle into That Good Night'

Endnotes

1   Carpe Diem from Horace to #yolo

[1]   http://www.dailymail.co.uk/news/article-2651658/For-time-Britains-favourite-D-Day-runaway-Bernard-Jordan-tells-amazing-story.html

[2]   http://forums.digitalspy.co.uk/showthread.php?t=2037992

[3]   Thoreau 1986, 135.

[4]   Special thanks to Dr Tim Smith-Laing for leading on this research, and also to Christopher Whalen, who made a significant contribution. The analysis focused primarily on English-language sources. The core data has been compiled in a Carpe Diem Database (Smith-Laing, Whalen and Krznaric 2015).

[5]   http://www.ons.gov.uk/peoplepopulationandcommunity/ birthsdeathsandmarriages/divorce/bulletins/ divorcesinenglandandwales/2013

[6]   http://www.dailymail.co.uk/sciencetech/article-2449632/How-check-phone-The-average-person-does-110-times-DAY-6-seconds-evening. html

[7]   http://brainblogger.com/2014/05/23/the-self-help-industry-helps-itself-to-billions-of-dollars/; https://www.theguardian.com/books/2013/ dec/28/self-help-books-literature-publishers-growth

[8]   https://www.youtube.com/watch?v=LRX5MiOG420

[9]   Inglehart and Welzel 2005, 135–145; http://www.worldvaluessurvey.org/ WVSContents.jsp?CMSID=Findings

[10]   Quoted in Cooper (2013, 44).

[11]   http://legacy.fordham.edu/halsall/basis/bede-book2.asp

[12]   Laing 1967, 37.

[13]   On the reception of Horace in the Renaissance see McGann (2007, 305–317).

14 Horace 2000, 34.
15 Smith-Laing, Whalen and Krznaric 2015.
16 http://www.dailyscript.com/scripts/dead_poets_final.html
17 Horace 2000, 145.
18 Earlier examples of carpe diem poetry include Shakespeare's 'O Mistress Mine, Where Are You Roaming', from *Twelfth Night*, and Lorenzo de' Medici's 'Trionfo', which begins, 'Youth is sweet and well/But doth speed away!/Let who will be gay,/To-morrow, none can tell'. http://www.elfinspell.com/MediciPoem.html
19 Anderson 1992, 115–122; Lill 1997, 109–110; Moldenhauer 1968, 189, 204.
20 McMahon 2006, 70-74; Eyres 2013, 181–193; Grimm 1963, 316–317.
21 This figure is based on data from 2005 to 2015 (Smith-Laing, Whalen and Krznaric 2015).
22 Ehrenreich 2006, 92, 97–117.
23 See, for example, the speech by the Marquis of Lansdown in the House of Lords on February 3rd, 1795, Parliamentary Register, p.533. Analysis based on Google Ngram word search, and Smith-Laing, Whalen and Krznaric (2015).
24 *The Times*, November 7th, 1933.
25 http://www.pbs.org/wgbh/amex/china/sfeature/nixon.html. Nixon claimed to be quoting a poem by Mao, but his words contained an uncanny echo of Horace. He used the phrase 'seize the moment' before his visit to China, and it even became the title for one of his books. See also William Safire's analysis of the changing political usage of Horace's carpe diem in the *New York Times*, December 24th, 2000.
26 https://www.youtube.com/watch?v=IZsy8YYRQxc

2 Dancing with Death

1   Duncan 1964, 66.
2   Quoted in Solomon et al (2015, 218).
3   Ariès 2008, 132.
4   http://deathcafe.com/what/. There is also a growing Death Over Dinner movement that is spreading internationally: http://deathoverdinner.org/
5   Paz 1967, 49.
6   http://www.romankrznaric.com/outrospection/2015/10/19/3935
7   Solomon et al 2015, 8–9, 45, 104; http://fivebooks.com/interview/sheldon-solomon-on-fear-of-death/
8   Yalom 1980, 41. My thinking on death, and other key carpe diem topics such as freedom, owes an enormous debt to the writings of Irvin Yalom, especially his book *Existential Psychotherapy*.
9   Solomon et al 2015, 87.
10 Solomon et al 2015, 97.

11 Yalom 1980, 53–54.
12 For this interpretation of Klimt's painting, see Néret (2015, 71) and Solomon et al (2015, 213).
13 http://news.stanford.edu/news/2005/june15/jobs-061505.html
14 Aurelius 2006, Book 7 Section 40.
15 Seneca 1932, Sections 1 and 7.
16 Irvine 2009, 200.
17 http://www.nbcnews.com/science/environment/apple-creates-34-2-million-metric-tons-greenhouse-gases-n345031; http://unstats.un.org/unsd/environment/air_greenhouse_emissions.htm
18 http://www.historyandtheheadlines.abc-clio.com/ContentPages/ContentPage.aspx?entryId=1171741
19 Kurosawa (1952).
20 Niemiec and Schulenberg 2001, 395.
21 Frankl 1987, 76.
22 Frankl 1987, 111.
23 http://www.firstshowing.net/2013/interview-about-time-writer-director-richard-curtis-on-happiness/
24 https://archive.org/stream/completenietasch10nietuoft/completenietasch10nietuoft_djvu.txt
25 Loeb 2013, 645–671.
26 Cox 2011, 101.
27 http://gutenberg.us/articles/h%C5%8Dj%C5%8Dki
28 http://www.washburn.edu/reference/bridge24/Hojoki.html
29 https://www.theguardian.com/stage/2016/jan/12/lindsay-kemp-david-bowie-ziggy-stardust-interview; http://thequietus.com/articles/09927-david-bowie-is-v-a-exhibition
30 Buckley 2005, 1.
31 Tolstoy 1960, 152.
32 Tolstoy 1960, 148.
33 http://bronnieware.com/regrets-of-the-dying/; Hennezel 2012, 5, 68–72.
34 Yalom 1980, 173–175.
35 Eagleman 2009, 104–105.

3 How Carpe Diem Was Hijacked

1 http://www.theguardian.com/society/2014/dec/14/britons-learned-art-last-minute-living
2 Ehrenreich 2006, 91.
3 Ehrenreich 2006, 79, 85.
4 Thompson 1968, 448.
5 Weber 1958, 166, 168.
6 Ehrenreich 2006, 99; Weber 1958, 157.
7 Camus 2005, 80; McMahon 2006, 104.

8   Thompson 1968, 450–451.

9   Foucault 1979, 298-306; Young 2008, 78.

10 Thanks to the economist Peter Antonioni for enlightening me on the idea of an 'info bomb'.

11 Burton 1838, 3.

12 http://www.digitalspy.co.uk/fun/news/a464219/75-percent-of-people-use-their-phone-on-the-toilet.html#~paG8CyVh1J6R2n

13 http://www.theguardian.com/science/2015/jan/18/modern-world-bad-for-brain-daniel-j-levitin-organized-mind-information-overload

14 Rosenthal 2005, 33–35.

15 https://medium.com/swlh/how-technology-hijacks-peoples-minds-from-a-magician-and-google-s-design-ethicist-56d62ef5edf3#.c7y7hiu9e

16 Kringelbach and Phillips 2014, 164–165; Baumeister and Tierney 2012, 104.

17 http://blog.vendhq.com/post/64901826173/encourage-impulse-buys-store-deeper-look-unplanned-purchases; http://www.sciencedirect.com/science/article/pii/S1057740802702325

18 Krznaric 2011, 130.

19 http://www.statista.com/topics/846/amazon/; http://uk.businessinsider.com/new-cirp-amazon-prime-numbers-2016-1?utm_source=feedly&utm_medium=webfeeds?r=US&IR=T

20 Katz 1994, 199.

21 Center for Applied Research 1999, 1.

22 Katz 1994, 146; Coombs 2014, 257–258; Lucas 2000, 149–164; Arsenault and Fawzy 2001, 63–76; Helstein 2003, 276–292; Penaloza 1998, 337–400.

23 Katz 1994, 39.

24 Kim and Short 2008, 43.

25 Berger 1972, 131; Ewen 1996, 3–4, 131–145.

26 Berger 1972, 131.

27 http://www.monbiot.com/2014/01/20/addicted-to-comfort/

28 Around 66% of people over the age of 16 in the UK list shopping as one of their favoured leisure activities; this is a higher percentage than for alternative activities such as reading, gardening or sport. http://www.ons.gov.uk/ons/rel/social-trends-rd/social-trends/social-trends-40/social-trends-40---lifestyles-and-social-participation-chapter.pdf. Some surveys reveal that UK adults spend 2.5 hours per week on window shopping and browsing (with a further two hours per week on essential grocery shopping). See http://www.dailymail.co.uk/femail/article-2295244/Brits-spend-18-days-year-shopping.html. US data shows average time spent shopping daily is around 45 minutes, with women spending more time than men. See http://www.bls.gov/news.release/archives/atus_06242016.pdf. Time spent shopping on smartphones in the US almost doubled

from 2013 to 2015. See http://uk.businessinsider.com/five-must-know-retail-trends-in-mobile-and-social-marketing-2016-4-24.

29 Adorno and Horkheimer 1997, 123.

30 Packard 1960, 11–17.

31 Many of the pleasures of television – both individual and collective – are explored in Moran (2013).

32 Average television watching time in the UK on a regular TV set is 3 hours and 40 minutes. See http://media.ofcom.org.uk/news/2015/cmr-uk-2015/, and https://www.thinkbox.tv/News-and-opinion/Newsroom/10032016-New-figures-put-TV-viewing-in-perspective. The latest US government data shows daily average TV time for people over 15 was 2.78 hours, out of a total 5.21 hours of leisure time. The figure for television time may well be an underestimate, as it excludes watching programmes on devices such as phones and tablets. See http://www.bls.gov/news.release/pdf/atus.pdf. Many studies give a higher figure for hours of TV watched, in both the US and European countries. See, for example, http://www.nielsen.com/us/en/insights/reports/2016/the-total-audience-report-q4-2015.html. See also http://www.economist.com/node/15980817 and Kubey and Csikszentmihalyi (2003, 50).

33 Based on total daily electronic media exposure of 9 hours and 51 minutes. See Nielson (2016, 16), http://www.nielsen.com/us/en/insights/reports/2016/the-total-audience-report-q4-2015.html

34 Kaiser Family Foundation 2010, 3.

35 Mander 1978, 24.

36 Debord 2010, 2; Kubey and Csikszentmihalyi 1990, 185.

37 Moran 2013, 3.

38 Based on an Italian study of over 500 couples: http://serenellasalomoni.com/2014/10/22/la-televisione-in-camera-spegne-la-libido/

39 Kubey and Csikszentmihalyi 2003, 53; Owen et al 2010, 4.

40 Orlowski 2007, 6.

41 http://www.commercialfreechildhood.org/sites/default/files/kidsandscreens_0.pdf

42 Veerman et al 2011, 1.

43 Dunstan et al 2010, 5; Paddock 2010, 1–4; Owen et al 2010, 105–113; http://www.health.harvard.edu/blog/too-much-sitting-linked-to-an-early-death-201401297004.

44 Kubey and Csikszentmihalyi 2003, 48–55; Baumeister and Tierney 2012, 4.

45 Kubey and Csikszentmihalyi 2003, 48–55; Crawford 2015, 8–10.

46 Bourdieu 1998, 7.

47 Kubey and Csikszentmihalyi 1990, 196, 200.

48 Kubey and Csikszentmihalyi 1990, 190–191, 213–214.

49 See, for instance, Rosenthal (2005, ix), Schwartz (2005, 2) and Greenfield (2012, 27).

4 The Art of Seizing Opportunities

[1]   Smith-Laing, Whalen and Krznaric 2015.

[2]   Angelou 2009, ix.

[3]   Angelou 2004, 232, 310, 460–464.

[4]   Angelou 2009, 1.

[5]   Angelou 2004, 416.

[6]   Angelou 2004, 510–511, 605, 1005.

[7]   Angelou 2004, 1163.

[8]   http://www.phrases.org.uk/meanings/412350.html

[9]   http://www.theguardian.com/news/oliver-burkeman-s-blog/2014/may/21/everyone-is-totally-just-winging-it

[10] http://www.dailyscript.com/scripts/Harold-and-Maude.htm

[11] Tedeschi and Calhoun 2004, 2.

[12] Tedeschi and Calhoun 2004, 6; Ring 1996, 187–190; Yalom 1980,36; Noyes 1980, 235; http://www.ted.com/conversations/2306/what_3_things_did_you_learn_wh.html

[13] Noyes 1980, 237–238; Yalom 1980, 33–40.

[14] https://www.youtube.com/watch?v=yPfe3rCcUeQ

[15] Solomon, Greenberg and Pyszczynksi 2015, 197.

[16] McCullin 1992, 187.

[17] McCullin 1992, 218.

[18] Morris and Morris 2012.

[19] Morris and Morris 2012; McCullin 1992, 15, 53.

[20] Morris and Morris 2012.

[21] https://www.theguardian.com/artanddesign/2005/aug/06/photography.art

[22] Marsh, James 2008.

[23] Adams 2001, 15–17.

[24] Sennett 1986, 34; Goffman 1956, 11–12.

[25] Personal communication 12.03.15.

[26] Sartre 1969, 59–60; Phillips 1981, 23–24; Vaneigem 2012, 114–116.

[27] Hogg and Vaughan 2005, 304.

[28] Krznaric, Whalen and Zeldin 2006, 328.

[29] Krznaric, Whalen and Zeldin 2006, 338, 340.

[30] Smiles 1968, 11; Josephson 1962, 10; Salecl 2010, 19–22.

[31] Zinn 1995, 248.

[32] Smiles 1968, 247.

[33] Morris 2006, 60.

[34] Zinn 1995, 248; Morris 2006, 65.

[35] Zinn 1995 249; Morris 2006, 27.

[36] Morris 2006, 16.

[37] Quoted in Moore (2008, 11).

[38] Machiavelli 1961, 91.

[39] Bellow 2001, 66, 90; Mathis 1965, 43.

[40] Marshall 2008, 311; Woodcock and Avakumović 1971, 119; Kropotkin 1978, 202.

[41] Kropotkin 1978, 221–229.

[42] Kropotkin 1978, 254.

[43] Kropotkin 1978, 256.

[44] Kropotkin 1978, 261.

[45] Sartre 1946, 14.

[46] Tweet by @richardbranson, November 21st, 2014.

[47] http://www.bbc.co.uk/news/education-26954901

[48] http://hdt.typepad.com/henrys_blog/2010/04/april-24-1859.html

5 The Hidden Virtues of Hedonism

[1] http://www.tandfonline.com/doi/abs/10.1300/J398v01n03_03

[2] Mill and Bentham 1987, 278; Veenhoven 2003, 437.

[3] Gilead 1985, 133–153; https://www.youtube.com/watch?v=m7e6RRtAZkw

[4] Beard 2010, 216; https://www.theguardian.com/culture/2005/oct/29/television; Edwards 1988, 134; Fagan 2002, 36.

[5] Ehrenreich 2006, 46–56; Walton 2002, 25.

[6] http://www.u.arizona.edu/~afutrell/republic/web%20readings/livy39week11.html

[7] McMahon 2006, 55; Seneca 1932, Section 7; Blackburn 2004, 44–45.

[8] McMahon 2006, 54–57; Klein 2015, 9.

[9] Blackburn 2004, 44–53; Sorabji, R., 2000, 55–75; http://plato.stanford.edu/entries/stoicism/; Prose 2003, 9–10.

[10] Blackburn 2004, 51; Dabhoiwala 2013, 7.

[11] St Augustine's moral thought was also influenced by the Greek Neoplatonists. Colish 1985, 143–144, 207.

[12] Walton 2002, 69, 147–151.

[13] Walton 2002, 140–141.

[14] Kringelbach 2009, 181.

[15] Blackburn 2004, 5; http://www.advocatesforyouth.org/publications/publications-a-z/409-the-truth-about-abstinence-only-programs

[16] http://www.tandfonline.com/doi/abs/10.1080/00224499.2011.565429; https://www.psychologytoday.com/blog/the-sexual-continuum/201112/how-often-do-men-and-women-think-about-sex

[17] Dabhoiwala 2013, 146–147.

[18] Gay 1984, 6; Foucault 1990, 3–5.

[19] Gay 1984, 3-5; Cannadine 1984, 1–9.

[20] Gay 1984, 461.

[21] Gay 1984, 82–83, 461.

[22] Gay 1984, 82–83, 461.

[23] Gay 1984, 90–96.

[24] Gay 1984, 81, 98, 107, 111, 133–137, 141, 144, 169, 172, 176, 197; Cannadine 1984, 1–9; Zeldin 1993, 295–297; Dabhoiwala 2013, 1–4.

[25] Burton 1963, 133–134.

[26] FitzGerald 2014, 7; Behtash 2012, 203.

[27] FitzGerald 2014, quatrain 35.

[28] For an interesting comparison of the *Rubáiyát* and Horace's Odes, see Mierow (1917, 19–21).

[29] Behtash 2012, 203–205, 211.

[30] http://www.gutenberg.org/files/470/470-h/470-h.htm

[31] Gray 2013, 28, 33; Behtash 2012; 213.

[32] Wilde 1985, 45–46, 66.

[33] http://law2.umkc.edu/faculty/projects/ftrials/wilde/Wildelibeltranowcross.html; Wilde 1985, 8; Muriqi 2007, 3.

[34] Comfort 1996, 7–11.

[35] Walton 2002, 9–10, 208–209.

[36] Quoted in Walton (2002, 145); Letcher 2006, 73–80.

[37] Walton 2002, 86–87.

[38] Walton 2002, 243.

[39] De Quincey 1862, v–vii.

[40] De Quincey 1862, 234, 268.

[40] Holmes 1989, 10.

[42] Holmes 1998, 354, 429, 502, 519; De Quincey 1862, 9–10; Walton 2002, 255.

[43] Wolfe 1989, 224.

[44] Hobsbawm 1995, 333.

[45] Grund and Breeksema 2013, 15.

[46] Shorto 2014, 287–301.

[47] Grund and Breeksema 2013, 3–4, 13, 16, 22, 47–48.

[48] Fisher 1963, 449.

[49] Fisher 1963, 452–456.

[50] Fisher 1963, 27–28.

[51] Walton 2002, 16.

[52] Pater 1924, 249–250.

6 Beyond the Now of Mindfulness

[1] This figure is based on data from 2005 to 2015 (Smith-Laing, Whalen and Krznaric 2015).

[2] http://www.soundstrue.com/podcast/transcripts/jon-kabat-zinn.php?camefromhome=camefromhome; http://www.salon.com/2014/12/06/mindfulness_truthiness_problem_sam_harris_science_and_the_truth_about_buddhist_tradition/

[3] See http://funktionellelidelser.dk/en/about/treatment/mindfulness/. For another example of the way that the concepts of mindfulness and carpe diem are fusing, see Langley (2013, Introduction).

4   Quoted in Orrell (2012, 223).
5   Cohen 2010, 110.
6   For a critique of the narrowness of the Kabat-Zinn approach to mindfulness, see Pagnini and Philips (2015, 288–289).
7   http://healthland.time.com/2012/01/11/mind-reading-jon-kabat-zinn-talks-about-bringing-mindfulness-meditation-to-medicine/; Kabat-Zinn 2004, xiii.
8   http://www.themindfulnessinitiative.org.uk/images/reports/Mindfulness-APPG-Report_Mindful-Nation-UK_Oct2015.pdf
9   Cohen 2010, 111; Crawford 2015, 3–27.
10   https://www.washingtonpost.com/lifestyle/magazine/pearls-before-breakfast-can-one-of-the-nations-great-musicians-cut-through-the-fog-of-a-dc-rush-hour-lets-find-out/2014/09/23/8a6d46da-4331-11e4-b47c-f5889e061e5f_story.html
11   My first encounter with Buddhist meditation was in my twenties, in sessions run by the Triratna Buddhist Order (what used to be known as the Friends of the Western Buddhist Order). I have also had some experience of the Karma Kagyu tradition of Tibetan Buddhism, and been especially influenced by the writings of Thich Nhat Hanh.
12   I actually took a second mindfulness course, but it was just as self-focused as the first.
13   Public conversation between Matthieu Ricard and the author, Amsterdam, February 2nd, 2015: https://www.youtube.com/watch?v=B287LxA4Lo4. In the original conversation he said 'five letters' by mistake, and actually meant six, so I have changed it to this in the quote to reflect his true intention.
14   Singer discusses some of her latest research findings here: https://www.youtube.com/watch?v=n-hKS4rucTY
15   Stanley 2012, 639.
16   http://www.bloomberg.com/news/articles/2014-05-28/to-make-killing-on-wall-street-start-meditating
17   Cohen 2010, 112; Stanley 2012, 631–641; Hickey 2010, 174, 178.
18   Salecl 2010, 148.
19   http://www.salon.com/2014/12/06/mindfulness_truthiness_problem_sam_harris_science_and_the_truth_about_buddhist_tradition/
20   Stanley 2012, 638.
21   http://karuna-shechen.org/
22   https://www.youtube.com/watch?v=HTfYv3IEOqM
23   https://www.youtube.com/watch?v=3nwwKbM_vJc
24   Kabat-Zinn 2004, 47, 57, 63.
25   The main finding of the study reveals a correlation between mindfulness and reported ethical consumption, but no clear causal relationship (Armstrong and Jackson 2015, 25–30).

26   Corkin 2013, xii, 234.
27   Corkin 2013, 235.
28   Kringelbach 2009, 215.
29   Frankl 1973, 20.
30   Quoted in Thomas (2009, vii).
31   Frankl 1973, 32.
32   Frankl 1987, 35, 79.
33   Frankl 1973, 32.
34   Frankl 1973, 35–36.
35   Frankl 1987, 65.
36   Frankl 1973, 40.
37   Frankl 1987, 98.
38   Frankl 1973, 23, 29, 31, 33, 49, 73.
39   As Jon Kabat-Zinn puts it, 'The future is a concept – a very useful
      concept. I'm not putting it down. The past, memory, is also a concept.
      But the only time that our lives are unfolding is now. And if we learn
      to inhabit the now more, with awareness, it is almost as if the universe
      becomes your teacher, because there's no boundaries to this.' https://www.
      youtube.com/watch?v=3nwwKbM_vJc
40   Tolle 2005, 28, 189.
41   Jamison 2004, 4.
42   Jamison 2004, 5–6.
43   Jamison 2004, 130–131.
44   Quoted in Jamison (2004, 11).
45   Partington, Partington and Olivier 2009, 176.
46   http://www.theskooloflife.com/wordpress/wp-content/uploads/
      stokedforlife.pdf. See also Wayne Lynch quoted in Stranger (1999, 269).
47   Krznaric 2006, 11–30.
48   Csikszentmihalyi 2002, 3.
49   Holmes 1989, 330; Coleridge 1991, 139–143.
50   Coleridge 1991, 145.
51   Quoted in Spangenburg and Moser (2004, 4–5).
52   Darwin 1977, 434.
53   See especially Book 2 Chapter 7. https://archive.org/stream/
      elementaryformso00durkrich/elementaryformso00durkrich_djvu.txt
54   https://newrepublic.com/article/106464/when-god-talks-back-vineyard-
      evangelical-church
55   Papadimitropoulos 2009, 71.
56   Canetti 1962, 19.
57   Krznaric 2015, xx, 3.
58   Freeman 2000, 1–7; see also Ehrenreich (2006, 24).
59   Quoted in (Gleick 2012, 149).

7 Recovering Our Spontaneous Selves

1   http://www.tikit.com/software/time-capture/
2   Smith-Laing, Whalen and Krznaric 2015.
3   http://rwe.org/chapter-vii-works-and-days/
4   Emerson 1995, 33.
5   http://www.theguardian.com/society/2014/dec/14/britons-learned-art-last-minute-living; http://lastminutecareers.com/spontaneity/
6   Przybylski et al 2013, 1841.
7   http://www.newstatesman.com/culture/2014/07/think-you-act-against-modern-cult-spontaneity
8   Przybylski et al 2013, 1846; http://mashable.com/2013/07/09/fear-of-missing-out/#vCQ_8vfMpaqB
9   Przybylski et al 2013, 1841, 1845.
10   Krznaric 2011, 7.
11   Fromm 1960, 222–223.
12   Berger 1965, 11.
13   Staller 2001, 6.
14   http://www.nytimes.com/1996/05/29/arts/organ-improvisation-as-an-art-form.html
15   This is similar to the idea of 'trained spontaneity', which appears in early Chinese thought (Puett and Gross-Loh 2016, 146).
16   Vasari 2008, 425.
17   Krznaric 2011, 253–279.
18   Johnstone 2007, 96.
19   Johnstone 2007, 92, 95.
20   Poynton 2013, 17.
21   Poynton 2013, 20.
22   Poynton 2013, 28.
23   Johnstone 2007, 99.
24   Hemingway 2000, 9.
25   Gannon and Pillai 2013, 559.
26   Levine 2006, 131–132.
27   Gannon and Pillai 2013, 558.
28   Quoted in Foster (2003, 74).
29   Quoted in Foster (2003, 81).
30   Mason 1995, 123–124; Foster 2003, 73.
31   http://www.independent.co.uk/sport/football/international/menezes-sets-brazil-quest-for-old-style-7466751.html
32   Robb 2004, 22–29.
33   Krznaric 2011, 186.
34   http://www.script-o-rama.com/movie_scripts/r/room-with-a-view-script.html
35   https://www.youtube.com/watch?v=wZsj8yuaBKA

8 Just Doing It Together

[1] Notes from Nowhere 2003, 173–195; Flesher Fominaya 2014, 50–80.

[2] Castells 2015, 12; Scott 2012, xviii–xix; Klein 2014, 459. I have discussed the place of social movement mobilisation in relation to other forms of political change in Krznaric (2007, 6–15).

[3] Zinn 1995, 380–383.

[4] Scott 2012, 141.

[5] Sarotte 2015, 26–27, 52, 91–93, 107–110, 115–118, 127, 134–141, 145–146.

[6] Kenney 2002, 3.

[7] Kenney 2002, 277.

[8] Sarotte 2015, 95.

[9] Sarotte 2015, 180.

[10] Kenney 2002, 1, 267.

[11] Kenney 2002, 15.

[12] Kenney 2002, 7, 9; Hobsbawm 2003, 279; Hobsbawm 1995, 479; Sarotte 2015, xx–xxi, 180; http://www.faz.net/aktuell/politik/15-jahre-danach-wer-zu-spaet-kommt-den-bestraft-das-leben-1191290.html; www.fed.cuhk.edu.hk/history/history2001/berlinandcoldwar.doc

[13] Castells 2015, 319; http://www.e-ir.info/2012/09/27/why-is-turnout-at-elections-declining-across-the-democratic-world/; http://blogs.lse.ac.uk/europpblog/2013/05/06/decline-in-party-membership-europe-ingrid-van-biezen/

[14] Castells 2015, 127.

[15] Castells 2015, 118.

[16] www.avaaz.org/en/about.php

[17] Ortiz el at 2013, 5–6, 31, 34.

[18] http://theconversation.com/hard-evidence-this-is-the-age-of-dissent-and-theres-much-more-to-come-52871

[19] Ortiz el at 2013, 13.

[20] Castells 2015, xv, 23, 132, 250–256; see also Mason's applications of Castells's ideas (Mason 2013, 130–131).

[21] Castells 2015, 275–276.

[22] Skocpol and Williamson 2011, 3, 4, 10.

[23] Skocpol and Williamson 2011, 5, 8, 11–12; Castells and Kumar 2014, 96.

[24] http://www.nytimes.com/2009/09/13/us/politics/13protestweb.html?_r=0

[25] Skocpol and Williamson 2011, 4–5; Castells 2015, 160–161; http://www.forbes.com/sites/bowmanmarsico/2015/11/19/how-weak-is-the-tea-party-really/#e19bacf52f2a

[26] Graeber 2013, 49.

[27] Castells 2015, 174.

[28] Van Gelder 2011, 8; Castells 2015, 251.

[29] Castells 2015, 251.

30 Graeber 2013, 240.
31 Van Gelder 2011, 28; https://m.youtube.com/watch?v=QXISGHLT0Og;
    see also Mason 2013, 37–38, 49,53.
32 Ehrenreich 2006, 259–260.
33 Graeber 2013, 255.
34 The carpe diem quality of Occupy in the US and beyond is perfectly
    captured by Castells: 'The rapid propagation of Occupy... shows the
    depth and spontaneity of the protest, rooted in the outrage felt by the
    majority of the population across the country and in society at large. It
    also shows the seizing of the opportunity by many to voice their concerns
    and to discuss alternatives in the midst of a generalized crisis of trust in
    the economy and in the polity' (Castells 2015, 166–169).
35 Green 2015, 16–17; Mason 2013, 275; https://www.opendemocracy.net/
    ourkingdom/eliane-glaser/postpolitics-and-future-of-left
36 Green 2015, 16; Van Gelder 2011, 11; Castells 2015, 196–197.
37 http://www.truth-out.org/opinion/item/4093:framing-occupy-wall-street
38 Castells 2015, 196.
39 http://papers.ssrn.com/sol3/papers.cfm?abstract_id=1943168
40 Morozov 2011, 186–187.
41 Mason 2013, 187.
42 Quoted in Morozov (2011, 196).
43 Flesher Fominaya 2015, 148; Van Gelder 2011, 16; Castells 2015,
    170.
44 Graeber 2013, 51.
45 Iglesias 2015, 1–10.
46 According to Castells, today's social movements 'are suited for their role
    as agents of change in the network society, in sharp contrast with the
    obsolete political institutions inherited from a historically superseded
    social structure' (Castells 2015, 262).
47 http://www.theguardian.com/politics/2016/jul/02/march-for-europe-eu-
    referendum-london-protest
48 Klein 2014, 20-22, 450-451, 458-459, 464.
49 Carpamus diem is the hortatory subjunctive and translates as 'let's seize
    the day'. Thanks to advice from Tim Smith-Laing on the intricacies of
    Latin grammar.
50 Arendt 1989, 12–14.

9 I Choose, Therefore I Am

1 Locke 1690, Chapter 2, Section 56.
2 McMahon 2006, 10–12.
3 McMahon 2006, 104, 176–177, 204.
4 Krznaric 2011, 88–91; McMahon 2006, 104, 176–177, 204, 219–221,
   356–359; Arendt 1989, 14–16; Haybron 2013, 19–23.

5   Philosopher Gary Cox's book on existentialism, for example, makes the link to carpe diem explicit, ending with the lines: 'Be a true existentialist, be authentic, seize your freedom, seize the day. *Carpe diem* as the noble Romans used to say.' (Cox 2011, 106).

6   Sartre 1946, 16.

7   Bakewell 2016, 15, 21.

8   De Beauvoir 2015, 14–15.

9   Fanon 1963, 22, 30. Not all existentialists took Sartre's radical position on Algeria. Camus, for instance, was much less sympathetic to the cause of independence (Zaretsky 2013, 84).

10 Sartre 1946, 16; de Beauvoir 2015, 78; Flynn 2006, 78–70. Unfortunately Sartre never got around to writing the book on ethics and existentialism that he had always promised, leaving his philosophy lacking a strong moral framework. De Beauvoir made much more effort in this field, evident in her book *The Ethics of Ambiguity*.

11 Russell 1984, 683.

12 Over the years Sen has regularly quoted Horace in his academic papers, and even gave him a mention in his Nobel Prize acceptance speech. However, I have found no record of him directly quoting Ode XI.

13 Sen 1999, xi, 14–15, 284.

14 Sen 1999, 282, 298.

15 These basics broadly reflect Sen's list of what he calls 'crucial instrumental freedoms': economic opportunities, political freedoms, social facilities, transparency guarantees and protective security (Sen 1999, xii).

16 De Beauvoir 1997, 445–447; Bakewell 2016, 216.

17 Seneca 1932, Section 16.

18 Quoted in Steel (2007, 67).

19 Steel 2007, 65.

20 Steel 2007, 65–66.

21 Steel 2007, 67, 73–84; see also Burka and Yuen (2008, xiii, 6, 19).

22 Schwartz 2005, 3.

23 Schwartz 2005, 5.

24 Kahneman 2011, 283–286; Kringelbach and Phillips 2014, 158–160.

25 Kahneman 2011, 130.

26 Smith 2007, 1–17; Adams 2001, 15–17.

27 http://www.monbiot.com/2014/01/20/addicted-to-comfort/

28 Beckett 2006, 87.

29 Frankl 1973, 108, 89, 39.

30 The idea of expressing choice in terms of what you are 'for' can be found in philosopher Ruth Chang's TED talk, 'How to Make Hard Choices'(2014): https://www.ted.com/talks/ruth_chang_how_to_make_ hard_choices?language=en

31 Quoted in Cox (2011, 5).

32 For a discussion of Sartre's concept of the 'fundamental project' see Sartre (1969, 564–567) and Bakewell (2016, 215).

33 Sartre 1946, 7, 9; Yalom 1991, 8.

34 Quoted in Arendt (1989, 175).

35 Chang 2014.

36 Camus 2005, 60–61; Flynn 2006, 72–78; Sartre 1978, 54–55; Sartre 1946, 14.

37 Burka and Yuen 2008, 289.

38 Krznaric 2012, 75–85.

39 Ibarra 2004, xii, 18.

40 For an enlightening critique of the Enlightenment tradition of rational, deliberative thought, see Gladwell (2006, 141), who argues that 'truly successful decision making relies on a balance between deliberate and instinctive thinking'.

41 The value of experiential learning has been well established for at least a century, going back to the writings of the philosopher John Dewey, and even earlier to Montaigne (Montaigne 1958, 343–406).

42 Nicholl 2005, 7.

43 Jay 2006, 10.

44 Emerson's journal, November 11th, 1842, http://www.perfectidius.com/Volume_6_1842-1844.pdf

45 http://www.mama.org/exhibits/modernist/sculpture/giacometti/. I do not know if Giacometti ever read Horace, but he was a great friend of Sartre's, who admired his elongated human forms as an expression of existentialism.

Epilogue: A Carpe Diem Mandala

1 Horace 2000, 108.

2 Baggini 2005, 135.

3 Yalom 1980, 8–9.

4 Lanier 2011, 16; www.edge.org/q2010/q10_9.html

5 http://www.nybooks.com/articles/2010/11/25/generation-why/

Further Reading

Adams, John (2001) *Risk* (London, Routledge).

Adorno, Theodor and Max Horkheimer (1997) *Dialectic of Enlightenment* (London, Verso).

Anderson, William S. (1992) 'Horace's Different Recommenders of "Carpe Diem" in C. 1.4, 7, 9, 11', *The Classical Journal*, Vol. 88 No.2: 115–122.

Angelou, Maya (2004) *The Collected Autobiographies of Maya Angelou* (New York, Modern Library).

Angelou, Maya (2009) *Letter to My Daughter* (London, Virago).

Arendt, Hannah (1989) *The Human Condition* (Chicago, University of Chicago Press).

Ariès, Philippe (2008) *The Hour of Our Death* (New York, Vintage).

Armstrong, Alison and Tim Jackson (2015) 'The Mindful Consumer: Mindfulness Training and the Escape from Consumerism', a report for Friends of the Earth, Big Ideas Project, London.

Arsenault, Darin J. and Tamer Fawzy (2001) 'Just Buy It: Nike Advertising Aimed at Glamour Readers: A Critical Feminist Analysis', *Tamara: Journal of Critical Postmodern Organization*, Vol. 1 Issue 2: 63–76.

Aurelius, Marcus (2006) *Meditations*, translated by Martin Hammond (London, Penguin).

Baggini, Julian (2005) *What's It All About? Philosophy and the Meaning of Life* (London, Granta).

Bakewell, Sarah (2016) *At The Existentialist Café: Freedom, Being and Apricot Cocktails* (London, Chatto & Windus).

Baumeister, Roy and John Tierney (2012) *Willpower: Why Self-Control is the Secret to Success* (London, Penguin).

Beard, Mary (2010) *Pompeii: The Life of a Roman Town* (London, Profile Books).

Beckett, Samuel (2006) *Waiting for Godot* (London, Faber & Faber).

Behtash, Esmail Z. (2012) 'The Reception of FitzGerald's Rubáiyát of 'Umar Khayyām by the Victorians', in A.A. Seyed-Gohrab (ed) *The Great Umar Khayyām: A Global Reception of the Rubáiyát* (Leiden, Leiden University Press): 203–14.

Bellow, Saul (2001) *Seize the Day* (London, Penguin).

Berger, John (1965) *Success and Failure of Picasso* (Harmondsworth, Penguin).

Berger, John (1972) *Ways of Seeing* (London, BBC Books and Harmondsworth, Penguin).

Blackburn, Simon (2004) *Lust* (Oxford, Oxford University Press).

Bourdieu, Pierre (1998) *On Television* (New York, New Press).

Buckley, David (2005) *Strange Fascination: David Bowie, The Definitive Story* (London, Virgin Books).

Burka, Jane and Lenora Yuen (2008) *Procrastination: Why You Do It, What to Do About It Now* (Cambridge MA, Da Capo Press).

Burton, Richard (1963) *The Perfumed Garden of the Shaykh Nefzawi* (London, Panther).

Burton, Robert (1838) *The Anatomy of Melancholy* (London, B. Blake).

Camus, Albert (2005) *The Myth of Sisyphus* (London, Penguin).

Canetti, Elias (1962) *Crowds and Power* (London, Victor Gollancz).

Cannadine, David (1984) 'The Victorian Sex Wars', *New York Review of Books*, February 2nd: 1–9.

Castells, Manuel (2015) *Networks of Outrage and Hope: Social Movements in the Internet Age* (Cambridge, Polity).

Castells, Manuel and Mukul Kumar (2014) 'A Conversation With Manuel Castells', *Berkeley Planning Journal*, Vol. 27 No.1: 93–99.

Center for Applied Research (1999) 'Nike's "Just Do It" Advertising Campaign', Philadelphia PA.

Chang, Ruth (2014) 'How to Make Hard Choices', TED Talk, https://www.ted.com/talks/ruth_chang_how_to_make_hard_choices?language=en

Cohen, Elliot (2010) 'From the Bodhi Tree, to the Analyst's Couch, then to the MRI Scanner: The Psychologisation of Buddhism', *Annual Review of Critical Psychology*, Vol. 8: 97–119.

Coleridge, Samuel Taylor (1991) *Coleridge Among the Lakes & Mountains* (London, The Folio Society).

Colish, Marcia L. (1985) *The Stoic Tradition from Antiquity to the Early Middle Ages, Volume II: Stoicism in Christian Latin Thought through the Sixth Century* (Leiden, E.J. Brill).

Collins, Michael and Stewart A. Carter (2001) 'Improvisation §II: Western Art Music' in Sadie Stanley and John Tyrrell (eds) *The New Grove Dictionary of Music and Musicians* (New York, Oxford University Press): 1–34.

Comfort, Alex (1996) *The Joy of Sex* (London, Mitchell Beazley).

Coombs, Danielle Sarver (2014) 'Nike: Goddess of Victory, Gods of Sport' in Danielle Sarver Coombs and Bob Batchelor, *We Are What We Sell: How Advertising Shapes American Life… And Always Has* (Santa Barbara, Praeger).

Cooper, Artemis (2013) *Patrick Leigh Fermor: An Adventure* (London, John Murray).

Corkin, Suzanne (2013) *Permanent Present Tense: The Man With No Memory, and What He Taught the World* (London, Allen Lane).

Cox, Gary (2011) *How to Be an Existentialist* (London, Continuum).

Crawford, Matthew (2015) *The World Beyond Your Head: How to Flourish in an Age of Distraction* (London, Viking).

Csikszentmihalyi, Mihaly (2002) *Flow: The Classic Work on How to Achieve Happiness* (London, Rider).

Dabhoiwala, Faramerz (2013) *The Origins of Sex: A History of the First Sexual Revolution* (London, Penguin).

Darwin, Charles (1977) *The Voyage of the 'Beagle'* (London, J.M. Dent & Sons).

De Beauvoir, Simone (1997) *The Second Sex* (London, Vintage).

De Beauvoir, Simone (2015) *The Ethics of Ambiguity* (New York, Open Road).

Debord, Guy (2010) *Society of the Spectacle* (Detroit, Black & Red).

De Quincey (1862) *Confessions of an English Opium-Eater: De Quincey's Works Volume I* (Edinburgh, Adam and Charles Black).

Duncan, Ronald (1964) *All Men Are Islands: An Autobiography* (London, Rupert Hart-Davis).

Dunstan, D.W., E.L. Barr, G.N. Healy, J. Salmon, J.E. Shaw, B. Balkau, D.J. Magliano, A.J. Cameron, P.Z. Zimmet, N. Owen (2010) 'Television Viewing Time and Mortality: The Australian Diabetes, Obesity and Lifestyle Study (AusDiab)', *Circulation* Vol. 121: 384–391.

Eagleman, David (2009) *Sum: Forty Tales from the Afterlives* (Edinburgh, Canongate).

Edwards, John (1988) *The Roman Cookery of Apicius* (London, Rider Books).

Ehrenreich, Barbara (2006) *Dancing on the Street: A History of Collective Joy* (New York, Metropolitan Books).

Emerson, Ralph Waldo (1995) *Essays and Poems* (London, J.M. Dent).

Ewen, Stuart (1996) *PR! A Social History of Spin* (New York, Basic Books).

Eyres, Harry (2013) *Horace and Me: Life Lessons from an Ancient Poet* (London, Bloomsbury).

Fagan, Garrett (2002) *Bathing in Public in the Roman World* (Ann Arbor, The University of Michigan Press).

Fanon, Frantz (1963) *The Wretched of the Earth*, with a preface by Jean-Paul Sartre (New York, Grove Press).

Fisher, M.F.K. (1963) *The Art of Eating* (London, Faber & Faber).

FitzGerald, Edward (2014) *The Rubaiyat of Omar Khayyam* (Oxford, Bodleian Library, University of Oxford).

Flesher Fominaya, Cristina (2014) *Social Movements and Globalization: How Protests, Occupations and Uprisings Are Changing the World* (Basingstoke, Palgrave Macmillan).

Flesher Fominaya, Cristina (2015) 'Debunking Spontaneity: Spain's 15-M/Indignados as Autonomous Movement', *Journal of Social, Cultural and Political Protest*, Vol.14 No.2: 142–163.

Flynn, Thomas A. (2006) *Existentialism: A Very Short Introduction* (Oxford, Oxford University Press).

Foster, Kevin (2003) 'Dreaming of Pelé: Football and Society in England and Brazil in the 1950s and 1960s', *Football Studies*, Vol. 6 No.1: 70–86.

Foucault, Michel (1979) *Discipline and Punish: The Birth of the Prison* (London, Penguin).

Foucault, Michel (1990) *The History of Sexuality: Volume 1, An Introduction* (London, Penguin).

Frankl, Viktor (1973) *Psychotherapy and Existentialism: Selected Papers on Logotherapy* (Harmondsworth, Penguin).

Frankl, Viktor (1987) *Man's Search for Meaning: An Introduction to Logotherapy* (London, Hodder & Stoughton).

Freeman, Walter J. (2000) 'A Neurobiological Role of Music in Social Bonding' in N. Wallin, B. Merkur and S. Brown (eds), *The Origins of Music* (Cambridge MA, MIT Press): 411–424.

Fromm, Erich (1960) *Fear of Freedom* (London, Routledge).

Gannon, Martin J. and Rajnandini Pillai (2013) *Understanding Global Cultures: Metaphorical Journeys Through 31 Nations, Clusters of Nations, Continents and Diversity* (Los Angeles, Sage).

Gay, Peter (1984) *Education of the Senses: The Bourgeois Experience, Victoria to Freud* (New York, Oxford University Press).

Gilead, Sarah (1985) 'Ungathering "Gather Ye Rosebuds": Herrick's Misreading of Carpe Diem', *Criticism: A Quarterly for Literature and the Arts*, Vol. 27 No.2: 133–153.

Gladwell, Malcolm (2006) *Blink: The Power of Thinking Without Thinking* (London, Penguin).

Gleick, James (2012) *The Information: A History, A Theory, A Flood* (London, Fourth Estate).

Goffman, Erving (1956) *The Presentation of Self in Everyday Life* (Edinburgh, University of Edinburgh Social Science Research Centre).

Graeber, David (2013) *The Democracy Project: A History. A Crisis. A Movement.* (London, Penguin).

Gray, Erik (2013) 'Common and Queer: Syntax and Sexuality in the *Rubáiyát*' in Adrian Poole, Christine van Ruymbeke, William H. Martin and Sandra Mason (eds) *FitzGerald's Rubáiyát: Popularity and Neglect* (London, Anthem Press): 27–43.

Green, Marcus E. (2015) 'Gramsci and Subaltern Struggles Today: Spontaneity, Political Organization, and Occupy Wall Street' in Mark McNally (ed) *Antonio Gramsci* (New York, Palgrave): 1–22.

Greenfield, Kent (2012) *The Myth of Choice: Personal Responsibility in a World Without Limits* (London, Biteback Publishing).

Grimm, R.E. (1963) 'Horace's "Carpe Diem"', *The Classical Journal*, Vol. 58 No. 7: 313–318.

Grund, Jean-Paul and Joost Breeksema (2013) 'Coffee Shops and Compromise: Separated Illicit Drug Markets in the Netherlands', Global Drug Policy Program, Open Society Foundations, New York.

Haybron, Daniel (2013) *Happiness: A Very Short Introduction* (Oxford, Oxford University Press).

Helstein, Michelle T. (2003) 'That's Who I Want To Be: The Politics and Production of Desire Within Nike Advertising to Women', *Journal of Sports and Social Leisure*, Vol. 27 No. 3: 276–292.

Hemingway, Ernest (2000) *Fiesta: The Sun Also Rises* (London, Vintage).

Hennezel, Marie de (2012) *Seize the Day: How the Dying Teach Us to Live* (London, Macmillan).

Hickey, Wakoh Shannon (2010) 'Meditation As Medicine: A Critique', *Crosscurrents*, Vol. 60 No. 2: 168–184.

Hobsbawm, Eric (1995) *The Age of Extremes: The Short Twentieth Century 1914–1991* (London, Abacus).

Hobsbawm, Eric (2003) *Interesting Times: A Twentieth-Century Life* (London, Abacus).

Hogg, Michael and Graham Vaughan (2005) *Social Psychology, 4th Edition* (Harlow, Pearson Education).

Holmes, Richard (1989) *Coleridge: Early Visions* (London, Hodder & Stoughton).

Holmes, Richard (1998) *Coleridge: Darker Reflections* (London, HarperCollins).

Horace (2000) *The Complete Odes and Epodes*, translated by David West (Oxford, Oxford University Press).

Ibarra, Herminia (2004) *Working Identity: Unconventional Strategies for Reinventing Your Career* (Cambridge MA, Harvard Business School Press).

Iglesias, Pablo (2015) 'Spain On Edge', *New Left Review*, Vol. 93 May–June: 1–10.

Inglehart, Ronald and Christian Welzel (2005) *Modernization, Cultural Change and Democracy: The Human Development Sequence* (Cambridge, Cambridge University Press).

Irvine, William (2009) *A Guide to the Good Life: The Ancient Art of Stoic Joy* (Oxford, Oxford University Press).

Jamison, Kay Redfield (2004) *Exuberance: The Passion for Life* (New York, Vintage).

Jay, Martin (2006) *Songs of Experience: Modern American and European Variations on a Universal Theme* (Berkeley, University of California Press).

Johnstone, Keith (2007) *Impro: Improvisation and the Theatre* (London, Methuen).

Josephson, Matthew (1962) *The Robber Barons: The Great American Capitalists 1861–1901* (London, Eyre & Spottiswoode).

Kabat-Zinn, Jon (2004) *Wherever You Go There You Are: Mindfulness Meditation for Everyday Life* (London, Piatkus).

Kahneman, Daniel (2011) *Thinking, Fast and Slow* (London, Allen Lane).

Kaiser Family Foundation (2010) 'Generation M2: Media in the Lives of 8- to 18-Year-Olds', Kaiser Family Foundation Study (Menlo Park, California).

Katz, Donald (1994) *Just Do It: The Nike Spirit in the Corporate World* (Holbrook MA, Adams Media Corporation).

Kenney, Padraic (2003) *A Carnival of Resistance: Central Europe 1989* (Princeton, Princeton University Press).

Kim, Yeong-Hyun and John Rennie Short (2008) *Cities and Economies* (Abingdon, Routledge).

Klein, Daniel (2015) *Every Time I Find the Meaning of Life They Change It* (London, Oneworld).

Klein, Naomi (2014) *This Changes Everything: Capitalism vs. The Climate* (New York, Simon & Schuster).

Kringelbach, Morten (2009) *The Pleasure Centre: Trust Your Animal Instincts* (Oxford, Oxford University Press).

Kringelbach, Morten and Helen Phillips (2014) *Emotion: Pleasure and Pain in the Brain* (Oxford, Oxford University Press).

Kropotkin, Peter (1978) *Memoirs of a Revolutionist* (London, The Folio Society).

Krznaric, Roman (2001) 'Mortgaged Democracy' in Paul Barry Clarke and Joe Foweraker (eds) *The Encyclopedia of Democratic Thought* (London, Routledge): 449–452.

Krznaric, Roman (2006) *The First Beautiful Game: Stories of Obsession in Real Tennis* (Oxford, Ronaldson Publications).

Krznaric, Roman (2007) 'How Change Happens: Interdisciplinary Perspectives for Human Development', an Oxfam Research Report (Oxford, Oxfam).

Krznaric, Roman (2011) *The Wonderbox: Curious Histories of How to Live* (London, Profile Books).

Krznaric, Roman (2012) *How to Find Fulfilling Work* (London, Macmillan).

Krznaric, Roman (2015) *Empathy: Why It Matters, and How to Get It* (London, Rider Books/Penguin Random House).

Krznaric, Roman, Christopher Whalen and Theodore Zeldin (eds) (2006) *Guide to an Unknown University* (Oxford, The Oxford Muse).

Kubey, Robert and Mihaly Csikszentmihalyi (1990) *Television and the Quality of Life: How Viewing Shapes Everyday Experience* (Hillsdale NJ, Lawrence Erlbaum).

Kubey, Robert and Mihaly Csikszentmihalyi (2003) 'Television is No Mere Metaphor', *Scientific American Mind*: 48–55.

Kurosawa, Akira (1952) *Ikiru* (film).

Laing, R.D. (1967) *The Politics of Experience and the Bird of Paradise* (Harmondsworth, Penguin).

Langley, Martha (2013) *The Mindfulness Workbook* (London, McGraw-Hill Education).

Lanier, Jaron (2011) *You Are Not a Gadget* (London, Penguin).

Letcher, Andy (2006) *Shroom: A Cultural History of the Magic Mushroom* (London, HarperCollins).

Levine, David (2006) *A Geography of Time: The Temporal Misadventures of a Social Psychologist* (Oxford, Oneworld).

Lill, Anne (1997) 'Carpe Diem: Hedonistic, Sceptical or Frightened', *Trames*, Vol. 1 (51): 109–124.

Locke, John (1690) *An Essay Concerning Human Understanding* (London, Eliz. Holt)

Loeb, Paul S. (2013) 'Eternal Recurrence' in Ken Gemes and John Richardson (eds) *The Oxford Handbook of Nietzsche* (Oxford, Oxford University Press).

Lucas, Shelley (2000) 'Nike's Commercial Solution: Girls, Sneakers and Salvation', *International Review for the Sociology of Sport*, Vol. 35 No.2: 149–164.

Machiavelli, Niccolò (1961) *The Prince* (London, Penguin).

Mander, Gerry (1978) *Four Arguments for the Elimination of Television* (New York, Quill).

Marsh, James (2008) *Man On Wire* (film).

Marshall, Peter (2008) *Demanding the Impossible: A History of Anarchism* (London, Harper Perennial).

Mason, Paul (2013) *Why It's Still Kicking Off Everywhere: The New Global Revolutions* (London, Verso).

Mason, Tony (1995) *Passion of the People? Football in South America* (London, Verso).

Mathis, James C. (1965) 'The Theme of Seize the Day', *Critique*, Vol.7: 43-5.

McCullin, Don (1992) *Unreasonable Behaviour: An Autobiography* (London, Vintage).

McGann, Michael (2007) 'The Reception of Horace in the Renaissance' in Stephen Harrison (ed) *The Cambridge Companion to Horace* (Cambridge, Cambridge University Press): 305–317.

McMahon, Darrin (2006) *Happiness: A History* (New York, Grove Press).

Mierow, Herbert Edward (1917) 'Horace and Omar Khayyam', *The Classical Weekly*, Vol.11 No.3 (October 15th): 19–21.

Mill, John Stuart and Jeremy Bentham (1987) *Utilitarianism and Other Essays* (London, Penguin).

Moldenhauer, Joseph J. (1968) 'The Voices of Seduction in "To His Coy Mistress": A Rhetorical Analysis', *Texas Studies in Literature and Language*, Vol. 10 No.2: 189–206.

Montaigne, Michel de (1958) *Essays* (Harmondsworth, Penguin).

Moore, Lucy (2008) *Anything Goes: A Biography of the Roaring Twenties* (London, Atlantic).

Moran, Joe (2013) *Armchair Nation: An Intimate History of Britain in Front of the TV* (London, Profile).

Morozov, Evgeny (2011) *The Net Delusion: How Not to Liberate the World* (London, Allen Lane).

Morris, Charles R. (2006) *The Tycoons: How Andrew Carnegie, John D. Rockefeller, Jay Gould, and J.P. Morgan Invented the American Supereconomy* (New York, Owl Books).

Morris, David and Jacqui Morris (2012) *McCullin* (film).

Muriqi, Luljeta (2007) 'Homoerotic codes in The Picture of Dorian Gray', A60 Literary Seminar, Department of English, Lund University.

Néret, Gilles (2015) *Gustav Klimt, 1862–1918*, (Cologne, Taschen).

Nicholl, Charles (2005) *Leonardo da Vinci: The Flights of the Mind* (London, Penguin).

Nielson (2016) 'The Total Audience Report', Quarter 4, 2015, http://www.nielsen.com/us/en/insights/reports/2016/the-total-audience-report-q4-2015.html

Niemiec, Ryan M. and Stefan E. Schulenberg (2011) 'Understanding Death Attitudes: The Integration of Movies, Positive Psychology, and Meaning Management', *Death Studies*, Vol. 5 No.5: 387–407.

Notes from Nowhere (ed) (2003) *We Are Everywhere: The Irresistible Rise of Global Anticapitalism* (London, Verso).

Noyes, Russell (1980) 'Attitude Change Following Near-Death Experiences', *Psychiatry*, Vol. 43 (August): 234–242.

Orlowski, Alexander P. (2007), 'Television Consumption and Civic Engagement Among 15 to 25 Year Olds', The Center for Information & Research on *Civic* Learning, Tufts University, Medford, MA.

Orrell, David (2012) *Economyths: How the Science of Complex Systems is Transforming Economic Thought* (London, Icon Books).

Ortiz, Isabel, Sara Burke, Mohamed Berrada and Hernán Cortés Saenz (2013) 'World Protests 2006–2013', Initiative for Policy Dialogue, Columbia University and Friedrich-Ebert-Stiftung New York, Working Paper 2013.

Owen, Neville, Genevieve N. Healy, Charles E. Matthews and David W. Dunstan (2010) 'Too Much Sitting: The Population-Health Science of Sedentary Behavior', *Exercise Sports Scientific Review*, Vol. 38 No. 3: 105–113.

Packard, Vance (1960) *The Hidden Persuaders* (Harmondsworth, Penguin).

Paddock, Catharine (2010) 'Prolonged TV Viewing Linked to Higher Risk of Death Even in Regular Exercisers', *Medical News Today*, January 12th.

Pagnini, Francesco and Deborah Philips (2015) 'Being Mindful About Mindfulness', *The Lancet Psychiatry* Vol.2 No.4 (April): 288–289.

Papadimitropoulos, Panagiotis (2009) 'Psychedelic Trance: Ritual, Belief and Transcendental Experience in Modern Raves', *Durham Anthropology Journal*, Vol. 16. No.2: 67–74.

Partington, Sarah, Elizabeth Partington and Steve Olivier (2009) 'The Dark Side of Flow: A Qualitative Study of Dependence in Big Wave Surfing', *The Sports Psychologist* Vol. 23: 170–185.

Pater, Walter (1924) *The Renaissance: Studies in Art and Poetry* (London, Macmillan).

Paz, Octavio (1967) *The Labyrinth of Solitude: Life and Thoughts in Mexico* (London, Allen Lane).

Penaloza, Lisa (1998) 'Just Doing It: A Visual Ethnographic Study of Spectacular Consumption Behavior at Nike Town', *Consumption, Markets and Culture*, Vol. 2 No.4: 337–465.

Phillips, D.Z. (1981) 'Bad Faith and Sartre's Waiter', *Philosophy*, Vol. 56 Issue 215: 23–31.

Poynton, Robert (2013) *Do Improvise: Less Push. More Pause.*

Better Results. A New Approach to Work (and Life) (London, Do Book Company).

Prose, Francine (2003) *Gluttony* (Oxford, Oxford University Press).

Przybylski, Andrew, Kou Murayama, Cody DeHaan and Valerie Gladwell (2013), 'Motivational, emotional and behavioural correlates of fear of missing out', *Computers in Human Behaviour*, Vol. 29, June: 1841–1848.

Puett, Michael and Christine Gross-Loh (2016) *The Path: A New Way of Thinking About Everything* (London, Viking).

Pugh, Martin (1990) *The Making of Modern British Politics* (Oxford, Basil Blackwell).

Rifkin, Jeremy (2014) *The Zero Marginal Cost Society: The Internet of Things, The Collaborative Commons, and the Eclipse of Capitalism* (New York, Palgrave Macmillan).

Ring, Kenneth (1996) 'Near-Death Experiences: Implications for Human Evolution and Planetary Transformation' in Lea W. Bailey and Jerry Yates (eds) *The Near-Death Experience: A Reader* (New York, Routledge).

Robb, Peter (2004) *A Death In Brazil: A Book of Omissions* (London, Bloomsbury).

Rosenthal, Edward (2005) *The Era of Choice: The Ability to Choose and its Transformation of Everyday Life* (Cambridge MA, MIT Press).

Russell, Bertrand (1984) *A History of Western Philosophy* (London, Unwin).

Salecl, Renata (2010) *Choice* (London, Profile Books).

Sarotte, Mary Elise (2015) *The Collapse: The Accidental Opening of the Berlin Wall* (New York, Basic Books).

Sartre, Jean-Paul (1946) *Existentialism Is a Humanism* https://www.marxists.org/reference/archive/sartre/works/exist/sartre.htm.

Sartre, Jean-Paul (1969) *Being and Nothingness* (London, Methuen).

Sartre, Jean-Paul (1978) *Sartre By Himself* (New York, Urizen Books).

Schwartz, Barry (2005) *The Paradox of Choice: Why More Is Less* (New York, Harper Perennial).

Scott, James (2012) *Two Cheers for Anarchism: Six Easy Pieces on Autonomy, Dignity, and Meaningful Work and Play* (Princeton, Princeton University Press).

Sen, Amartya (1999) *Development As Freedom* (New York, Alfred A. Knopf).

Seneca, Lucius Annaeus (1932) 'On the Shortness of Life', translated by John W. Basore, Loeb Classical Library (London, William Heinemann).

Sennett, Richard (1986) *The Fall of Public Man* (London, Faber & Faber).

Shorto, Russell (2014) *Amsterdam: A History of the World's Most Liberal City* (New York, Vintage).

Skocpol, Theda and Vanessa Williamson (2011) *The Tea Party and the Remaking of Republican Conservatism* (New York, Oxford University Press).

Smiles, Samuel (1968) *Self-Help: The Art of Achievement Illustrated by Accounts of the Lives of Great Men* (London, Sphere Books).

Smith, Roderick (2007) 'Carpe Diem: The Dangers of Risk Aversion', The 2007 Lloyd's Register Educational Trust Lecture (London, The Royal Academy of Engineering).

Smith-Laing, Tim, Christopher Whalen and Roman Krznaric (2015) *Carpe Diem Database* (electronic file, unpublished).

Solomon, Sheldon, Jeff Greenberg and Tom Pyszczynski (2015) *The Worm at the Core: On the Role of Death in Life* (London, Allen Lane).

Sorabji, Richard (2000) *Emotion and Peace of Mind: from Stoic Agitation to Christian Temptation* (Oxford, Oxford University Press).

Spangenburg Ray and Kit Moser (2004) *Carl Sagan: A Biography* (Westport CT, Greenwood Press).

Staller, Natasha (2001) *A Sum of Destructions: Picasso's Cultures and the Creation of Cubism* (New Haven, Yale University Press).

Stanley, Steven (2012) 'Mindfulness: Towards A Critical Relational Perspective', *Social and Personality Psychology Compass*, Vol. 6 No. 9: 631–641.

Steel, Piers (2007) 'The Nature of Procrastination: A Meta-Analytic and Theoretical Review of Quintessential Self-Regulatory Failure', *Psychological Bulletin* Vol. 133 No.1: 65–94.

Stranger, Mark (1999) 'The Aesthetics of Risk: A Study of Surfing', *International Review for the Sociology of Sport*, Vol. 34 No. 3: 265–276.

Tedeschi, Richard G. and Lawrence G. Calhoun (2004) 'Posttraumatic Growth: Conceptual Foundations and Empirical Evidence', *Psychological Inquiry*, Vol. 15 No.1: 1–18.

Thomas, Keith (2009) *The Ends of Life: Roads to Fulfilment in Early Modern England* (Oxford, Oxford University Press).

Thompson, E.P. (1968) *The Making of the English Working Class* (Harmondsworth, Penguin).

Thoreau, Henry David (1986) *Walden and Civil Disobedience* (New York, Penguin Books).

Tolle, Eckhart (2005) *The Power of Now: A Guide to Spiritual Enlightenment* (London, Hodder & Stoughton).

Tolstoy, Leo (1960) *The Death of Ivan Ilych and Other Stories* (New York, Signet).

Vaneigem, Raoul (2012) *The Revolution of Everyday Life* (Oakland CA, PM Press).

Van Gelder, Sarah (ed) (2011) *This Changes Everything: Occupy Wall Street and the 99% Movement* (San Francisco, Berrett-Koehler).

Vasari, Giorgio (2008) *The Lives of the Artists* (Oxford, Oxford University Press).

Veenhoven, Ruut (2003) 'Hedonism and Happiness', *Journal of Happiness Studies*, Vol. 4: 437–457.

Veerman, J. Lennert, Genevieve N. Healy, Linda J. Cobiac, Theo Vos, Elisabeth A. H. Winkler, Neville Owen and David W. Dunstan (2011) 'Television Viewing Time and Reduced Life Expectancy: A Life Table Analysis', *British Journal of Sports Medicine*, doi:10.1136/bjsm.2011.085662.

Walton, Stuart (2002) *Out of It: A Cultural History of Intoxication* (London, Penguin).

Ward, Colin (2004) *Anarchism: A Very Short Introduction* (Oxford, Oxford University Press).

Weber, Max (1958) *The Protestant Ethic and the Spirit of Capitalism* (New York, Charles Scribner's Sons).

Wilde, Oscar (1985) *The Picture of Dorian Gray* (London, Penguin).

Wolfe, Tom (1989) *The Electric Kool-Aid Acid Test* (London, Black Swan).

Woodcock, George and Ivan Avakumović (1971) *The Anarchist Prince: Peter Kropotkin* (New York, Schocken Books).

Yalom, Irvin (1980) *Existential Psychotherapy* (New York, Basic Books).

Yalom, Irvin (1991) *Love's Executioner: and Other Tales of Psychotherapy* (London, Penguin).

Young, Damon (2008) *Distraction* (Durham, Acumen).

Zaretsky, Robert (2013) *A Life Worth Living: Albert Camus and the Quest for Meaning* (Cambridge MA, Belknap Press).

Zeldin, Theodore (1993) *A History of French Passions, Volume 1: Ambition, Love and Politics* (Oxford, Oxford University Press).

Zinn, Howard (1995) *A People's History of the United States, 1492– Present* (New York, HarperPerennial).

Image Credits

Robin Williams in *Dead Poets Society*, 14, © AF archive/Alamy Stock Photo.

Death and Life by Gustav Klimt, 25, © FineArt/Alamy Stock Photo.

Steve Jobs, 27, © AF archive/Alamy Stock Photo.

Ikiru, 32, © Photos 12/Alamy Stock Photo.

David Bowie applying Ziggy Stardust makeup, 39, © Roger Bamber/Alamy Stock Photo.

Death dice, 44, © Roman Krznaric.

Fight Between Carnival and Lent, 49, © Artepics/Alamy Stock Photo.

Display of trainers, 58, © Nik Taylor Sport/Alamy Stock Photo.

Maya Angelou, 71, © Everett Collection Historical/Alamy Stock Photo.

Don McCullin, 78, © epa European pressphoto agency b.v./Alamy Stock Photo.

Ashley Madison, 96, © Maurice Savage/Alamy Stock Photo.

Hieronymus Bosch's *The Garden of Earthly Delights*, 102, © World History Archive/Alamy Stock Photo.

Mabel Loomis Todd, 108, © Todd-Bingham Picture Collection (MS 496E). Manuscripts and Archives, Yale University Library.

Surfing action, 141, © Buzz Pictures/Alamy Stock Photo.

Acknowledgments

This book has been created not just by its author, but by its readers. Rather than take up the offer of a regular publishing deal, I made a seize-the-day decision and opted to crowdfund the book instead. I owe enormous thanks to the over 480 people who gave their incredible support to the project, and am especially grateful to those who made major contributions, including Berry Liberman, Danny Almagor and Richard Raworth. There was also a group of intrepid readers who signed up to be Editorial Advisors, giving comments on chapter drafts. They all deserve special thanks for their incisive thoughts: Anne Fawcett, David Hare, Dom Emery, Jon Emery, Kath Boddy and Teresa Elwes.

None of it could have happened without the fabulous team at the crowdfunding publisher Unbound: my editor John Mitchinson, Dan Kieran, DeAndra Lupu, Phil Connor, Amy Winchester, Jimmy Leach, Isobel Frankish, Georgia Odd and Tamsin Shelton. Mark Bowsher made a superb video for the crowdfunding campaign and Mark Ecob created a breathtaking cover. Huge thanks to my wise and wonderful agent Maggie Hanbury and my fantastic US publisher Marian Lizzi, as well as my US agent Robin Straus, Harriet Poland, Ruth Killick, and the team at ILA. I've also been lucky to have Sophia Blackwell's masterful editorial scalpel work over the text.

This is the first time I've ever worked with researchers on a book project: Tim Smith-Laing and Chris Whalen both used their sharp brains and scholarly nous to brilliant effect. Another first was holding dinner debates on the text with various friends and experts; thanks to good-humoured critiques from Adam Swift, Gina Cowen, Ita Mac Carthy, James Attlee, Martin Kalungu-Banda, Martin Stott, Rebecca Wrigley, Sophie Roell and Sue Gerhardt.

Conversations with Matthieu Ricard, Nigel Warburton and Sheldon Solomon were invaluable, as were comments from David Lewis, Lisa Gormley and Quentin Spender. I also received help and advice from Angelika Lueckert, Cecilia Macfarlane, Danielle Coombs, George Monbiot, Gijs van Hensbergen, John-Paul Flintoff, Peter Antonioni, Sophie Raworth, Ted Hunt and Uri Gordon.

My partner Kate Raworth gave me extraordinary support – reading chapters, challenging ideas, providing inspiration, solace and sustenance – all while writing her own book at the same time. Thank you for all the varieties of love you bring to my life. And to our children, Casimir and Siri, it's now time for us all to seize the day together.

Index

Supporters

Unbound is a new kind of publishing house. Our books are funded directly by readers. This was a very popular idea during the late eighteenth and early nineteenth centuries. Now we have revived it for the internet age. It allows authors to write the books they really want to write and readers to support the books they would most like to see published.

The names listed below are of readers who have pledged their support and made this book happen. If you'd like to join them, visit www.unbound.com.

Rebecca Abrams
Alhassan Adam
Frederika Adam
Christine Adams
Laurence Adams
Ellie Agrebi
Jo Ahern
Danny Almagor
Gareth Andrews
Manolis Andriotakis
Jessica Arroyo
Alec Ash
Charlotte Ashbee
James Attlee
Reuben Avis-Anciano
Nenad Bach

Nick Baker
Nick & Tash Baker
Alan Baker & Shelley Costa
Jason Ballinger
Jack & Reuben Baltzer
Adele Barlow
Anthony Barnett
Adela Barrio
Michael Barylak
Austin Barzetti
Atty Bax
Andy Bell
Sonia Bell
Charlie Bennett
Tina Bernstein
Angelica Berrie

Heather Bignold
Kate Bingham
Carolyn Deere Birkbeck
Jamie Blanck
Stefan Blaser
Eva Blechova
Ben Bleet
Kath Boddy
Iain Bonehill
Bil Bonnice
Richard Bradley
Mary Ellen Bratu
Anne Braybon
Teresa Brayshaw
Pip Brennan
Caroline Brimmer
Johanna Brinton
Julieann Brooker
Bryan Brown
Sarah Brown
Michael Bryan
Anthony Bunge
Beatriz Burin
Ipek S. Burnett
Jennie Butterworth
Abel Sampériz Callís
Tracey Camilleri
Aifric Campbell
Reinaldo Campos
Susan Canney
Marina Cantacuzino
Antonio Cantafio
Alicia Carey
Clare Carswell
Ita Mac Carthy
Gwynn Carver
Colin Cather
Elaine Chambers
Tom Chatfield
Andy Checker

Sarah Chilvers
Al Chisholm
Nobel Chowdhury
Christa Christensen
Anne Clark
Kevin Clisham
Annie Cogdell
Maurice Coles
David Conlisk
Wendy Constance
Alan Constantine
Carol Coombes
Sarah Corbett
Sarah Cornell
John Coss
Daphne Cotton
Fluffhead Cottontail
Kevin Covert
Gina Cowen
John Crawford
Daniel Crewe
Kate Croucher
Niall Curran
Natalie Dalkiran
Rajan Datar
Edward Davey
Brian Davidson
Nia Davies
Carina de Geest
Rachael de Moravia
Joanna Dennison
Lisa Denny
Surbhi Deva
Wayne Diamond &
    Catherine Barber
Kate Dodgson
Samiro Douglas
Tom Douglas
Genevieve Douglass
Juliet Dowsett

281

Anne Doyle
Brian Doyle
Felix Drewes
Paul Driver
Fuchsia Dunlop
Jane Durney
Christopher Eddie
Maggie Edelstein
Owen Edmondson
Scott Elliott-Brand
Sarah Ellis
Teresa Elwes
Jo Ely
Jon Emery
Jan Erola
Judith Escribano
James Etheridge
Ross Evans
Alissa Everett
Katie Faddy
Anne P. Fawcett
Sarah Fawssett
Dianali Rodríguez Fernández
Charles Fernyhough
Susannah Field
FiveBooks.com
John-Paul Flintoff
Maya Floyd
Chris Forse
Jilly Forster
Paul Forster
Emma Louise Fung
Lynda Fussell
Anita Galeazzi
Alex Yeung Galland
Hilary Gallo
Chris Gaskell
Peter Gatbonton
Esme Gaussen
Andrew Gaynor

Ted Geier
Andrew George
Sue Gerhardt
Gal Gibson
Ed Gillespie
Richard Gipps
Eliane Glaser
Elaine Godden
Danielle Goldstone
Carl Gombrich
Family Gormley & Ray
Marc Goulart
Jane Gould
Alistair Goulding
Jacqueline Graham
Peggptty Graham
Emmanuelle Granados
John Gray
Judith Green
Judy Greenwood
Bertina Greven
Mini Grey
Nanda Griffioen
Goranka Gudelj
Helena Gutmane
Siri Haavie
Tony Hagan
Megan Halligan
Matt Hameroff
Michael and Irena Hamilton
Emma Hancock
Stephen Hancock
Jacques Handelé
Rick Hanson
David Hare
Emily Harris
Sharon Harvey
Ronnie Hausheer
Frances Haysey
Tim Healing

Andrew Hearse
David Hebblethwaite
Adriana Heinzen
Caspar Henderson
Benjamin Hennig
Alex Busby Hicks
Kat Busby Hicks
Faith Hill
Julia Hobsbawm
Liz Hodgson
Marijke Hoek
Matt Holland
Janet Holmes à Court AC
Alexis Hombrecher
Andy Homden
Sharon Horbyk
Valerie Houillon
Carol Howard
Stephen Humphreys
Abigail Hunt
Michele Hutchison
Robert Hutchison
Jeff Hutner
Warrick Isaachsen
Nina Iskra
Tony Ivanda
William Jarett
Murray Jason
Derek Jenkins
Jon Jenkins
Luke Jenner
Abi Johnson
Peter Johnson
Alice Jolly
David Jones
Sandra Joyce
Joey Katona
Tom Keith
Robert Kelsey
Dan Kieran

Ruth Killick
Seung Kuk Kim
Patrick Kincaid
Iain King
Isabel Melo King
Sarah Knott
Michaela Knowles
Jean Knox
Emma Konopka
Roselle Kovitz
Casimir Krznaric
Peter Krznaric
Siri Krznaric
Todd Landman
Eileen Laurie
Elizabeth Eva Leach
Peter Lefort
Luke Leighfield
Andy Letcher
Alexandra Lewis
David Lewis
Berry Liberman
Stewart Licudi
Larissa Lily
Don Limn
Jorge Limon
Jakob Lingg
James Lloyd
Nick Lloyd
Victoria Lloyd-Hughes
Kaj Lofgren
Eric Lonergan
Iain Lorriman
Karen Lott
Livia Lucheroni
Angelika Lueckert
Dragana Lukic
Sofija Lukic
Kate Lunn
Xiong Luong

Mark Lynas
Andrew Macheta
Rob Machin
Karen Macmillan
YES! Magazine
James Maitland-Smith
Danijel Majhan
Gosia Makarczuk
Jubin Mama
Jill Mann
Ben Margolis
Fernando Martins
Roshana May
Colin McArthur
Monica McCarthy
Jeannine McCartney
Sally McColl
Jonathan McFarland
Alison McIntosh
Hannah McLeod
Kathryn McNicoll
Tyler McNish
Britta Meier
Nicki Meier
Vânia C. Mendes
Forrest Metz
Giannantonio Mezzetti
J.B. Miller
Jonny Miller
May Miller-Dawkins
John Mitchinson
Ronald Mitchinson
Virginia Moffatt
Marjolein Moonen
Dylan Mordike
Miguel Olmedo Morell
Eka Morgan
Annalise Moser
Rod Mountain
Richard Mulcahy

Paul Murphy
Ron Mutton
Lina Nahhas
Vijay Nathwani
Carlo Navato
LaWaune Netter
Jan Neufeld
Frank Newhofer
Alexander Nirenberg
Julia Noble
Caroline Norris
Marjan Novak
Dermot O'Kane
Rachael O'Meara
Cathy O'Neill
Kimba OftheJungle
Gregory Olver
Will Ord
Irina Paert
Lucia Palmero
Ilaria Parodi and Massimo Balestri
Adah Parris
Ken Parsonage
Clare Patey
Rosie Pearson
Jadranka Boban Pejić
Toby Peregrine-Jones
Philippa Perry
Dan Peters
Jamie Pett
New Philosopher
Roger Pilgrim
Jennifer Pirtle
Karey Pohn
Justin Pollard
Dior Popko
Gerard Popko
Hallina Popko
Jason Popko
Chase Popko-Fowler

Tom Povey

Geesje Prins

Ben Pritchard

Philip Pullman

Janet Rabinowitz

David Rappuhn

Jenny Raworth

Kate Raworth

Richard Raworth

Louise Ray

Michael Ray

Lea Redmond

John Reed

Michele Ren

Fernanda Resende

Martin Reynolds

Tony Richards

Heikki Rintakumpu

George Roberts

Michael Robertson

Jonny Rodgers

Tobias Rodrigues

Phil Rogacki

Ben Ronaldson

Katrena Rose

Kitty Ross

Philip Rostant

Mark Russell

Fran Ryan

James Sabry

Manish & Claire Sadarangani

Graham Salisbury

Christoph Sander

Linda Sarah

Tebby Saunders

Vicky Saunders

Cynthia Savage

Sebastian Schleussner

The School of Life Antwerp

The School of Life Brasil

Anna Schroeder

Cordula Schuh

Robin Sen

Taryn Sexton

David Shaftel

Divyesh Shah

Nicole Shannon

Suzie Sheehy

Belinda Sherlock

Jackie Shonerd

Craig Simmons

Anjali Singh

Andrew Smith

Mary Smith

Gary Snapper

Cheryl Snell

Ben Solanky

Dave Sox

Utz Spaeth

Quentin Spender

John Sprackland

Julie St Clair Hoare

Kirsty Stanley

Richard Stanley

Garry Stannard

Rob Stead

Robin Steele

Jennifer Steven

David Stevens

Kitty Stewart

Martin Stott

Andrea Stringhini

Michelle Sutherland

Adam Swift

Sophia Swithern

Selma Tafro

Courtney Talbot

Paul Talbot

Doudy & Clea Tang

Marcia Tassinari

Sol Tatlow
Tot Taylor
Frank Michael Tedesco
Claire Thomas
Richard Thomas
Branden Thornhill-Miller
Rufus Thurston
Nat Tsolak
Irwin Turbitt
Lydie van de Laar – RebootTime
Frank Van Den Steen
Gijs van Hensbergen
Frank Vanaudenaerde
Craig Vaughton
Januschka Veldstra
Mark Vent
Mark Vernon
Nicolas Victoir
Caroline Vu
Christopher Wakling
Robert Walker
Stephen Walker
Martin Walsh
Mark Ware
Hugh Warwick
Laura Watcham
Colleen Waterston
Julie Watters

Charlotte Weatherley
Don Weir
Joshua Welensky
Christopher Whalen
Andrew Whitmore
Donie Wiley
Alex Wilks
Derek Williams
Andrew Wilson
John Wilson
Rob Wilson
Robyn Wilson-Smith
Ruth Winden
Jonathan Winter
Sarah Wisson
Hanna Wiszniewska
Jeff Wolfin
Gabrielle Wong
Rebecca Wrigley
Gerald Wyatt
Phil Yates
Peter Yeo
Jenny Yeong
Zachary York
Philip Young
Bella Zanesco
Cristina Zanetti